The U.S.–China Trade War

The U.S.–China Trade War

GLOBAL NEWS FRAMING AND
PUBLIC OPINION IN THE DIGITAL AGE

Edited by Louisa Ha and Lars Willnat

MICHIGAN STATE UNIVERSITY PRESS | *East Lansing*

Michigan State University Press
East Lansing, Michigan 48823–5245

Library of Congress Cataloging-in-Publication Data
Names: Ha, Louisa, editor. | Willnat, Lars, 1964– editor.
Title: The U.S.–China trade war : Global news framing and public opinion in the digital age edited by
Louisa Ha and Lars Willnat.
Description: East Lansing : Michigan State University Press, [2022] |
Series: US–China relations in the age of globalization | Includes bibliographical references.
Identifiers: LCCN 2021016779 | ISBN 978-1-61186-421-2 (paperback ; alk. paper) | ISBN 978-1-60917-
688-4 (PDF) | ISBN 978-1-62895-454-8 (epub) | ISBN 978-1-62896-448-6 (Kindle)
Subjects: LCSH: United States—Foreign economic relations—China—Press coverage. | China—Foreign
economic relations—United States—Press coverage. | Tariff—United States—Press coverage. | United
States—Commercial policy—Press coverage. | China—Commercial policy—Press coverage.
Classification: LCC HF1456.5.C6 U5264 2022 | DDC 337.73051—dc23
LC record available at https://lccn.loc.gov/2021016779

Cover design by Erin Kirk.
Cover art by Tampatra.

Visit Michigan State University Press at *www.msupress.org*

ON THE INTERSECTION OF EDGE BALL AND COURTESY:
NOTES ON SCHOLARSHIP IN THE AGE OF GLOBALIZATION

Like America or France or Brazil, China is a nation-state riven with fault-lines along region and race, ethnicity and education, linguistics and libido, gender and more general divisions. The US media tends to portray Chinese society as monolithic—billions of citizens censored into silence, its activists and dissidents fearful of retribution. The "reeducation" camps in Xinjiang, the "black prisons" that dot the landscape, and the Great Firewall prove this belief partially true. At the same time, there are more dissidents on the Chinese web than there are living Americans, and rallies, marches, strikes, and protests unfold in China each week. The nation is seething with action, much of it politically radical. What makes this political action so complicated and so difficult to comprehend is that no one knows how the state will respond on any given day. In his magnificent *Age of Ambition*, Evan Osnos notes that "Divining how far any individual [can] go in Chinese creative life [is] akin to carving a line in the sand at low tide in the dark." His tide metaphor is telling, for throughout Chinese history waves of what Deng Xiaoping called "openness and reform" have given way to repression, which can then swing back to what Chairman Mao once called "letting a hundred flowers bloom"—China thus offers a perpetually changing landscape, in which nothing is certain. For this reason, our Chinese colleagues and collaborators are taking great risks by participating in this book series. Authors in the "west" fear their books and articles will fail to find an audience; authors in China live in fear of a midnight knock at the door.

This series therefore strives to practice what Qingwen Dong calls "edge ball": Getting as close as possible to the boundary of what is sayable without crossing the line into being offensive. The image is borrowed from table tennis and depicts a shot that barely touches the line before ricocheting off the table; it counts as a point and is within the rules, yet the trajectory of the ball makes it almost impossible to hit a return shot. In the realm of scholarship and politics, playing "edge ball" means speaking truth to power while not provoking arrest—this is a murky game full of gray zones, allusions, puns, and sly references. What this means for our series is clear: Our authors do not censor themselves, but they do speak respectfully and cordially, showcasing research-based perspectives from their standpoints and their worldviews, thereby putting multiple vantage points into conversation. As our authors practice "edge ball," we hope our readers will savor these books with a similar sense of sophisticated and international generosity.

—Stephen J. Hartnett

Contents

PART 3. Media Coverage of the Trade War in China

Introduction

The U.S.–China Trade War as a Case Study of U.S.–China Relations

Louisa Ha and Lars Willnat

O n March 2, 2018, U.S. President Donald Trump tweeted, "When a country (USA) is losing many billions of dollars on trade with virtually every country it does business with, trade wars are good, and easy to win." Since then, it has become apparent that trade wars are not easy to win. In fact, it appears the U.S.–China trade war has slowed U.S. economic momentum, frozen business investments, and chilled economic growth to 2.3 percent in 2019 (Mutikani, 2020). The economic dispute between China and the United States has, in fact, snowballed into the "biggest trade war in economic history" (*New York Times*, 2018), leaving both nations reeling. In the U.S. vice-presidential debate on October 7, 2020, Democratic candidate Kamala Harris blamed the Trump administration for starting a trade war that has cost the United States 300,000 jobs: "Farmers have experienced bankruptcy, because of it. We are in a manufacturing recession" (Page, 2020, 40:45).

Thus, a closer look at how the U.S. and Chinese news media interpreted and framed the trade war for their respective audiences will help to better understand the effects of professional journalism and user-generated content on public opinion in international conflicts—and will provide a clearer picture of how these effects might differ due to differences in political and media systems. Accordingly, this book addresses media coverage of the U.S.–China trade war as a case study of U.S.–China relations.

As of January 2021, the trade war is frozen in place, with little progress in sight. At the G7 Summit held in February 2021, President Biden stressed the need to forge an alliance with Europe to ensure "long-term strategic competition" with China, especially in the areas of cyberspace, artificial intelligence, and biotechnology (Sanger, 2021). As the Biden administration begins to recalibrate economic and political relations with China, the U.S.–China trade war likely will become a topic of intense negotiation again. When that happens, critics of the trade war will point to an overwhelming amount of data showing that the trade war damaged the economies of both nations (Archana, 2020). Gerhard (2021) estimates that Americans have paid $68 billion in tariffs imposed on Chinese imports, and the U.S. China Business Council reported a loss of 245,000 American jobs at the peak of the trade war (Reuters, 2021). The tariffs also slowed down China's economic growth and reduced some of the Chinese imports to the United States (Wallace, 2019).

While the economic impact of the U.S.–China trade war is slowly becoming clear, this study offers the first detailed analysis of how both legacy and social media in China and the United States portrayed the trade war during its most dramatic phase between 2018 and 2019. Our analyses show how the media in both nations established "frames" that offered significant differences in perspectives regarding the trade war, oftentimes working at cross-purposes with their respective national governments. Our analyses also show that public discussions of the trade war in China and the United States were driven by a number of factors that had little to do with economics and more with questions of nationalism and sense of self (Boylan et al., 2021). We argue that individuals in both nations approached the trade war through highly emotional frames of (mis)understanding steeped in longstanding narratives about the other nation.

In terms of the historical context of our study, U.S.–China trade relations began to accelerate when the United States extended "permanent normal trade relations" (equivalent to "most favored nation") to China in 1999, which helped China to join the World Trade Organization (WTO) in 2001. This was seen as a move by the United States to ensure that China complied with international trade rules and lowered trade barriers for U.S. companies (U.S.–China Security Review Commission, 2002; Lipton, 2018). As a result, the trade volume between the two countries grew from about $121 billion in 2001 to $636 billion by 2017 (Amadeo, 2019). As detailed in Steven Beckman and Stephen Hartnett's "The China Knot," the trade war culminated in a series of conflicts triggered by this massive increase in economic relations between the United States and China. The Chinese government's initiatives to expand its manufacturing and technological innovation capacities, in particular, have caught the United States' attention because they are seen as a threat to its superpower status.

Within China's recent economic developments, the Belt and Road Initiative (BRI), which started in 2013, stands as an audacious and game-changing program. The BRI proposes to link China with other Asian, European, and African countries using the ancient Silk Road concept to create a large free-trade zone. This initiative aims to build a global economic network for trade and development by establishing new trade routes, constructing infrastructure, and establishing transportation links (Chatzsky & McBride, 2019a). Critics have noted that the BRI amounts to an unprecedented program of debt-trap development, complete with deep ties to China's political and military ambitions (Clarke, 2020).

Likewise, in 2015, the proposition Made in China 2025, led by China's State Council, demonstrated China's determination to become the world's manufacturing superpower. Made in China 2025 is the first stage of a broader strategy in China's ten-year plan to transform the nation into the world's leading manufacturer of high-tech products. This national strategic plan aims to manufacture 70 percent of all products used in ten technology sectors such as aerospace, semiconductors, and biotechnology by 2025. The Chinese government's commitment to assist Chinese firms involved in the plan through state-directed investment funds and preferential access to credit from state banks likely will pose a direct threat to the United States' technological leadership (Chatzsky & McBride, 2019b). Like the BRI, Made in China 2025 alarms American critics, who see the plan as amounting to a state-sponsored pursuit of an unhealthy global monopoly over key manufacturing sectors (Greer, 2018).

In both cases, China's plans for economic growth are seen by American critics as warning signs that China is not content to play along with the WTO and other international bodies, instead seeking to create a new world order directed by Beijing. As U.S. trade representative Robert Lighthizer expressed in 2018, "China's government is aggressively working to undermine America's high-tech industries and our economic leadership through unfair trade practices and industrial policies like Made in China 2025" (Office of the U.S. Trade Representative, 2018, para. 3).

The establishment of the Asian Infrastructure Investment Bank (AIIB) in 2016 further challenged U.S. financial leadership in the world. The mission of the AIIB, which has 103 members from around the world and is based in Beijing, is to improve social and economic outcomes in Asia (AIIB, 2019). In 2020, the bank committed between four to five billion dollars for twenty to thirty development projects in countries such as Bangladesh, Nepal, and India, related to sustainable infrastructure, cross-border connectivity, and private capital mobilization (AIIB, 2020). For China's government, the AIIB provides an opportunity to insinuate itself into developing regional nations by leveraging its economic clout; to American critics, the AIIB is nothing less than an attempt to dethrone the dollar as the default international currency.

The U.S. tariffs imposed on China in 2018 were meant to diminish the United States' trade deficit with China. They were also a clear indication of America's frustrations with China over the AIIB, the BRI, Made in China 2025, and other key issues of global leadership and power. However, to the Trump administration's disappointment, even after implementing the trade tariffs, the trade deficit between China and the United States increased from about $376 billion in 2017 to $419 billion in 2018 (Amadeo, 2019). One of the reasons why the tariffs failed to reduce the U.S. trade deficit with China was the fact that while U.S. technology products were in high demand in China, U.S. manufacturers could not benefit from this demand because they were not allowed to export these products to China (due to trade blockages imposed by both the United States and China). As a consequence of the trade war, manufacturing and employment decreased, while production costs increased in the United States (Seipel, 2019). Recognizing these negative economic trends, the U.S. administration's narrative shifted toward pressuring China into importing agricultural goods and implementing structural changes, such as removing state subsidies to increase the cost of Chinese goods so that their prices would not be as competitive. As detailed by Beckman and Hartnett and by Hamilton Bean in "China's Foreign Direct Investment Expansion: News Coverage of U.S.–China Economic and Security Commission Reports," the Trump administration's trade war was based on shaky economic foundations, amounting more to angry symbolism than reasoned trade practice.

Nonetheless, President Trump's trade war with China was welcomed by political groups in the United States that have been critical of China for many years, such as the right-wing U.S. foreign policy advisory group, Committee on the Present Danger: China. The committee stated its mission as "help[ing] defend America through public education and advocacy against the full array of conventional and non-conventional dangers posed by the People's Republic of China." The committee also noted that "Communist China represents an existential and ideological threat to the United States and to the idea of freedom—one that requires a new American consensus regarding the policies and priorities required to defeat this threat" (Committee on the Present Danger: China, 2019, para. 3). The committee consists of prominent current and former politicians, such as former secretary of state George Shultz, former director of the CIA, James Woolsey, and former House Speaker Newt Gingrich. With close connections to the Trump White House, Congress, and federal agencies, this group significantly influenced the U.S. government's policy toward China (Swanson, 2019). The committee's revival from the Cold War signals that China has replaced Russia as the main enemy among hawkish U.S. politicians who fear China's alleged danger to the United States (Militarist Monitor, 2019). Moreover, Trump's top economic officials, Peter Navarro (director of trade and manufacturing policy), Wilbur Ross (secretary of commerce), and Larry Kudlow (director of the United States National Economic Council), were all known to support an aggressive foreign stance toward China (Aleem, 2017; Kawanami & Harada, 2018; Schneider-Pedsinger, 2017). Trump's trade war was, in part, a product of this advocacy by anti-China Cold War Warriors.

U.S. legislators also fueled the trade war with numerous bills targeted at China. Since 2018, more than 366 bills were tabled in the U.S. Congress related to China, Hong Kong, Taiwan, Tibet, and the Xinjiang Autonomous Region of China, breaking all previous records (Kennedy, 2020). For example, the Hong Kong Democracy and Human Rights Act of 2019 supported the autonomy of Hong Kong and undermined China's sovereignty over Hong Kong. The passing of the Uyghur Act on December 3, 2019, calling for tough sanctions on Beijing over the re-education camps in Xinjiang province, added to the political and economic tensions between the two countries.

The U.S. hawks' hostility toward China, perhaps best illustrated in the "China threat" narrative that dominates reports by the U.S.–China Economic and Security Review Commission (see Bean in this volume), coincided with the rise of political hardliners in China. Although there have always been nationalist voices in China critical of Western imperialism, relations between China and the United States had been relatively cordial during the rule of Chinese presidents Jiang Zemin and Wu Jintao, who emphasized learning from and collaborating with the West. President Xi Jinping's rise to power and his vision of the "China Dream," which links international economic expansion policies with patriotism and the embrace of traditional Chinese culture, ended China's "friendly competition" with the United States (Liu, 2015). In fact, some Western observers see President Xi's China Dream as an attempt to revive the old glory of the Middle Kingdom through global expansion (French,

2017). Many Chinese hardliners believe that concessions to U.S. demands related to the trade war, such as reducing state ownership of large companies or eliminating state subsidies, could lead to China's demise. For example, Rear Admiral Luo Yuen stated that China must stand firm against U.S. pressure during the trade war (Luo, 2018). In his 2018 speech, Luo explained that the ideological differences between China and the United States are so fundamental that it would be foolish to expect that the United States will allow China to continue to grow economically. China's reluctance to agree to U.S. demands related to the trade war also might be due to not wanting to follow Japan's footsteps, which conceded to U.S. demands during the U.S.–Japan trade war in the late 1980s. As a consequence, Japan entered into a prolonged recession that plunged it into two decades of economic stagnation (Landers, 2018; Tai, 2018).

However, there are moderates in each country who would like to improve bilateral relations rather than seeing them as a zero-sum game. In his latest report on U.S.–China relations for the Center for Strategic and International Studies, national security expert Anthony H. Cordesman (2019a) discussed the cooperation, competition, and conflict between the two countries. He reminded U.S. policymakers that they should understand how China's history over the past two hundred years has influenced the current administration's strategy in pursuing the Chinese dream of becoming a strong and prosperous country. Instead of advocating for China's suppression, Cordesman offered a more nuanced view of China's military power:

> Serious warfighting of any kind between China and the United States will probably cost the winner more than victory is worth, and both nations already have the capability to inflict devastating nuclear countervalue damage on the other state. The only way to win is not to play (Cordesman, 2019b, p. 3).

Similarly, Graham Allison (2017), former U.S. assistant secretary of defense, argued that in order to avoid war between China and the United States, radical attitudinal changes are required in both countries' leaders and people (also see Lieberthal & Wang, 2014).

In short, the trade war was welcomed by hardliners in the United States and China, cheering on their respective nations, while moderates sought a path of understanding and cooperation. But what did the people of China and America think of the trade war? How was their thinking influenced by both legacy and new social media? And how did the people and media in both countries support, contradict, or otherwise respond to their respective national governments? Before we tackle these questions, we offer a brief summary of how each nation's government viewed the conflict.

The Trade War as a Dispute about Fair Trade

As of this book's writing, the United States and China have held thirteen rounds of trade talks since the beginning of the trade war in early 2018—none of which has solved the dispute. Both the United States and China maintain their views of what "fair trade" actually means. In March 2018, the Trump administration argued that

> China has implemented laws, policies, and practices, and has taken actions related to intellectual property, innovation, and technology that may encourage or require the transfer of American technology and intellectual property to enterprises in China or that may otherwise negatively affect American economic interests. These laws, policies, practices, and actions may inhibit United States exports, deprive United States citizens of fair remuneration for their innovations, divert American jobs to workers in China, contribute to our trade deficit with China, and otherwise undermine American manufacturing, services, and innovation. (Executive Office of the U.S. President, 2018, p. 1)

While China has not acknowledged these arguments as the causes of the trade deficit, it has agreed to engage in trade negotiations with the United States. The Chinese position, as argued in its White Paper, *Facts of the Trade Friction and China's Position*, is that the U.S. trade deficit with China is due to the United States' high consumption and low savings rate; China's exports to the United States that are mostly consumer goods, while the majority of U.S. exports to China consists of more specialized products such as airplanes, integrated circuits, and agricultural products; the fact that the U.S.–China trade is a typical international division of labor; restrictions on exports of sophisticated U.S. technologies to China; and the use of the U.S. dollar as a global currency (ISOC, 2018).

In a second White Paper, *China's Position on the China-US Economic and Trade Consultations*, China blames the United States for raising trade tariffs multiple times. According to the report, the United States repeatedly raised U.S. tariffs on Chinese exports even "after China agreed to increase import of agricultural goods and energy products from the United States [and] to reduce the deficit and resolve the conflict through negotiation in early 2018." The report argues that Trump continued to implement the tariffs, even "after the December 2018 G20-summit where both Xi and Trump agreed to pause the tariffs and resume negotiations" (ISOC, 2019, section 2). It also makes clear that China places the blame for the trade dispute squarely at America's feet, pointing both to longstanding economic factors and President Trump's erratic handling of international relations.

While the trade war was covered in the news media of both nations, the ongoing trade negotiations between the United States and China were covered less prominently in the U.S. news media—mainly because other domestic issues, such as the confirmation hearings of Supreme Court Justice nominee Brett Kavanaugh, dominated the headlines. In contrast, the Chinese news media covered the trade negotiations more extensively, yet most reports were brief because the government kept the negotiations secret and mentioned them only when it needed to deny unilateral statements made by the United States. Thus, while the trade war attracted significant news coverage, the actual trade negotiations received only limited media attention in each nation.

Nonetheless, U.S. President Trump and China's Vice Premier Liu He signed a "phase one" trade agreement on January 15, 2020. In the agreement, Trump agreed to relax some of the tariffs he imposed on Chinese imports, while Beijing promised to buy more American products. The implementation of the trade agreement was subject to review in August 2020 but was postponed due to the COVID-19 pandemic. To provide a better understanding of the developments that characterized the U.S.–China trade war, table 1 provides a list of the main events that occurred between January 2018 and January 2020.

Making Sense of News Representations of the Trade War

This book analyzes how the U.S. and Chinese media covered the trade war as a political and economic conflict. To this end, we compare the U.S. and Chinese media's coverage of the trade war within the media environments of both countries, which are both characterized by thriving multiplatform news delivery systems and native digital news brands. Our authors present detailed empirical studies

TABLE 1. Timeline of the U.S.–China Trade War, January 2018 to January 2020

JANUARY 22, 2018	President Trump placed a 30 percent tariff on foreign solar panels, to be reduced to 15 percent after four years. China, the world leader in solar panel manufacturing, protested the tariffs. That same day, tariffs of 20 percent were placed on washing machines for the first 1.2 million units imported during the year.
MARCH 22, 2018	President Trump ordered 25 percent tariffs on steel imports and 10 percent on aluminum. Trump asked the United States Trade Representative (USTR) to investigate applying tariffs on US$50–60 billion worth of Chinese goods, stating that the proposed tariffs were "a response to the unfair trade practices of China over the years," including theft of U.S. intellectual property. Over 1,300 categories of Chinese imports were listed for tariffs, including aircraft parts, batteries, flat-panel televisions, medical devices, satellites, and various weapons.
APRIL 2, 2018	China responded by imposing retaliatory tariffs on 128 products imported from America, including aluminum, airplanes, cars, pork, and soybeans (which have a 25 percent tariff), as well as fruit, nuts, and steel piping (15 percent). On April 5, 2018, Trump responded by saying that he was considering another round of tariffs on an additional $100 billion of Chinese imports. The next day the World Trade Organization received a request from China for consultations on new U.S. tariffs.
MAY 15, 2018	Vice Premier Liu He, the top economic adviser to the president of China, Xi Jinping, visited Washington for further trade talks.
MAY 20, 2018	Chinese officials agreed to "substantially reduce" America's trade deficit with China by committing to "significantly increase" its purchases of American goods. As a result, treasury secretary Steven Mnuchin announced that "we are putting the trade war on hold."
MAY 29, 2018	The White House announced that it would impose a 25 percent tariff on $50 billion of Chinese goods with "industrially significant technology"; the full list of affected products was to be announced by June 15, 2018. It also planned to impose investment restrictions and enhanced export controls on certain Chinese individuals and organizations to prevent them from acquiring U.S. technology. China said it would discontinue trade talks with Washington if it imposed trade sanctions.
JUNE 15, 2018	Trump declared that the United States would impose a 25 percent tariff on $50 billion of Chinese exports, out of which $34 billion would start July 6, 2018, with a further $16 billion to begin later. China's Commerce Ministry accused the United States of launching a trade war and said China would respond in kind with similar tariffs for U.S. imports, starting on July 6, 2018. Three days later, the White House declared that the United States would impose additional 10 percent tariffs on another $200 billion worth of Chinese imports if China retaliated against these U.S. tariffs.
JUNE 19, 2018	China retaliated almost immediately, threatening its own tariffs on $50 billion of U.S. goods, and claimed the United States had "launched a trade war."

JULY 6, 2018	American tariffs on $34 billion of Chinese goods came into effect. China imposed retaliatory tariffs on U.S. goods of similar value. The tariffs accounted for 0.1 percent of the global gross domestic product. On July 10, 2018, the United States released an initial list of the additional $200 billion of Chinese goods that would be subject to a 10 percent tariff. China vowed to retaliate with additional tariffs on American goods worth $60 billion annually two days later.
AUGUST 8, 2018	The Office of the United States Trade Representative published its finalized list of 279 Chinese goods, worth $16 billion, to be subject to a 25 percent tariff from August 23, 2018. China responded with its own tariffs of equal value on August 23, 2018.
AUGUST 14, 2018	China filed a complaint with the World Trade Organization (WTO), claiming that U.S. tariffs on foreign solar panels clashed with WTO ruling and had destabilized the international market for solar PV products.
AUGUST 22, 2018	U.S. treasury undersecretary David Malpass and Chinese commerce vice minister Wang Shouwen met in Washington, D.C., in a bid to reopen negotiations. Meanwhile, on August 23, 2018, the United States' and China's promised tariffs on $16 billion of goods took effect. Four days later, China filed a new WTO complaint against the United States regarding the additional tariffs.
SEPTEMBER 17, 2018	The United States announced its 10 percent tariff on $200 billion worth of Chinese goods would begin on September 24, 2018, increasing to 25 percent by the end of the year. They also threatened tariffs on an additional $267 billion worth of imports if China retaliated, which China promptly did on September 18, with 10 percent tariffs on $60 billion of U.S. imports. So far, China either imposed or proposed tariffs on $110 billion of U.S. goods, representing most of its imports of American products.
DECEMBER 6, 2018	The planned increases in tariffs were postponed after Trump and Xi met at the G20 Summit meeting in Chile, and a truce was announced for ninety days. The White House stated that both parties would "immediately begin negotiations on structural changes with respect to forced technology transfer, intellectual property protection, non-tariff barriers, cyber intrusions, and cyber theft."
JUNE 29, 2019	The U.S. Department of Commerce stated that in 2018 the U.S. trade deficit with China reached $621 billion, the highest it had been since 2008.
AUGUST 5, 2019	The U.S. Department of Treasury officially declared China as a currency manipulator after the People's Bank of China allowed the yuan to depreciate 2 percent to its 2008 level.
SEPTEMBER 1, 2019	The United States imposed the first batch of tariffs of 15 percent on $300 billion of Chinese goods. China imposed the first batch of 10 percent or 5 percent on $75 billion of U.S. goods.
SEPTEMBER 26, 2019	The *Wall Street Journal* reported that Chinese retaliatory tariffs on lumber and wood products had caused hardwood lumber exports to China to fall 40 percent during 2019, resulting in American lumber mills slashing employment. A USDA spokesperson said the organization had provided the industry $5 million in aid through its Agricultural Trade Promotion Program.
OCTOBER 7, 2019	Citing human rights issues, the United States Department of Commerce put twenty Chinese public security bureaus and eight high-tech companies on the Export Administration Regulations entities blacklist. Like Huawei, which was sanctioned on an identical blueprint for national security reasons, the entities would need U.S. government approval before they could purchase components from U.S. companies.

OCTOBER 11, 2019	Trump announced that the United States and China had reached a tentative agreement for the "first phase" of a trade deal, with China agreeing to buy up to $50 billion in American farm products and to accept more American financial services in their market, and with the United States agreeing to suspend new tariffs scheduled for October 15.
DECEMBER 13, 2019	The United States and China concluded the "phase one" trade deal in which China agreed to increase its import of U.S. agricultural products and the U.S. would gradually eliminate its tariffs on Chinese goods.
JANUARY 13, 2020	The U.S. Treasury Department dropped its designation of China as a currency manipulator two days before the two sides were due to sign a preliminary trade agreement.
JANUARY 15, 2020	China and the United States signed the "phase one" trade agreement at the White House.

Note: The fifteen events listed in 2018 are analyzed in the media content analysis chapters in Parts 2 and 3.

Sources
CGTN. (2019, December 13). China, US agree on the text of phase one trade deal. https://news.cgtn.com/news/2019-12-13/China-U-S-agree-on-text-of-phase-one-trade-deal-MoKVBhf8je/index.html
Wong, D., & Koty, A. C. (2020, August 25). The US-China trade war timeline. China Briefing. https://www.china-briefing.com/news/the-us-china-trade-war-a-timeline/

conducted in the United States and China and offer readers a comparative look at how U.S. and Chinese news media covered the conflict.

In China, there is high competition for audiences between the official party media and the more commercially oriented native digital news media. This unique media environment requires a new understanding of how news content is presented in a Communist nation with a diverse media system that is driven by both political and economic demands. One of this book's major contributions is offering readers a data-driven analysis of China's emerging media ecosystem, which describes how China's media are evolving in exciting ways, with users drawing from party-run legacy media, social media apps affiliated with these legacy outlets, and alternative social media sources. Contrary to old stereotypes of China as a drab and monolithic sphere of communication, our data reveal civic spaces full of lively debate and occasional criticism of the government.

In the United States, partisan media have covered the U.S.–China trade war from various ideological perspectives. While commercial U.S. television broadcasters have dominated news production for many decades, cable news networks, such as the conservative Fox News and the liberal MSNBC, have gained large audiences in recent years (Espinoza, 2019). Consequently, news coverage of the U.S.–China trade war was highly partisan. Conservative media supported Trump's trade war policies, while the liberal media presented a more skeptical view of the trade war.

At the same time, this partisan coverage of the trade war was characterized by the rhetorical habits of much of the U.S. media establishment, which routinely portrays China in a negative light (Peng, 2004; Wei et al., 2017). However, recent studies have found that English-language social media networks present China more positively and with more diverse images than the mainstream U.S. news media (Xiang, 2013). Therefore, it remains unclear whether public perceptions of the U.S.–China trade war actually were dominated by negative media coverage or more diverse images of the conflict that emerged on social media.

Across these concerns of media partisanship and the differences between mainstream and social media, this book demonstrates how Chinese and American journalists write for their domestic audiences while simultaneously using the trade war to build broader narratives about the status of U.S.–China relations. This book also recognizes that many news consumers in the United States and China have migrated online. According to the latest report of the China Internet Network Information Center (CNNIC, 2020), China had 940 million internet users in 2020, amounting to about 67 percent of its total population. Among them, 77.1 percent received news through the internet, of whom 77.2 percent consumed news on their mobile phones. In the United States, news websites and social media have become popular news sources for the American public, surpassed only by television (Shearer, 2018).

While the internet has increased Chinese citizens' access to diverse news sources and information, China's official media have unique advantages over digital information sources. These advantages are mostly due to the fact that China's official media have inherited professional news production teams and government licenses to cover major political news and international affairs. Thus, China's official media not only enjoy exclusive access to government information but also can cover foreign affairs with more resources than their digital counterparts.

The government's media convergence policy also enables party-controlled news media to compete with other native digital media brands through their online and social media accounts (Weibo and WeChat), albeit while working within the party's tightly controlled argumentation norms (see Dodge, 2020; Yang & Wei, 2021). Overall, the internet and social media have become essential sources of news for both American and Chinese audiences and therefore greatly influence how the citizens of these nations understand foreign affairs.

The Framing of Global News and Public Opinion

Most people are dependent on the mass media for information about international affairs. As a result, the media can play an important role in shaping mass perceptions of other nations. Studies have found that exposure to global news coverage not only increases knowledge of international affairs but also can significantly influence public perceptions of foreign countries (Albritton & Manheim, 1983, 1985; Manheim & Albritton, 1984; Perry, 1987). Such perceptions, in turn, have important implications in several areas, ranging from attitudes about foreign policy to the practice of public diplomacy (Bartels, 1995; Brewer et al.,2003; Manheim, 1991, 1994; Peffley & Hurwitz, 1992).

Current research on how the media might influence perceptions of foreign affairs is based on the premise that audiences either learn about the importance of international issues from the media, which might subsequently influence which topics people consider important when thinking about foreign countries (*agenda-setting*), or they are guided by the media to see a foreign affairs issue from a particular frame of reference, which might subsequently alter the way they think about a foreign nation (*framing*). The agenda-setting hypothesis proposes that "not only do people acquire factual information about public affairs from the news media, readers and viewers also learn how much importance to attach to a topic based on the emphasis placed on it in the news" (McCombs, 2002, p. 1). Applied to the study of international affairs, this means that the news media can set the agenda for the public's attention to a small number of issues around which perceptions of foreign nations form. The theory suggests that international news coverage of the trade war focused audience attention on this economic dispute and drew attention to related issues, such as the U.S. trade deficit with China or the theft of American intellectual property. Such an agenda-setting function of the news media can influence public opinion and affect foreign policy decisions (Soroka, 2003).

Likewise, the ways the U.S. and Chinese media "framed" news about the trade war likely affected how audiences in China and the United States understood this economic conflict and U.S.–China relations. Frames represent storylines or "organizing ideas" (Gamson, 1992, p. 3) that guide how people understand the world and form judgments. According to Entman (1993, p. 52), media framing consists of "select[ing] some aspects of a perceived reality and mak[ing] them more salient in a communicating text, in such a way as to promote a particular problem definition, causal interpretation, moral evaluation, and/or treatment recommendation." Particularly relevant in the case at hand is the likelihood that the U.S. and Chinese media might have framed the trade war in ways that aligned with their respective governments' economic and political interests. Overall, both agenda-setting and framing are important theoretical frameworks for our cross-national analysis of international news about the U.S.–China trade war.

Working within this theoretical framework, we hypothesized that the state-controlled media in China would be likely to report only official government positions regarding the conflict, hence stoking nationalism and mobilizing public support for opposing U.S. sanctions. On the other hand, we believed China's commercial digital news media might pursue different strategies tethered less tightly to the government's position. Moreover, we assumed that Chinese social media platforms would enable users to consider alternative views of the political and economic relationships between the two nations.

Based on our theoretical and historical grounding, we therefore began our study expecting to find at least three different modes of agenda-setting and framing in China's news coverage of the trade war. As expected, our data pointed to party-run outlets towing the party line, party-affiliated social media platforms taking a more ambivalent stance, and commercially driven news apps offering alternative perspectives.

The coverage of the U.S.–China trade war in the U.S. media, by contrast, was strongly influenced by President Trump. Although President Trump frequently called the press "fake news" and "the enemy of people," he also sought to marshal the media in a manner that matched the characteristics of war journalism, aiming squarely at achieving political and economic victory for the United States. In fact, Vice President Mike Pence commended U.S. journalists for supporting the U.S. government during the trade war, noting that "it's also great to see more journalists reporting the truth without fear or favor, digging deep to find where China is interfering in our society, and why ... And we hope that American and global news organizations will continue to join this effort on an increasing basis" (Frum, 2019, para. 8).

Media Effects on Public Perceptions of China and the United States

The escalating trade war between the United States and China contributed to a significant drop in how favorable Americans viewed China. Public opinion polls conducted in early 2019 showed that only 41 percent of Americans had a favorable view of China, down by 12 percentage points from the previous year (Gallup, 2019). The Covid-19 pandemic only exacerbated this negative trend, with President Trump's repeated references to the "Chinese virus" fueling racism and xenophobia toward Chinese and other people of Asian descent. The pandemic's devastating death toll and Trump's attempts to blame China for the global spread of coronavirus predictably affected Americans' perceptions of China. A survey conducted by the Pew Research Center in March 2020 indicated that only 26 percent of Americans held favorable views of China, the most negative rating for China since Pew began asking this question in 2005. These negative views were especially pronounced among Republicans, who were more worried about the trade deficit and job losses to China than Democrats and Independents (Devlin et al., 2020).

Similarly, polls conducted in China (Willnat et al., 2016; Willnat et al., 2019) showed that favorable opinions of the United States dropped from 50 percent in 2016 to about 40 percent in 2017—a dramatic shift that was likely caused by President Trump's anti-China policies during his first year in office. As shown in the third chapter, "National Images as Integrated Schemas: How Americans and Chinese Think about Each Other and the U.S.–China Trade War," by Lars Willnat, Shuo Tang, Jian Shi, and Ning Zhan, the United States' favorability ratings dropped even further in 2019, with only approximately 37 percent of the Chinese people holding favorable views of the United States.

Overall, these dramatic shifts in overall favorability toward China indicate that the U.S.–China trade war and the worldwide pandemic significantly affected how Americans saw China. The media likely played a significant role in these attitude changes because most people rely on the media to learn about international affairs. In the United States, news coverage of the trade war and related social media posts increased after Trump's announcements on May 5, 2019, that he was raising tariffs on $200 billion worth of Chinese products; coverage then spiked again around August 1, 2019, when Trump stated that the United States would impose additional tariffs on another $300 billion worth of Chinese goods. Similarly, increased coverage of the trade war in the Chinese news media in May 2019 was accompanied by a large spike in Weibo posts related to the trade war that month. Weibo posts on the trade war increased by 34 percent from 2018 to 2019. Thus, increased media coverage of the trade war in the United States and China was matched by increased chatter about the economic dispute on social media in both nations. Consequently, our authors ask whether increased public discussions of the trade war on social media affected how American and Chinese news consumers perceived the trade war.

Political Polarization and Partisan News Coverage of the U.S.–China Trade War

While there is strong evidence for the proposition that the U.S. media played an important role in shaping American perceptions of China and the U.S.–China trade war, one of the biggest concerns regarding President Trump's tenure in the White House has been his impact on how the U.S. public views the news media. According to surveys conducted just before the 2016 presidential election, only 32 percent of Americans had either "a great deal" or "a fair amount of trust" in the news media (Swift, 2016). However, more recent survey data suggest that trust in the news media increased to 41 percent in 2019 (Brenan, 2019). While trust in news media has improved among Republicans and Democrats, there remains a significant gap in trust across the political aisles, with only 15 percent of Republicans and 69 percent of Democrats trusting the news media in 2019.

These polarized perceptions can be mostly explained by the fact that Republicans and Democrats have fundamentally different views of the U.S. news media. For example, Republicans are considerably less likely to personally identify with news coverage than Democrats. According to a recent Pew survey (Gottfried & Grieco, 2019), 73 percent of Republicans felt misunderstood by the news media, regardless of their media habits and demographic characteristics. By contrast, only about 40 percent of Democrats felt misunderstood by the news media. Overall, these gaps in perceptions of the news media between Democrats and Republicans reflect the American public's growing political polarization in recent years (Westwood et al., 2019).

Most researchers (Müller et al., 2017; Pasquino, 2008) agree that the news media's polarizing messages have contributed to an increasingly toxic political divide in the United States. Moreover, the growing fragmentation of the U.S. media landscape, especially on cable television (Prior, 2005), has made it considerably easier for audiences to consume partisan news closely aligned with their political views and beliefs. Recent polls have shown that audiences on the far-right and far-left of the political spectrum rely on very different news sources closely aligned with their respective political views (Fletcher, 2017; Gottfried et al., 2017; Miller, 2017; Mitchell et al., 2014). A multi-year study of political polarization by the Pew Research Center, for example, indicated that Republicans tend to use Fox News as their sole news source, whereas Democrats rely on a broader range of news sources with more liberal viewpoints. Approximately 60 percent of the Republicans surveyed stated that they trusted Fox News as a news source and obtained their political news from this network in the past week. By contrast, 70 percent of the Democrats surveyed stated that they trusted CNN, and about 50 percent indicated that they obtained their political news from CNN in the past week (Jurkowitz et al., 2020).

In contrast to Americans, Chinese media audiences generally report high confidence and trust in their news media. Research conducted in China suggests that Chinese citizens maintain relatively positive views of the news media. For example, a national survey conducted in 2017 found that approximately 70 percent of Chinese people believed that their news media are doing at least a "good" job of informing the public. About 75 percent of Chinese people had either "a great deal" or "a fair amount" of trust in the Chinese news media to report the news "accurately and fairly" (Willnat et al., 2018).

It is important to remember, though, that how American and Chinese audiences view the news media is driven by each media system's specific characteristics. While the U.S. news media outlets tend to be politically diverse and free of government control, the Chinese news media outlets are politically much more homogeneous and controlled by the state. Consequently, U.S. coverage of foreign policy issues is politically more diverse and contentious than the foreign coverage found in the Chinese news media. Moreover, Chinese foreign affairs coverage is closely aligned with the Chinese government's policies and positions and seldom deviates from official viewpoints. Meanwhile, although conservative news media outlets and news commentators in the United States showed an extreme willingness to support President Trump's national and international actions and policies, liberal U.S. media outlets grew increasingly critical of the Trump administration's efforts to isolate the United States on the international stage (see Ray & Lu, "U.S. Television News Coverage of the Trade War: Partisan Media vs. Nonpartisan Media," in this volume).

Analyses of how the U.S. and Chinese media covered the trade war must therefore consider each nation's political landscape and how the media function within each system. Moreover, U.S. and Chinese media audiences differ significantly in their political orientations, making direct comparisons difficult. While U.S. media audiences are politically divided—a fact that significantly shapes their media consumption and their views of the news media—Chinese media audiences are more politically homogenous. Consequently, Chinese might be less likely than Americans to evaluate their news media through a political lens and may be more likely to align politically with foreign news found on the pages of *People's Daily* or other official news media outlets in China. The analyses presented in parts 2 and 3 of this book address these questions with a nuanced examination of how the U.S. and Chinese legacy media, social media, and public opinion reacted to the U.S.–China trade war.

Social Media Use and Perceptions of the U.S.–China Trade War

Although the U.S. news media are characterized by a broad political spectrum that ranges from conservative to liberal, our analyses show that American audiences encountered considerably less news coverage on the trade war than their Chinese counterparts. Social media, which has become ubiquitous in the United States and China, filled this gap with a large amount of real and fake news. As of September 2020, approximately 77 percent of Chinese citizens had access to the internet, and more than 725 million Chinese netizens consumed news online (CNNIC, 2020). In the United States, where internet penetration reached 90 percent in 2019, about 34 percent of U.S. adults said they preferred to get their news online. While television remained the most popular news source, 20 percent of adults frequently get news from social media (Geiger, 2019).

Owing to the growing use of social media for news consumption, the potential effects of social media use on people's trust in traditional news media have become an important topic in media research. Ardèvol-Abreu and Gil de Zúñiga (2017) found that people who used social media were less likely to trust traditional media. However, Kim and Choi (2017) demonstrated that social media use reduced trust in traditional media only among nonpartisan news consumers, while partisan news consumers were unaffected. Experimental findings by Turcotte et al. (2015) suggested that recommendations from friends on social media can significantly boost people's trust in the news media. People who discuss the news with others on social media might be more inclined to question the news stories they see in the mainstream media. Moreover, scholars and practitioners are increasingly concerned about the growing amount of misinformation on social media and how it has boosted negative public perceptions of the mainstream news media. President Trump's extensive use of Twitter to attack the U.S. news media as "fake news" likely contributed to such an effect (Brummette et al., 2018; Whipple & Shermak, 2020).

These adverse effects of social media use on people's perceptions of traditional news media have not been found in China. For example, Li and Zhang (2018) found that Chinese social media users trust traditional media (newspapers, TV, and radio) significantly *more* than either online media (news portals and news websites) or social media (social networking sites, blogs, and microblogs). While such effects were not the focus of our research, our data indicate that more social media use in the United States is associated with decreased trust in the legacy media and the government, whereas more social media use in China correlates with more trust in both entities.

Overall, it is clear that a cross-national study of the role of the media in the U.S.–China trade war is complex because it involves two very different media systems and because both professional news and user-generated content influence the way audiences in China and the United States understand this economic conflict. Thus, today's international news coverage carries special meaning because professional journalists have been joined by citizen journalists, online influencers, and ordinary users, who each play an important role in shaping the public discourse of foreign affairs.

Unquestionably, it has become considerably easier for engaged audiences to stay more informed and involved in economic and foreign affairs. Simultaneously, both citizens and journalists can use war journalism frames to escalate the economic rivalry between the United States and China, either by supporting the tariffs or by condemning the other country's trade practices. Alternatively, both parties can use peace journalism frames to promote peaceful solutions to the conflict by reflecting on the justifications of their respective nations' trade policies (Galtung, 1996; 2003). Thus, elements of war and peace journalism likely affected how audiences in the United States and China perceived the trade war. In order to explore these potential effects, this book focuses on how the media in each nation have covered the trade war—using agenda-setting, framing, the foreign policy market equilibrium model, and notions of war versus peace journalism—and asks how this coverage has influenced their respective audiences.

Organization of the Book

This book represents a collaboration between sixteen U.S. and Chinese scholars who examine the U.S.–China trade war with both national and cross-national comparative perspectives. The chapters are based on research projects conducted by the two editors and one of the contributors. They include three national surveys conducted in 2019 (two in the United States and one in China); content analyses of U.S. and Chinese TV newscasts, online versions of elite newspapers, a mobile news app, and social media posts published in 2018; a rhetorical analysis of government documents and news coverage; and a computer-based topic modeling and content analysis of U.S. tweets related to the U.S.–China trade war.

While most of the analyses are quantitative, we also included a qualitative analysis of the U.S.–China Economic and Security Commission Reports (Bean, "China's Foreign Direct Investment Expansion") and a mixed-methods analysis of how Americans discussed the trade war on Twitter (Louisa Ha, Rik Ray, Frankline Matanji & Yang Yang, "How News Media Content and Fake News about the Trade War Are Shared on Twitter: A Topic Modeling and Content Analysis"). We hope these different research approaches provide a comprehensive look at how traditional media delivered the news on digital platforms and how social media conveyed or challenged official positions regarding the U.S.–China trade war; moreover, we ask how both legacy and social media shaped the public's understanding of this trade dispute, both in China and the United States, and how they affected public perceptions of the United States and China overall.

The book is divided into three parts. Part 1 focuses on the political and economic contexts that led to the U.S.–China trade war and how this dispute influenced public perceptions of the "other" nation both in China and the United States. In the first chapter, "The China Knot," Beckman and Hartnett discuss the origins of the U.S.–China trade deficit based on international trade theory; they demonstrate how American frustrations with China, based in part on white workers' distress due to globalization, led to the rise of Donald Trump and the trade war. In "China's Foreign Direct Investment Expansion," Bean focuses on how the U.S.–China Economic and Security Review Commission's reports on China's foreign direct investments fueled a "China threat" narrative, and how *China Daily* responded to the commission's reports. In "National Images as Integrated Schemas," Willnat, Tang, Shi, and Zhan offer a cross-national comparison of how the national image of China and the United States affected public opinion and support for the trade war in each country.

Part 2 analyzes the news coverage of the trade war in the United States, how news media use affected American perceptions of the trade war, and how Americans discussed this issue on social media. In "U.S. Television News Coverage of the Trade War," Ray and Lu demonstrate how pro-Trump partisan TV news outlets in the United States covered the trade war by using provocative narratives against China, while nonpartisan TV news generally provided more balanced reporting of this issue. Zhang, Ha, and Bi's analysis of the American public's perceptions of the trade war, in "How Media Use and Perceptions of Chinese Immigrants and Mainland Chinese Affect Americans' Attitudes toward the U.S.–China Trade War," shows that those who used partisan conservative media were considerably more supportive of the trade war than those who consumed less partisan media. In addition, the perceived competition of Chinese immigrants for social welfare benefits and perceived loss of jobs to mainland Chinese led to higher support of the trade war. Using computational and manual content analyses, Ha, Ray, Matanji, and Yang examine, in "How News Media Content and Fake News about the Trade War Are Shared on Twitter," how American Twitter users and automated bots amplified news about the trade war on social media.

Part 3 examines the ways the Chinese news media covered the trade war, how Chinese and U.S. media differ in their news coverage of the trade war, how the Chinese discussed this issue on social media, and how Chinese social media align with mainstream news media on frames about the trade war. In "How the Chinese News Media Present the U.S.–China Trade War," Chen and Guo analyze China Central Television, the party newspapers *People's Daily* and *Global Times*, and the news app *The Paper* to illustrate how party and commercial media outlets covered the trade war in China. In "Comparing U.S. and Chinese Media Coverage of the U.S.–China Trade War," Ha and her colleagues compare news coverage of the trade war between the United States and China to show that the Chinese news media were more likely to engage in peace journalism than the U.S. media—and that the media in both nations contained few instances of war journalism. Part 3 concludes with "How Weibo Influencers and Ordinary Posters Responded to the U.S.–China Trade War," by Ha, Chen, Guo, and Lyu, who analyze posts about the trade war on Weibo, China's largest microblogging platform. The authors find a high degree of alignment between the views of the trade war presented by Chinese news media and Weibo users' opinions.

The book concludes this analysis of the U.S.–China trade war with a summary of the findings and a discussion of the complementary and competing roles of professional and user-generated media in the growing political and economic disputes between the United States and China. But despite our focus on war journalism framing strategies throughout the book, we hope our contribution will help fuel the purposes of peace journalism: increasing understanding and minimizing conflict in the interests of international peace.

REFERENCES

Albritton, R. B., & Manheim, J. B. (1983, December 1). News of Rhodesia: The impact of a public relations campaign. *Journalism and Mass Communication Quarterly*, 622–28.

Albritton, R. B., & Manheim, J. B. (1985). Public relations efforts for the third world: Images in the news. *Journal of Communication, 35*(1), 43–59.

Aleem, Z. (2017, April 6). I read Trump's trade adviser's anti-China book: It's wilder than you can imagine. *Vox*. https://www.vox.com/world/2017/4/6/14697762/china-trump-trade-navarro

Allison, G. (2017). *Destined for war: Can America and China escape Thucydides's Trap?* Houghton Mifflin Harcourt.

Amadeo, K. (2019, December 14). US trade deficit with China and why it's so high. *The Balance*. https://www.thebalance.com/u-s-china-trade-deficit-causes-effects-and-solutions-3306277

Archana, V. (2020). Who will win from the trade war? Analysis of the US–China trade war from a micro perspective. *China Economic Journal, 13*(3), 376–93, https://doi.org/10.1080/17538963.2020.1785073

Ardèvol-Abreu, A., & Gil de Zúñiga, H. (2017). Effects of editorial media bias perception and media trust on the use of traditional, citizen, and social media news. *Journalism and Mass Communication Quarterly, 94*(3), 703–24.

Asian Infrastructure Investment Bank (AIIB) (2019). *About AIIB*. https://www.aiib.org/en/about-aiib/index.html

Asian Infrastructure Investment Bank (AIIB) (2020). *Approved projects*. https://www.aiib.org/en/projects/approved/index.html

Bartels, L. (1995). The American public's defense spending preferences in the post–Cold War era. *Public Opinion Quarterly, 58*, 479–508.

Boylan, B. M., McBeath, J., & Wang, B. (2020). US–China Relations: Nationalism, the Trade War, and COVID-19. *Fudan Journal of Humanities and Social Sciences, 14*, 23–40. https://doi.org/10.1007/s40647-020-00302-6

Brenan, M. (2019). Americans' trust in mass media edges down to 41%. *Gallup*. https://news.gallup.com/poll/267047/americans-trust-mass-media-edges-down.aspx

Brewer, P. R., Graf, J., & Willnat, L. (2003). Priming or framing: Media influence on attitudes toward foreign countries. *Gazette, 65*(6), 493–508.

Brummette, J., DiStaso, M., Vafeiadis, M., & Messner, M. (2018). Read all about it: The politicization of "fake news" on Twitter. *Journalism and Mass Communication Quarterly, 95*(2), 497–517.

Chatzky, A., & McBride, J. (2019a, May 21). China's massive Belt and Road Initiative. *Council of Foreign Relations*. https://www.cfr.org/backgrounder/chinas-massive-belt-and-road-initiative

Chatzky, A., & McBride, J. (2019b, May 13). Is 'Made in China 2025' a threat to global trade? *Council of Foreign Relations*. https://www.cfr.org/backgrounder/made-china-2025-threat-global-trade

Clarke, M. (2020, May 28). Why is there so much furor over China's Belt and Road Initiative? *The Conversation*. https://theconversation.com/why-is-there-so-much-furore-over-chinas-belt-and-road-initiative-139461

CNNIC (2020, September). Statistical report on internet development in China. http://www.cnnic.com.cn/IDR/ReportDownloads/202012/P020201201530023411644.pdf

Committee on the Present Danger: China (2019). *About the Committee*. https://presentdangerchina.org/about-us/

Cordesman, A. H. (2019a, October 1). Overview of China and the United States: Cooperation, competition, and/or conflict. *Center for Strategic and International Studies*. https://www.csis.org/analysis/china-and-united-states-cooperation-competition-andor-conflict

Cordesman, A. H. (2019b). Part I. China's national strategy. In *China and the United States: Cooperation, competition, and/or conflict*. Center for Strategic and International Studies. https://csis-prod.s3.amazonaws.com/s3fs-public/publication/190807_china_and_US_part1.pdf

Devlin, K., Silver, L., & Huang, C. (2020, April 21). U.S. views of China increasingly negative amid coronavirus outbreak. *Pew Research Center*. https://www.pewresearch.org/global/2020/04/21/u-s-views-of-china-increasingly-negative-amid-coronavirus-outbreak/

Dodge, P. (Ed.). (2020). *Communication convergence in contemporary China*. Michigan State University Press.

Entman, R. (1993). Framing: Toward clarification of a fractured paradigm. *Journal of Communication, 43*, 51–8.

Espinoza, R. (2019, September 24). ABC and NBC split network news ratings crown for 2018–19 TV season. *Forbes*. https://www.forbes.com/sites/russespinoza/2019/09/24/abc-and-nbc-split-network-news-ratings-crown-for-2018-19-tv-season/#4451392f7cd9

Executive Office of the United States President. (2018). Findings of the investigation into China's acts, policies, and practices related to technology transfer, intellectual property and innovation under section 301 of the Trade Act of 1974. https://ustr.gov/sites/default/files/enforcement/301Investigations/301%20Draft%20Exec%20Summary%203.22.ustrfinal.pdf

Fletcher, R. (2017). Digital news report. *Reuters Institute*. http://www.digitalnewsreport.org/survey/2017/polarisation-in-the-news-media-2017/

French, H. (2017). *Everything under the heavens: How the past helps shape China's push for global power*. Knopf.

Frum, D. (2019, December 14). Trump's trade war was futile. *The Atlantic*. https://www.theatlantic.com/ideas/archive/2019/12/trump-got-tough-on-china-it-didnt-work/603637/

Gallup. (2019). *Americans' favorable views of China take 12-point hit.* https://news.gallup.com/poll/247559/americans-favorable-views-china-point-hit.aspx

Galtung, J. (1996). *Peace by peaceful means: Peace and conflict, development and civilization.* SAGE.

Galtung, J. (2003). Peace journalism. *Media Asia, 30*(3), 177–80.

Gamson, W. A. (1992). *Talking politics.* Cambridge University Press.

Geiger, A. W. (2019, September 11). Key findings about the online news landscape in America. *Pew Research Center.* https://www.pewresearch.org/fact-tank/2019/09/11/key-findings-about-the-online-news-landscape-in-america/

Gerhard, B. (2021, February 7). Biden can save Americans billions of dollars by ending Trump's trade war with China now. *Business Insider.* https://www.businessinsider.com/biden-must-end-trumps-trade-war-with-china-remove-tariffs-2021-2

Gottfried, J., Barthel, M., & Mitchell, A. (2017). Trump, Clinton voters divided in their main source for election news. *Pew Research Center.* https://www.journalism.org/2017/01/18/trump-clinton-voters-divided-in-their-main-source-for-election-news/

Gottfried, J., & Grieco, E. (2019, January 18). Nearly three-quarters of Republicans say the news media don't understand people like them. *Pew Research Center.* https://www.pewresearch.org/fact-tank/2019/01/18/nearly-three-quarters-of-republicans-say-the-news-media-dont-understand-people-like-them/

Greer, T. (2018, December 6). One belt, one road, one big mistake. *Foreign Policy.* https://foreignpolicy.com/2018/12/06/bri-china-belt-road-initiative-blunder/

ISOC (Information Office of the State Council of the PRC) (2018, September 25). *The facts and China's position on China-US trade friction.* http://english.scio.gov.cn/whitepapers/2018-09/25/content_63998615.htm

ISOC (2019, June 2). *China's position on the China-US economic and trade consultations.* http://www.scio.gov.cn/zfbps/32832/Document/1655934/1655934.htm

Jurkowitz, M., Mitchell, A., Shearer, E., & Walker, M. (2020, January 24). U.S. media polarization and the 2020 election: A nation divided. *Pew Research Center.* https://www.journalism.org/2020/01/24/u-s-media-polarization-and-the-2020-election-a-nation-divided/

Kawanami, T. & Harada, I. (2018, March 16). China hawk in Kudlow. *Nikkei Asian Review.* https://asia.nikkei.com/Politics/International-relations/White-House-brings-in-another-China-hawk-in-Kudlow

Kim, H, & Choi, Y.-J. (2017). Political discussion, political news, and internet use: Factors of media trust in South Korea. *Communication Research Report, 34*(3), 211–20.

Kennedy, S. (2020, September 11). Thunder out of Congress on China. *Trustee China Hand,*

Center for Strategic and International Studies. https://www.csis.org/blogs/trustee-china-hand/thunder-out-congress-china

Landers, P. (2018, December 13). The old U.S. trade war with Japan looms over today's dispute with China. *Wall Street Journal.*

Li, X., & Zhang, G. (2018). Perceived credibility of Chinese social media: Toward an integrated approach. *International Journal of Public Opinion Research, 30*(1), 79–101.

Lieberthal, K., &. Wang, J. (2014). An overview of the U.S.-China relationship. In N. Hachigian (Ed.), *Debating China: The U.S.-China Relationship in Ten Conversations* (pp. 1–20). Oxford University Press.

Lipton, G. (2018 August 14). The elusive 'better deal' with China. *The Atlantic.* https://www.theatlantic.com/international/archive/2018/08/china-trump-trade-united-states/567526/

Liu, M. (2015). *The China dream: Great power thinking and strategic posture in the post-American era.* CN Times Books.

Luo, Y. (2018, December 28). What is the US-China trade war? Why and what do to? [in Chinese]. https://mp.weixin.qq.com/s/g9ErmRWHHl-su-sal0pvCA

Manheim, J. B. (1991). *All of the people, all the time: Strategic communication and American politics.* M. E. Sharp.

Manheim, J. B. (1994). Strategic public diplomacy: Managing Kuwait's image during the Gulf Conflict. In W. L. Bennett and D. L. Paletz (Eds.), *Taken by storm: The media, public opinion, and foreign policy in the Gulf War* (pp. 131–48). University of Chicago Press.

Manheim, J. B., & Albritton, R. B. (1984). Changing national images: International public relations and media agenda setting. *American Political Science Review, 78,* 641–57.

McCombs, M. (2002, June). The agenda-setting role of the mass media in the shaping of public opinion [Paper presented in Mass Media Economics 2002 Conference]. London School of Economics. http://sticerd.lse.ac.uk/dps/extra/McCombs.pdf

Militarist Monitor. (2019, September 21). *Committee on the Present Danger.* https://militarist-monitor.org/profile/committee_on_the_present_danger/

Miller, K. (2017). *As hyper-conservative media surged, Republicans' trust in news cratered.* TechCrunch.com. https://techcrunch.com/2017/03/19/as-hyper-conservative-media-surged-republicans-trust-in-news-cratered/

Mitchell, A., Gottfried, J., Kiley, J., & Matsa, K. E. (2014). Political polarization & media habits. *Pew Research Center.* https://www.journalism.org/2014/10/21/political-polarization-media-habits/

Mutikani, L. (February 5, 2020). U.S. trade deficit narrows in 2019 for first time in six years. *Reuters.com.* https://www.reuters.com/article/

us-usa-economy/u-s-trade-deficit-narrows-in-2019-for-first-time-in-six-years-idUSKBN1ZZ1WP

Müller, P., Schemer, C., Wettstein, M., Schulz, A., Wirz, D. S., Engesser, S., & Wirth, W. (2017). The polarizing impact of news coverage on populist attitudes in the public: Evidence from a panel study in four European democracies. *Journal of Communication, 67*(6), 968–92.

New York Times. (2018, July 6). How the 'biggest trade war in economic history' is playing out. *New York Times.*

Office of the US Trade Representative. (2019, June 15). *USTR issues tariffs on Chinese products in response to unfair trade practices.* https://ustr.gov/about-us/policy-offices/press-office/press-releases/2018/june/ustr-issues-tariffs-chinese-products

Page, S. (2020, October 8). Read the full transcript of vice-presidential debate between Mike Pence and Kamala Harris. *USA Today.*

Pasquino, G. (2008). Populism and democracy. In D. Albertazzi and D. McDonnell (Eds.), *Twenty-first century populism: The spectre of western European democracy* (pp. 15–29). Palgrave Macmillan.

Peffley, M., & Hurwitz, J. (1992). International events and foreign policy beliefs: Public responses to changing Soviet–US relations. *American Journal of Political Science, 36,* 431–461.

Peng, Z. (2004). Representation of China: An across time analysis of coverage in the New York Times and Los Angeles Times. *Asian Journal of Communication, 14*(1), 53–67.

Perry, D. K. (1987). The image gap: How international news affects perceptions of nations, *Journalism Quarterly, 64,* 416–21.

Prior, M. (2005). News vs. entertainment: How increasing media choice widens gaps in political knowledge and turnout. *American Journal of Political Science, 49*(3), 577–92.

Reuters. (2021, January 14). *U.S.-China trade war has cost up to 245,000 U.S. jobs: Business group study.* https://www.reuters.com/article/us-usa-trade-china-jobs/us-china-trade-war-has-cost-up-to-245000-us-jobs-business-group-study-idUSKBN29J2O9

Sanger, D. E. (2021, February 23). Biden declares 'America is back' on international stage. *New York Times.*

Schneider-Petsinger, M. (2017, March 2). *Wilbur Ross is in the driver's seat on US trade policy—For now.* Chatham House. https://www.chathamhouse.org/expert/comment/wilbur-ross-driver-s-seat-us-trade-policy-now

Seipel B. (2019, December 27). Fed study: Trump tariffs backfired, caused job losses and higher prices. *The Hill.* https://thehill.com/policy/finance/476100-fed-study-trump-tariffs-backfired-caused-job-losses-and-higher-prices

Shearer, E. (2018, December 10). Social media outpaces print newspapers in the U.S. as a news source. *Pew Research Center.* https://www.pewresearch.org/fact-tank/2018/12/10/social-media-outpaces-print-newspapers-in-the-u-s-as-a-news-source/

Soroka, S. N. (2003). Media, public opinion, and foreign policy. *Harvard International Journal of Press/Politics 8*(1), 27–48.

Swanson, A. (2019, July 20). A new red scare is reshaping Washington. *New York Times.*

Swift, A. (2016, September 14). Americans' trust in mass media sinks to new low. *Gallup.* https://news.gallup.com/poll/195542/americans-trust-mass-media-sinks-new-low.aspx

Tai, C. (2018, October 20). What Japan can teach China about the American art of (trade) war. *South China Morning Post.* https://www.scmp.com/week-asia/politics/article/2169427/what-japan-can-teach-china-about-american-art-trade-war

Donald Trump [@RealDonaldTrump]. (2018, March 2). *Trade wars are good, and easy to win* [Tweet; @RealDonaldTrump is no longer available]. https://twitter.com.

Turcotte, J., York, C., Irving, J., Scholl, R., & Pingree, R. (2015). News recommendation from social media opinion leaders: Effects on media trust and information seeking. *Journal of Computer-Mediated Communication, 20*(5), 520–35.

U.S.–China Security Review Commission. (2002). *Report to Congress.* https://www.uscc.gov/annual-report/2002-annual-report-congress

Wallace, C. (2019, August 9). Trade war hurting China's economy. *Forbes.* https://www.forbes.com/sites/charleswallace1/2019/08/09/trade-war-hurting-chinas-economy/?sh=1adc82f34035

Wei, R., Lo, V. H., & Golan, G. (2017). Examining the relationship between presumed influence of US news about China and the support for the Chinese government's global public relations campaigns. *International Journal of Communication, 11*, 2964–81.

Westwood, S. J., Peterson, E., & Lelkes, Y. (2019). Are there still limits on partisan prejudice? *Public Opinion Quarterly, 83*(3), 584–97.

Whipple, K. N., & Shermak, J. L. (2020). The enemy of my enemy is my tweet: How #NotTheEnemy Twitter discourse defended the journalistic paradigm. *Journalism & Mass Communication Quarterly, 97*(1), 188–210.

Willnat, L., Tang, S., & Zhang, H. (2016). Friend or foe: The role of media in how Americans and Chinese perceive each other [in Chinese]. *Journalism Bimonthly, 6*, 47–58.

Willnat, L., Tang, S., Zhang, H., & Shi, J. (2018). *How Chinese and Americans think about journalists and the media: A comparative look at perceived roles and values.* Annual Conference of the Association for Education in Journalism and Mass Communication (AEJMC), Washington, DC.

Willnat, L., Tang, L., Shi, J., & Zhan, N. (2019). *National images as integrated schemas: How news and national images shape perceptions of the Sino-U.S. trade war*. Annual Conference of the Midwest Association for Public Opinion Research (MAPOR), Chicago, IL.

Xiang, D. (2013). China's image on international English language social media. *Journal of International Communication, 19*(2), 252–71.

Yang, G., & Wei, W. (Eds.). (2021). *Engaging social media in China: Platforms, publics, and production*. Michigan State University Press.

PART 1

Economic and International Contexts

The China Knot

A Brief History of U.S.–China Trade Relations Leading to the Trade War

Steven Beckman and Stephen J. Hartnett

O n June 29, 1998, U.S. President Bill Clinton spoke to students at Beijing University (or Peking University). Clinton was committed to bringing China into the world of trade partners, yet he faced a bruising political fight over the question of China's joining the World Trade Organization (WTO). For those in favor of globalization, the thought of China entering the WTO sparked dreams of billions of new consumers, the opening of new financial and cultural markets, and, perhaps, global economic integration nudging China to accelerate its "opening and reform" in politics as well as economics. For opponents of this process, enabling China to join the WTO amounted to granting the People's Republic of China (PRC) a pass on its ongoing human rights controversies and forging an unholy compromise fueled by corporate, rather than national, interests (Hartnett, 2021). Fully aware of the fault-lines, Clinton said to his audience, "As you build a new China, America wants to build a new relationship with you. We want China to be successful, secure, and open, working with us for a more peaceful and prosperous world." In a line that encapsulates

This research was supported through a grant from the U.S. Department of Education, through its Centers for International Business, Education, and Research at the University of Colorado Denver. This research does not necessarily represent the policies of the U.S. Department of Education. For this assistance, the authors thank CU Denver CIBER director, Dr. Manuel Serapio.

Clinton's thinking from this period, he pledged, "we can clearly accomplish so much more by walking together rather than standing apart" (Clinton, 1998a).

Envisioning globalization as a form of mutual enrichment and alliance-building, Clinton imagined America and China "working toward a common destiny" (Clinton, 1998b). That same day, while visiting the U.S. Embassy in Beijing, the president thanked his assembled team for doing the on-the-ground labor of proving that "engagement is working." An upbeat Clinton focused on the need to convey "the message of cooperation and optimism" (Clinton, 1998c). From this perspective, supporting globalization meant inviting former adversaries and once-underdeveloped nations into a seamless market with shared values (Friedman, 2005; Hartnett & Stengrim, 2006).

Clinton's dream was realized when the PRC joined the WTO in 2001. Yet ever since then, the United States has felt betrayed by the results, for coaxing China into the WTO has not led to a new world of open markets and liberal governments. Rather, as Minxin Pei (2008) argues in *China's Trapped Transition*, gaining access to international markets has strengthened the Communist Party's stranglehold over the nation's economy, making its political control virtually unassailable and its international relations less flexible, not more (see Mann, 2007). Hence, the dominant view in the United States is that the PRC used its entry into the WTO to manipulate global trade flows in ways that hurt international partners while strengthening China's Communist regime. As articulated by U.S. Vice President Mike Pence in a speech attacking China:

> After the fall of the Soviet Union, we assumed a free China was inevitable. Heady with our optimism at the turn of the 21st century, America agreed to give Beijing open access to our economy, and we brought China into the World Trade Organization. Previous administrations made this choice in the hope that freedom in China would expand in all its forms ... But that hope has gone unfulfilled (Pence, 2018, paragraph 3).

Understanding the U.S.–China "trade war" requires beginning with this sense of dashed hopes, for Trump's actions in 2016 and after were the manifestation of twenty years of American frustration. This anger was so raw, the sense of conflict so sharp, that Trump, Pence, and their supporters warned that China's trade practices were leading toward "a new Cold War" (see Pence, 2018; Perlez, 2018; Rogin, 2018).

For Trump and the Republican hawks driving his economic and foreign policies, the problems go to the core of the Chinese economic and political systems. In *Death by China*, one of Trump's top trade advisors, Peter Navarro (2011) writes:

How can any . . . scholar credibly defend a totalitarian regime that knowingly sells products that maim and kill us, hacks our computers to pirate our intellectual property, launches mercantilist attacks upon our economy to steal our jobs, uses planet earth like a giant ashtray, treats its own workers like a bunch of slaves, and is arming itself to the teeth so it can sink our navy and shoot our satellites out of the sky and have its way with the world? (chapter 15, pp. 215–16).

Navarro is one among the champions of "China threat" discourse, which has been pushed in a raft of books with titles like *The Beijing Consensus: How China's Authoritarian Model Will Dominate the Twenty-First Century* (Halper, 2010), *The China Threat: How the People's Republic Targets America* (Gertz, 2000), and *When China Rules the World* (Jacques, 2009). From this perspective, the only solution to the China "knot" is to cut all ties. As Bown and Irwin note (2019):

To satisfy the United States, China would have to end forced technology transfers, stop stealing intellectual property, curtail subsidies to state-owned enterprises, abandon industrial policies designed to gain technological dominance, stop harassing foreign firms operating in China, and begin to open markets that the government deliberately closed to give control to domestic firms. In other words, the United States wants China to turn its state-dominated economic system into a market based one overnight. . . . The goal is . . . the economic decoupling of the United States and China (pp. 133–134).

If we consider this oscillation from President Clinton's optimism in the late 1990s through "China threat" discourse and President Trump's angry isolationism in 2020—with Bown and Irwin's summary encapsulating the arguments made by hawkish Republicans—we can see that the "trade war" is a much larger argument about contrasting modes of governance, different forms of trade, and clashing expectations about the norms and practices of international relations.

To understand how these debates have gone so wrong, leading to Trump's "trade war" and China's strong nationalist responses, this chapter reviews our two nations' recent economic history. As we will see, much of the difficulty stems from Americans hoping China would not only modernize rapidly, but would do so along routes modeled by other democratic, or at least democratizing nations (see Gilley, 2004; Nathan & Diamond, 2013). Yet the Communist Party never intended to pursue this model, meaning the Americans and Chinese have been talking past each other. While the other chapters in this book explore the nuances of this economics-based miscommunication, this chapter lays the foundation for that work by tracking some of the key aspects of U.S.–China trade relations.

U.S.–China Trade: Main Forces Prior to the WTO

Following the mass-produced starvation of the Great Leap Forward and then the Cultural Revolution (Dikötter, 2011), hunger drove the villagers of Xiaogang to secretly adopt private plots in the hopes of producing more food (Lei, 2019). Because it took these first steps away from state-managed Communism toward capitalism, Xiaogang became the birthplace of rural economic reform in China. But even while exploring new market techniques, each villager pledged to maintain all commitments to the PRC in terms of crops delivered and prices accepted. Still, within this new local farming model, any additional output not claimed by the Party could be used or sold by the villagers as they saw fit. Knowing these transformations carried great risks, the villagers pledged to raise each other's families should some be arrested. However, the experiment in Xiaogang proved successful, and so "mixed markets" soon spread to other regions of China.

After China's economic reform in the 1980s, anyone dependent on goods provided through the system of state-controlled prices and quantities continued to receive them. An urban worker seeking food at state-controlled prices could still do so, but she could also buy additional goods, beyond the state allotment, on the private market. These goods sold on open markets at privately set prices were new options that led to consistent economic growth (Lau et al., 2000). While this mixed market experiment led to increased production, it also fueled corruption, as people tried to acquire state goods at state prices, not for their use, but to sell them at higher private market prices for a profit (Wu, 2005). As a consequence, the moral simplicity of Mao-era Communism was fracturing into Deng-era confusions that led both to increased production and wealth but also to the first cracks in the old "iron rice bowl" system.

Filling the iron rice bowl first required extracting the rice through a household registration system, codified in 1958, which identified rural or urban workers and severely restricted their mobility. Modeled on a similar system used in the Soviet Union, rural workers' chief function was to provide food for the cities (Chan,

2010). As private markets gradually developed, a new urban-rural divide emerged. Urban workers had better access to education and health care and were free to seek employment in private firms in the cities. Rural workers, on the other hand, needed permission to live in cities, creating a pool of 700 to 800 million rural workers subject to discrimination. This pool of less educated and poorly paid workers provided low-wage labor to state-owned enterprises, township and village enterprises, and the export sector (Chan, 2010). This system of better-paid urban workers and low-wage rural workers prompted Navarro (above) to claim China treats its workers "as a bunch of slaves." More recently, some rural workers in China have been encouraged by the Chinese government to move to cities, freeing land for development (Zhan, 2017), and creating a new segment of urban dwellers the Party hopes will drive increased domestic consumption (Conley, 2018).

Across these issues, what is striking is watching China modernize rapidly while managing the world's largest national population. The evolutions noted here, regarding how markets stabilize prices, how workers adjust to new modes of production, and how cities and their surrounding countrysides build new relations that are both competitive and supportive, unfolded in America from roughly the middle of the eighteenth century. But in China they have occurred only since the 1980s, leading to dizzying transformations inside the nation-state (Osnos, 2015). At the same time, by marshaling its enormous rural workforce, China has managed to engage in international trade with a depressed wage structure. These low wages made its products incredibly cheap and provided the foundation for the grievances that would blossom into Trump's trade war.

Globalization adds another layer of forces to consider. Opening trade with China coincided with dramatic global changes driven by declining transportation costs. Krugman and Venables's (1995) international trade theory imagines two regions, North and South, that form a center and a periphery. Compressed to a few essential elements, the theory finds that globalization is defined by three main stages. In the first stage, transportation costs are so high that production is located near the point of sale, hence accounting for small-scale production of goods in workshops throughout the United States and China. Steamships and railroads usher in the second stage. Manufacturing plants produce more efficiently at a higher scale near large, wealthy concentrations of customers with poorer regions importing, and not producing, manufactured goods. These few manufacturing locations enjoy high wages and grow rapidly as they create and attract skilled workers and investors; the periphery imports the cheap mass-produced goods from abroad and produces mostly agricultural goods resulting in lower wages, fewer investment opportunities, and slower growth. The theory predicts a center and periphery without assuming exploitation, political domination, colonies, or large firms. The source of the center's power derives from the size of the market and the wide variety of goods and jobs available, which attract new firms and workers. As this productive capacity grows, it creates a cascade of opportunities, so the emerging urban centers drain the countryside of people and resources.

Eventually, as the wage gap between the two regions grows and transport costs fall even more with container ships and airlines, it becomes more profitable to locate manufacturing in the low-wage countryside and to ship products to the large markets. This shift in manufacturing facilities to low-wage areas defines the third stage, which, as Krugman and Venables warn, comes with consequences: "The final phase of the process of globalization described by our model, in which the spread of industry to the South reduces relative and perhaps absolute Northern wages, obviously corresponds to the fears of many commentators on the world economy" (p. 874). Researchers have documented the separation into poor and rich areas in the second stage (Pritchett, 1997) and the declining difference between rich and poor areas as manufacturing spreads globally in the third stage (Rodrik, 2013). To translate this theory for our purposes, China grew quickly during its post-Mao "opening and reform" period by marshaling low-wage rural workers, who produced goods that were highly competitive on emerging global markets, especially in the United States. This process hurt workers in the United States, whose high wages and job-related benefits made them less competitive, even while they enjoyed China's cheaper goods.

Thinking globally, this process was reproduced in multiple developing nations, resulting in job creation abroad, cheaper goods on the global market, and declining jobs for high-wage workers in the developed nations that were now shipping their manufacturing facilities overseas. If we use an index of international investment and money flows provided by Reinhart and Rogoff (2009, p 156), then the period from 1840 to 1946 marked the phase when a few geographic locations became manufacturing and cultural centers. Then, from 1946 to roughly 1980, markets slowly recovered from the devastation of World War II and the destruction of international shipping, banking, and trade regulations by building such post-War institutions as the World Bank, the IMF, the WTO, and so on. Beginning roughly around 1980, the index shows a return to prewar patterns as capital flows resume. But, given the lower transport costs, manufacturing slowly began to move to lower-wage countries.

This resulted in tremendous profits for the corporations able to take advantage of both international markets and low-wage rural workers, yet also slowly eroded manufacturing in developed nations.

Precisely as predicted by Krugman and Venables, these global movements of production capacity helped developing nations while undermining the working classes of the developed nations. As Rodrik (2017) warned, only concerted international responses by governments could render globalization fair and just. But with governments lacking the will and international bodies lacking the authority to manage the process, even while international elites leapt at the chance to exploit it, "globalization would deepen societal divisions, exacerbate distributional problems, and undermine domestic social bargains" (Rodrik, p. ix). Over the past two decades, the consequences of this process have accumulated in America's former industrial areas, where workers lost jobs because of these international factors, even while their former employers reaped immense profits (Stiglitz, 2002). Trump sought to capitalize on the resentment these processes created by naming China as the cause of America's pain. Trump's strategy was largely successful, as voters who switched from supporting Obama to Trump in 2016 "exhibit greater racial hostility, more economic insecurity, and more negative attitudes towards trade agreements and immigration" (Rodrik, 2020, p. 7).

China's Admission to the WTO

The shift in manufacturing from the United States (as the center) to China (as the former periphery) hit the United States most painfully in its former industrial centers, creating the "rust belt blues" (Stern, 2016). These same forces affected China differently because international markets enabled China's state-run industries to pursue new opportunities. However, globalization also forced the Chinese government to work with an international array of lawyers, bankers, and politicians. Indeed, China's entry into the WTO implied accepting decisions made by a group of international judges following an agreed-upon set of rules, not party doctrine, and accepting a set of global prices created by markets that were not subject to party decree. At a time when the Chinese government was already under severe stress, especially following China's international ostracization following the events of 1989, joining the WTO seemed to signal its willingness to begin ceding some economic control. For example, China used low-interest loans to state-owned enterprises

(SOEs) to control the economy, but rapid growth was achieved by converting some SOEs to private enterprises (Storesletten & Zilibotti, 2014). These transformations appeared to foreshadow China eventually choosing between economic growth and party control. No wonder then that the United States saw China's WTO membership as a commitment to market economics, declining party control, and hence a step toward Clinton's dream of a common destiny.

But this was never China's intention. In fact, Premier Zhu proclaimed to President George W. Bush in 1998 that China was *corporatizing* state assets, not *privatizing* them (Wu, 2016). On this interpretation, WTO membership would expand, not contract, state power as state corporations gained access to global markets (Pei, 2008; Yan, 2002). Using this corporatist model within the WTO's framework, China's global visibility, membership in international institutions, and global leadership potential all increased. The Constitution of the PRC states how the people of China retain control of assets through their representatives in the state: "The State encourages, supports and guides the development of the non-public sectors of the economy and, in accordance with law, exercises supervision and control over the non-public sectors of the economy" (chapter 1, article 11). In short, the Chinese government figured out a way to take advantage of the trade benefits of joining the WTO while maintaining its authoritarian control at home.

President Trump has made China-bashing a key part of his isolationist rhetoric. Yet, it is important to remember that the United States has long understood that wages in China and other developing countries were remarkably low and would challenge American workers. For example, in the 1999 meeting of the WTO, the United States pressed unsuccessfully for labor standards in the form of minimum wages and nondiscrimination, ostensibly to lend assistance to the workers of the world (Irwin, 2020), but also to protect its labor markets. Applied to China, these standards would have encouraged fundamental changes in its labor markets, perhaps most importantly in how the government regulated migration between urban and rural areas. Of course, the Chinese government was opposed to acceding to such demands. Economists thinking globally also opposed this move to regulate international wages and work-conditions along models provided by the United States and other developed nations. Krugman (1997), for example, argued against applying First World economic criteria to developing nations such as China:

> The advantages of established First World industries are still formidable. The only reason developing countries have been able to compete with those industries

is their ability to offer employers cheap labor. Deny them that ability, and you might well deny them the prospect of continuing industrial growth, even reverse the growth that has been achieved. And since export-oriented growth, for all its injustice, has been a huge boon for the workers in those nations, anything that curtails that growth is very much against their interests. A policy of good jobs in principle, but no jobs in practice, might assuage our consciences, but it is no favor to its alleged beneficiaries (p. 3).

The "injustice" of export-oriented growth is that the workers are paid little, but investors will not build factories in the rural periphery unless they can derive substantial profit from doing so. Wealth in New York, Paris, or London is generated by low wages in Sri Lanka, China, or Mexico. In this sense, Peter Navarro has it wrong—it is the global development process that pays workers little, not Chinese "slavery."

The paradox is that only allowing the process to continue offers any realistic hope of higher wages. Developing nations with low wages will, at least following Krugman's theory, evolve and eventually become labor markets more like those already formed in Europe and America. This is the reality behind Krugman's argument that the reduction of Northern wages is due to the spread of industry to the South. If markets are allowed to operate unimpeded and without redistribution, local labor markets in developed nations will suffer, while global elites and labor in developing countries prosper. This logic sounds harsh to Americans who have lost their jobs or seen their wages stagnate. Yet, the fact is that from 1980 to 2015, the bottom 50 percent of Chinese workers experienced real income gains averaging 4.6 percent per year (Alvaredo et al., 2018), while providing American consumers with affordable goods. As we will discuss below, the consequences of this process have been devastating for working-class Americans.

China's Trade Practices after Joining the WTO and Debates about Economic Models

WTO judges hear complaints about unfair trade practices and render decisions. Two main categories, dumping and state support of private businesses, dominate their agendas. Should WTO judges rule in favor of a particular country, that country is entitled to impose a tariff to offset any unfair trade practices. In contrast, the opposing country is not allowed to retaliate with tariffs of their own. However, the WTO cannot punish any country directly. Member nations comply with WTO decisions because they value the WTO as a mediating body. However, what is considered fair or unfair is determined entirely by each member nation.

In practice, then, the WTO facilitates international commerce while lacking the powers to enforce judgments. The nonprofit consumer advocacy organization, Public Citizen, even argued that "the WTO has functioned principally to establish rules for the global economy that benefit transnational corporations at the expense of national and local economies; workers, farmers, and indigenous peoples; health and safety; and the environment" (Public Citizen, 2020, para. 2). Moreover, these same "rules" have worked to the benefit of member nations. For example, Irwin (2020) has shown that from 1946 to 2000, WTO member nations enjoyed 43 percent more trade than non-member nations. Within this framework, dumping is the complaint most likely to be successful; it is therefore the complaint most often used.

Dumping

Dumping is defined as an export that has been priced below the domestic price. The difference between the two prices is the "dumping margin." For example, if the price for a good made in China is $10, but the product is sold in the United States for $8, then the dumping margin is $2, justifying an "anti-dumping duty" of $2. Such a duty would be a tariff applied by the U.S. government on products imported from China that have been found to violate the WTO anti-dumping rules. The original justification for these dumping policies was to deter predatory pricing, which is pricing below cost to drive out competitors and reap monopoly profits through higher prices later. This justification has fallen into disfavor, as illustrated by a U.S. Supreme Court decision that finds "predation is implausible" (Hemphill & Weiser, 2017, p. 2048).

An alternate explanation is provided by Brander and Krugman (1983): Large, imperfectly competitive firms have an established customer base in their home markets, which tolerate a higher price, while a lower foreign price helps create a customer base abroad. Under this interpretation, dumping duties defend the home market against foreign competition. What is interesting in these norms is the sense of *intentionality*, as if prices are set by firms to acquire market share as intentional acts of what Brander and Spencer (1984) call "trade warfare." But this thinking is difficult to apply to China because Chinese companies have access to low-interest loans, cheap land, and low-cost materials—including labor—meaning that Chinese prices are virtually guaranteed to be below the cost of a similar U.S.-made product.

While the inherent price differential between American and Chinese products may seem unfair, it is a common problem with non-market economies. To correct such imbalances in international wages and prices, the WTO allows member nations to calculate the dumping margin by determining a fair price based upon figures derived from a "surrogate" country. In the 2012 Chinese steel wheel case, for example, the surrogate country was Indonesia. The dumping margins calculated by the U.S. Department of Commerce ranged from 45 percent to 190 percent, justifying tariffs in equal magnitude (Irwin, 2020). Thus, while manufacturers with direct or indirect government support may produce cheaper goods, this balancing mechanism raises the price of those goods in the consumer markets of developed nations. This hurts consumers yet protects market share and workers in those markets.

Upon entering the WTO in 2001, China agreed to be designated a non-market economy for fifteen years, therefore rendering it subject to WTO dumping suits based on constructed value (Wu, 2016). China faced a disproportionate number of such suits, which severely affected its export of commodities (Irwin, 2020). After 2016, China sued the WTO to be considered a market economy but withdrew the suit when it became clear that the ruling would not be favorable (Miles, 2019). As these examples show, much of America's anger at China reflects these immensely complicated wage variations in international markets. However, regulating domestic wages is far beyond the WTO's authority, leaving it unable to manage these conflicts. And so, as a consequence, the Trump administration bypassed the WTO and, claiming "national security" was at risk, levied its tariffs, ostensibly to stop alleged Chinese "dumping."

State Support of Businesses

The WTO considers state support for businesses that export products unfair and allows the importing country to impose "countervailing duties" (CVDs) in the form of tariffs designed to offset this support. In addition, private companies can give each other discounts; no CVD is allowed in this case. The WTO then must determine if the support provided by one company to another is directly or indirectly linked to the government—a process that became more complex after China joined the WTO. The thinking here is that if, say, General Motors is trying to produce cars as an independent entity, then it is not fair to expect it to compete with a similar company that enjoys large subsidies from the Chinese government. From the American perspective, such government support amounts to an unfair trade practice. From the Chinese perspective, this practice makes perfect sense: Why wouldn't the government of a developing nation do everything in its power to help its domestic producers succeed? The conflict hinges on differing notions of what constitutes a proper relationship between the government and markets, with the U.S. model expecting a wide margin of separation between the two and the Chinese model based on a much tighter relationship.

We should note that while the division between independent corporations and supporting government entities is exceptionally murky in China, it is by no means clear in the United States. For example, Boeing receives indirect subsidies on its civilian aircraft because the military versions are purchased through government contracts, while Airbus receives direct subsidies from the European Union. This question of how direct and/or indirect support from the government impacts specific corporations has been the source of many suits and countersuits (Irwin, 2020). Particularly around new media technologies, artificial intelligence, and other R&D-rich industries, American corporations enjoy tight and deep relations with the U.S. government. In fact, as Jia and Nieborg (2022) note, we are entering a new phase of global capitalism wherein Chinese and American corporations now invest in each other, trade with each other, and even launch joint ventures supported by one or both governments. These examples raise another issue, as many of the firms are too large to be considered competitive and the struggle may well be over sizeable profits with governments helping their "national champions" extract what they can (Irwin, 2020). It is important for readers to understand that these debates about how state support to private entities skews markets is not just a matter of clashing national interests. Rather, global capitalism is evolving in ways that render state interests, corporate interests, and both worker and consumer benefits increasingly murky.

Nonetheless, in China's responses to these questions, the PRC has never wavered from trying to put the Party's interests first. For example, if, in response to the threat of WTO-imposed CVDs, China was to privatize its state assets, then government control of the economy would be eroded. Instead, the Party moved toward corporatizing state assets in 2003 with a series of reforms designed to maintain rapid growth and government control (Wu, 2016). Three organizations were created during these reforms: the State-Owned Assets Supervision and Administration Commission (SASAC), which was placed in charge of all SOEs; the Central Huijin, which bailed out the four state banks mired in non-performing loans to often corrupt SOEs and took majority ownership in exchange; and the National Development and Reform Commission (NDRC), which creates the five-year plans, sets prices of key resources (such as electricity, oil, natural gas, and water), administers the anti-monopoly law, approves large public and private projects, and coordinates industrial policies. The Communist Party appoints the heads of all three agencies.

Through these agencies, the Party has sought to reap the benefits of global trade while maintaining its strict political control at home. However, this is not an easy task as the divisions between state and private firms have become blurred as state banks make loans to private firms, private and state firms have ownership stakes in each other, and most have party committees in their leadership (Russo, 2019). Despite Trump-like arguments about a unified Chinese market invading America, these examples indicate that capitalism is evolving in complex and even baffling ways in China as well. In summary, ever since "opening and reform" began in the 1980s—and especially since China joined the WTO in 2001—the Chinese government has begun exploring different strategies of corporatist modeling, in which labor markets, producers, and consumers evolve in a capitalist direction under firm government control. To the Chinese, this makes perfect sense; to the Americans, this arrangement points to unfair economic practices meriting strong tariffs and CVDs to try to level the playing field.

Intellectual Property and Allegations of Theft

Within U.S.–China trade relations, the issue of intellectual property rights is the most hotly debated one, with most American observers alleging that the Chinese government engages in a clear pattern of theft (Hartnett, 2011; Krekel et al., 2009). Intellectual property agreements were first added to the list of WTO responsibilities in a series of negotiations conducted between 1986 and 1994, collectively known as the Uruguay Round. As part of the "grand bargain," developed countries won assurances that patents and copyrights would be enforced, even in developing countries, while developing countries were promised lower tariffs on their agricultural imports (Irwin, 2020). The United States, in particular, pressed for the enforcement of patents and the collection of royalties and licensing fees for pharmaceuticals, motion pictures, music, and software, hence seeking to protect its advantages in high-tech and other advanced R&D fields, cultural production, and medical research. To the Americans, this policy made great sense; to China and other rapidly developing nations—India and Brazil in particular—the "grand bargain" felt like an imperial defense strategy by which the United States sought to prevent developing nations from evolving their own domestic markets in these areas. This debate has been particularly heated regarding life-saving pharmaceuticals. In this case, U.S.-based corporations have argued that their products should be sold at market prices, for the R&D behind their products cost billions of dollars. But selling AIDs-related drugs in the developing world at U.S.-based market prices would lead to mass death, as impoverished consumers cannot afford the drugs. The issue is so pressing that the WTO now allows "compulsory licensing," whereby local pharmaceutical firms, often in Brazil or India, may compel foreign producers to share their technology to enable sales in developing countries (Irwin, 2020). In this case, the WTO facilitated a decision-making process where social justice took precedence over corporate profits; at the same time, this "compulsory licensing" set a precedent whereby developing nations could force developed nations to share their intellectual property rights.

Whereas U.S.-based entities have long complained about such arrangements, particularly regarding the cost of doing business in China, the number of intellectual property disputes with China has decreased since China developed its own intellectual properties. Now, most intellectual property disputes occur outside the WTO's purview. For example, China pressures foreign companies to share their trade secrets and technology with their Chinese partners as a condition for approving investments in China. Of course, foreign companies are reluctant to share information with state-affiliated firms for fear the information will leak to competitors. However, even Chinese investments in the United States and Europe are seen as partly motivated by an attempt to acquire technology that will be shared by the state throughout China.

These fears are heightened because state ownership of private firms in China is often hidden in complex ownership chains (Wübbeke et al., 2016). As Yang and Wei (2021) and Hoyng and Chong (2022) have argued, we may be witnessing a new phase of globalization in which the former questions of wages, transportation, and commodity pricing give way to new concerns about the "platformization" and "financialization" of communication and technology infrastructures that transcend national borders and raise serious questions about national sovereignty. For these reasons, intellectual property disputes that raise national security issues fall outside the WTO's purview.

For example, Huawei is a Chinese manufacturer of telecommunications equipment whose CFO is currently detained in Canada under an extradition request from the United States for violating sanctions against Iran (Whalen, 2019). However, the primary concern is the possibility for China to eavesdrop through Huawei's equipment on a wide range of U.S. businesses, private individuals, and government agencies. As a result, President Trump has called for a ban of Huawei's participation in Western 5G networks (Kennedy, 2020). Yet outright bans of all Huawei devices are likely to be counterproductive, as global supply chains stretch across the United States, Europe, South Korea, and Japan. Moreover, if the United States bans Chinese telecommunications and technology products, China will have additional reasons to subsidize local production—a move that would also undermine U.S. companies' access to the Chinese market. The Huawei case shows how local economic practices overlap with international markets and national security issues (Wan & Reckard, 2020), creating a labyrinth of mutual interdependence but also areas of conflict.

Currency Manipulation to Achieve a Trade Surplus

On April 22, 2015, Trump tweeted that "China has a backdoor into the Trans-Pacific Partnership (TPP). The deal does not address currency manipulation. China is laughing at us" (Taylor, 2018). Shortly after taking office, Trump abandoned the TPP because he feared China would join later and then use currency manipulation to maintain a trade surplus. The basic idea is that an underpriced currency makes Chinese goods cheaper for Americans while making American goods expensive for Chinese, contributing to the U.S. trade deficit with China. The proposition that developing countries benefit from currency manipulation early in the development process has strong academic support. For example, Rodrik (2008) found an undervalued Chinese currency in the 1990s coincided with more rapid economic growth in China. While several other developing countries have shown strong economic growth due to undervalued currencies, Rodrik (2008) argues that China, in particular, benefitted from a trade surplus in its transition to a market economy.

Krugman and Venables's (1995) trade theory offers another possible explanation for currency imbalances between China and the United States: the lower value of the currency speeds the relocation of firms from the United States to China by making Chinese land and machinery cheaper (for debates on Foreign Direct Investment, or FDI, see Bean, in this book). Rodrik's (2008) estimates imply that currency undervaluation leads to growth benefits until per capita income reaches the level of Spain or Taiwan, at which point an undervalued currency becomes counterproductive. Given that China's per capita income has historically been well below that level, China has benefitted from undervaluation. The question remains, though, whether China's currency is currently undervalued. Liu and Woo (2018) estimate that China's currency was undervalued by about 20 percent as recently as 2011, but it has averaged out to zero between 2014 and 2017. Thus, as in the case of Chinese wages, which were once incredibly low but have begun to rise, China's initial entry into international markets was fueled by currency manipulations that have since begun to move toward international standards.

Thus, China has modernized its domestic economy on a remarkably tight schedule, meaning that while its wage structure and currency were once indicative of an underdeveloped nation, they are now moving closer to international standards. It offers no relief to unemployed Americans, but what China needs to continue this welcome progress is not more bullying from Trump or pressure from the WTO, but simply the time for its markets to continue maturing.

The Devastating Effects of Globalization on America's Working Class

Compared to the "golden period" from 1946 to 1980, when wages in the United States grew consistently, Krugman and Venables's (1995) trade theory leads us to expect stagnating wages for the less skilled from roughly 1980 to the present. Avaredo et al. (2018) provide data on these two periods for American incomes: Following World War II, the income of the bottom 50 percent of Americans, adjusted for inflation, rose 102 percent between 1946 and 1980, but then only increased 1 percent between 1980 and 2014. The top 1 percent, on the other hand, saw gains of 47 percent between 1946 and 1980 and an astonishing 204 percent between 1980 and 2014. The relationship between degrees of globalization and polarization of income in the United States is striking and explains the rise of movements such as Occupy Wall Street and charges that the "1 percent" amount to a new plutocracy. The stagnation of workers' incomes in developed countries is a global phenomenon consistent with the Krugman and Venables's (1995) trade theory. It explains the rise of anger-driven nationalism across Europe, where the once robust working class has seen its living standard decline. Based on economic data collected from 1988 to 2008, Milanovic (2016) shows zero income growth for the lower-middle class of the industrial world—even as global incomes rose by an average of 50 percent during this period. Overall then, globalization has led to three interrelated effects: Income for workers in developing nations has risen dramatically over the past decades, while workers in the developed nations saw their wages stagnate and their standard of living crater. In addition, a new global elite has seen their incomes explode, producing a new class of international tycoons who benefit the most from globalization processes.

Because China has had one of the fastest-growing economies in the world, it perfectly illustrates each of these three effects of globalization. It therefore comes as no surprise that President Trump based his "America first" rhetoric in large part on bashing China. While such an assault may seem extreme, some economists have provided useful evidence supporting such an international economic outlook. For example, Autor et al. (2013) show that job losses in a community create persistent local unemployment. While manufacturing jobs are a declining percentage of the American labor force as robots replace workers and the economy shifts to services, the authors find that trade with China explains about 25 percent of the manufacturing jobs lost, contributing to "public ambivalence toward globalization and specific anxiety about increasing trade with China" (p. 2159). A key part of the problem, they explain, is that whereas earlier generations of Americans took advantage of mobility to find new jobs in new markets, worker mobility has dramatically decreased, meaning that the unemployed are less likely to find work by moving.

The concepts of globalization and polarization are illustrated clearly by Davis and Hilsenrath (2016), who focus on Hickory, a small city in North Carolina that was hard-hit by what Autor et al. (2013) call the "China syndrome." The community specialized in furniture production, believing the product's bulky nature would keep transport costs high and thereby protect it from competition with China. However, when transportation costs fell, production shifted swiftly to China. Skilled workers left, wages stagnated, and an attempt to reintroduce a specialized furniture firm failed. The United States had experienced job losses from imports before, but competition with China was different due to its low wages, cheap currency, government help, and huge population. Similar economic downturns occurred in communities across the United States, with profound political implications.

As a result, Trump won eighty-nine primaries in the one hundred counties most affected by trade with China (Davis & Hilsenrath, 2016). Hacker and Pierson (2019) explain the rise of populism in the United States and the appeal of Donald Trump as follows:

If economic resources are vastly unequal, and the conservative party is politically aligned with the small circle of winners, something besides economics must be offered as a rationale for voting conservative. Political survival depends on introducing new divisions into the political bloodstream. And in modern politics the list of candidates for an alternative cleavage, a political divider between "us" and "them," is short and grim: nationalism; sectional loyalties; racial, ethnic, religious or cultural divisions; demonization of government and political elites; and fear of immigrants. (p. 6)

Trump took these complicated questions of international economics and weaponized them, in essence blaming the multilayered consequences of globalization on China. His tactic simplified a complex network of forces to offer Americans a target for their anger, thus replacing a sense of international solidarity with xenophobia and racism.

To understand why this strategy worked, it is important to analyze the consequences of the three key findings noted above: rising wages internationally, a declining standard of living among the working classes of the developed world, and the simultaneous rise of a new global elite. The most compelling data has been provided by Case and Deaton (2015 and 2017), who have shown that the stresses on the white working class in the United States are so strong that middle-aged white people are dying at increasing rates due to suicide, drugs, and alcohol poisoning. The primary interest here is whether this distress can be linked to globalization and income inequality. According to Case and Deaton (2015), the overall mortality rate for American white non-Hispanics (WNH) rose from 1999 to 2013. This increase in mortality has been particularly strong among those with no more than a high school degree, precisely the population most likely to be affected by competition with foreign labor. For the forty-five to forty-nine-year-old age group, the WNH mortality rate per 100,000 people rose from 491.2 in 1999 to 620.1 in 2015. The annual variations in WNH death rates are inversely related to annual income changes, again suggesting a link to globalization (Case & Deaton 2017). In short, Case and Deaton argue that working-class Americans are literally dying because of the negative effects of globalization on the U.S. labor market. Responding to this crisis, President Trump called upon angry white voters in the name of "America First" (Trump, 2017). While this was a short-sighted strategy, the economic facts behind the anger and the frustration of those who had lost their jobs or suffered from declining wages were real. This explains why many Americans came to view China as a national threat to their health and well-being.

Trump's Furious Response

Rather than using the WTO's dispute settlement mechanism, Trump pursued his objectives by invoking national security. The U.S. tariffs of 25 percent on steel and 10 percent on aluminum imposed in March 2018 allegedly served national security, but were imposed on imports from Canada, the European Union, Mexico, and South Korea, with only 6 percent of tariffed imports originating in China (Bown & Kolb, 2020). Obviously, tariffs on steel imported from Canada have no clear national security justification and are opposed by the U.S. industry and unions. In this case, Trump's retaliatory tariffs, launched in the name of national security and supposedly targeting China, made little economic sense yet appealed to the anger of his base. To Trump's supporters, the tariffs look like a strong response to China, yet one study (Lee and Varas, 2020) shows they "increased annual consumer costs by roughly $57 billion annually," hence hurting the constituency Trump claimed to be helping.

While the "trade war" was therefore politically useful for stoking Trump's "America First" rhetoric, even while it proved harmful to American consumers, the U.S. president may have had another goal in mind: weakening the norms of international oversight. Indeed, by invoking national security as the reason for his tariffs, Trump avoided oversight from the WTO and any potential interference from the U.S. International Trade Commission (Bown & Irwin, 2019). This sidestepping of such oversight indicates a sharp break from previous administrations. Moreover, when the Trump administration allowed the number of appellate judges to fall below the required minimum, it essentially ended the dispute settlement process within the WTO. Consequently, any potential interference on U.S. trade disputes with other countries from the WTO has been eliminated since December 10, 2019 (Bown & Keynes, 2020).

The fact that Trump shook up the existing WTO bureaucracy, quit the TPP, withdrew from NAFTA, and pulled out of innumerable other treaties was strongly supported by Republican enablers. But did Trump achieve his economic goals? He clearly believed the trade deficit was a "bad thing" (Palmer, 2020) and waged his trade war to reduce the trade deficit with China. Yet, by August 2020, the trade deficit exceeded even the 2008 level (series BOPGTB, available on the Federal Reserve Economic Database). As many economic scholars have pointed out (Palmer, 2020), tariffs have little effect on the trade deficit, meaning Trump's policies were doomed to fail from the start. This failure is based on basic economic theory, in which a trade deficit simply means that we buy more products from other nations than we sell to them. This is only possible if these nations lend us the difference by buying our stocks, bonds, and treasury bills. Persistent trade deficits are partly due to the fact that other nations keep investing in the U.S. dollar as a global currency. From this perspective, it is difficult to see trade deficits as something negative.

Overall then, the problem is not the trade deficit but the inequality generated by the shift in manufacturing from developed to developing countries. Consequently, Trump's trade war was tragically misdirected. U.S. trade with China is projected to shrink by about half if the 2020 "phase one" tariffs are maintained. However, the overall effect of the tariffs on American GDP is estimated to be near zero as trade is diverted to other Asian countries (Li et al., 2020). Thus, Trump's trade war may have achieved his political goal of feeding right-wing populism and anti-China anger, but it did not reverse the inequalities associated with this phase of globalization.

Moreover, the trade war weakened the system of trade agreements and adjudication processes meant to maintain trade peace (Bown & Irwin, 2019). This leads us to the following two key points: First, while Trump's trade war is believed to have hurt China's economy at about –1.7 percent of real GDP, his trade tariffs cost American consumers billions of dollars because they were forced to pay higher prices for imported goods from China (Li et al., 2020). Second, by waging war on the WTO, the TPP, and other economic intermediaries, he damaged the international mechanisms built to ensure a fair and reliable global economy. No wonder, then, that trade expert Scott Kennedy told the *South China Morning Post* that "Trump's China trade policy is a failure of epic proportions" (Birmingham, 2020).

Conclusion

The lines of evidence offered here come with the humble caveat that new theories and data will likely lead to revisions of some or all of the ideas discussed herein. Still, by way of summary, until about 1980, manufacturing was concentrated in the developed world, making it difficult for developing countries to grow (Pritchett, 1997). But transportation costs are now low enough that manufacturing is shifting to developing countries where low wages contribute to higher profits for the international elite (Rodrik, 2013), as predicted by Krugman and Venables's (1995) theory. Workers in the developed world have seen wage stagnation as a result, while the global rich have done exceedingly well (Alvaredo et al., 2018; Milanovic, 2016). These conditions have, in turn, produced a wave of working-class anger in the United States, which Trump turned into hostility toward China. As President Barack Obama and others argued throughout the past decade, the United States could have reduced domestic inequality and increased growth through aggressive income and wealth redistribution plans (Berg et al., 2018). Instead, right-wing populism based on public fears related to immigration and international trade allowed conservative groups, closely allied with the wealthy, to prosper throughout the developed world (Hacker & Pierson, 2019; Rodrik, 2020). The United States exhibits the stress partially through the rising mortality rates of white non-Hispanics (Case & Deaton, 2017), which has driven an alarming upswing in anti-immigrant, racist, and xenophobic rhetoric so harsh that commentators have begun speculating about the ghosts of fascism (Crick, 2021).

As the largest nation of the past periphery, China is emerging as the most likely challenger to the United States. Its transition from socialism to some form of capitalism seems to be headed toward state capitalism (Wu, 2016) that will preserve the power of those in charge (Pei, 2008; Wu, 2005; Yan, 2002). The belief that the Chinese state works through its corporations to acquire foreign technology makes Western firms fearful about sharing their technology (Wübbeke et al., 2016). Moreover, fears that advanced communication technologies allow eavesdropping on government agencies has led to widespread support for isolating Chinese high-tech firms from sensitive activities (Kennedy, 2020). What is noteworthy here is that even as Trump sought to weaponize these processes to stoke white nationalism, the Chinese government made the situation worse by resorting to its own versions of strident nationalism and refusing to implement any sense of transparency in its handling of both domestic and international markets, particularly around social media and other lucrative communication technologies (Dodge, 2020).

Thus, cutting the China "knot" is not a solution because it is unlikely to work. The "phase one" tariffs are predicted to have little or no effect on the GDP of the United States as trade is diverted to other Asian countries (Li et al., 2020). Better strategies for dealing with the reality of a powerful China would include the more intentional redistribution of wealth in the United States, to deal with the inequality generated by this phase of globalization, working on mutually gratifying trade agreements to encourage reforms in China, and respecting the traditional limits on presidential power while giving international organizations more authority in mediating international trade disputes.

At the same time, a more rhetorically astute Chinese government should do everything in its power to help mitigate the consequences addressed herein. China has enjoyed the benefits of global trade, including the vast system of banking, shipping, and legal norms built by the United States since World War II, to say nothing of being handed virtually unlimited access to American markets. Yet, the Chinese government seems to think that negotiating in good faith, and compromising occasionally, will be perceived by domestic audiences as a sign of weakness. But just as Trump's "America First" rhetoric makes no sense in the face of globalization, it is clear that Xi Jinping's strident new nationalism fundamentally misunderstands the nature of international relations in an age of globalization. No nation can go it alone. Just as American consumers have come to rely on cheap Chinese products, Chinese producers heavily depend on robust American markets to fuel their continued growth.

Consequently, we find ourselves in a situation of mutually assured financial destruction (Fallows, 2008). Neither the United States nor China can prosper without the other, and harm to one party will produce harm in the other, rendering trade wars an unhelpful response to the nuances of global economics. Therefore, reasonable minds will want to find ways for the United States and China to grow and prosper together, but only if both parties can negotiate agreements that strike their respective populations as fair. For Americans, this would mean stopping the racist China-bashing and forging new relationships around R&D and other high-tech markets. China, on the other hand, should address legitimate U.S. concerns about dumping, currency manipulations, and SOEs, which all tilt the economic balance in China's favor. As Lieberthal and Wang (2012) have argued, both sides need to build trust through open and honest negotiations. Only a mutually beneficial approach to U.S.–China trade relations will ensure that Trump's rage against China will fall on deaf ears. However, if China continues to pursue market advantages without concern for their international consequences, there will be a high political price to pay.

REFERENCES

Alvaredo, F., Chancel, L., Piketty, T., Saez, E., & Zucman, G. (Eds.). (2018). *World inequality report 2018*. Harvard/Belknap Press.

Autor, D. H., Dorn, D., & Hanson, G. H. (2013). The China syndrome: Local labor market effects of import competition in the United States. *American Economic Review, 103*(6), 2121–68.

Baldwin, R. (2013). Trade and industrialization after globalization's second unbundling: How building and joining a supply chain are different and why it matters. In R. C. Feenstra & A. M. Tyler, *Globalization in an age of crisis: Multilateral economic cooperation in the twenty-first century* (pp. 165–212). University of Chicago Press.

Berg, A., Ostry, J. D., Tsangarides, C. G., & Yakhshilikov, Y. (2018). Redistribution, inequality, and growth: New evidence. *Journal of Economic Growth, 23*(3), 259–305.

Birminghan, F. (2020, October 22). Donald Trump promised a tough China policy, but few think it worked. *South China Morning Post.*

Bown, C. P., & Irwin, D. A. (2019). Trump's assault on the global trading system: And why decoupling from china will change everything. *Foreign Affairs, 98,* 125.

Bown, C. P., & Keynes, S. (2020). Why Trump shot the Sheriffs: The end of WTO dispute settlement 1.0 [working paper 20-4]. *Peterson Institute for International Economics.* https://www.piie.com/publications/working-papers/why-trump-shot-sheriffs-end-wto-dispute-settlement-10

Bown, C., & Kolb, M. (2020). Trump's trade war timeline: An up-to-date guide. *Peterson Institute for International Economics,* 1–17. https://www.piie.com/blogs/trade-investment-policy-watch/trump-trade-war-china-date-guide

Brander, J., & Krugman, P. (1983). A 'reciprocal dumping' model of international trade. *Journal of International Economics, 15*(3–4), 313–21.

Brander, J. A., & Spencer, B. J. (1984). Trade warfare: Tariffs and cartels. *Journal of International Economics, 16*(3–4), 227–242.

Case, A., & Deaton, A. (2015). Rising morbidity and mortality in midlife among white non-Hispanic Americans in the 21st century. *Proceedings of the National Academy of Sciences, 112*(49), 15078–83.

Case, A., & Deaton, A. (2017). Mortality and morbidity in the 21st century. *Brookings Papers on Economic Activity, 2017*(1), 397–476.

Chan, K. W. (2010). The household registration system and migrant labor in China: Notes on a debate. *Population and Development Review, 36*(2), 357–64.

Clinton, W. J. (1998a, June 29). Remarks and a question-and-answer session with students at Beijing University. *American Presidency Project.* https://www.presidency.ucsb.edu/documents/remarks-and-question-and-answer-session-with-students-beijing-university-beijing-china

Clinton, W. J. (1998b, June 29). Remarks by the president in presenting a collection of American books, Beijing University, [China] [folder 1] [2]. *Clinton Digital Library,* National Security Council, Speechwriting Office, and Paul Orzulak. https://clinton.presidentiallibraries.us/items/show/11243 [fifth document in this file, p. 9 of 90]

Clinton, W. J. (1998c, June 29). Remarks to the U.S. embassy community, Beijing, China. China Trip—Embassy Remarks, 6/29/98. *Clinton Digital Library,* National Security Council, Speechwriting Office, and Antony Blinken. https://clinton.presidentiallibraries.us/items/show/9860

Conley, D. S. (2018). China's fraught food system: Imagining ecological civilization in the face of paradoxical modernity. In S. J. Hartnett, L. B. Keränen, & D. S. Conley (Eds.), *Imagining China: Rhetorics of Nationalism in an Age of Globalization* (pp. 175–204). Michigan State University Press.

Constitution of the People's Republic of China. http://www.npc.gov.cn/zgrdw/englishnpc/Constitution/2007–11/15/content_1372962.htm

Crick, N. (Ed.). (2021). *The rhetoric of fascism.* University of Alabama Press.

Davis, B., & Hilsenrath, J. (2016, August 12). Deep, swift China shock drove Trump's support. *Wall Street Journal.*

Dikötter, F. (2011). *Mao's great famine: The history of China's most devastating catastrophe, 1958–1962.* Bloomsbury.

Dodge, P. S.-W. (2020). Introduction: Communication convergence and "the core" for a new era. In P. S.-W. Dodge (Ed.), *Communication convergence in contemporary China: International perspectives on politics, platforms, and participation* (ix–xxxii). Michigan State University Press.

Fallows, J. (2008, January–February). The $1.4 Trillion Question. *The Atlantic.* https://www.theatlantic.com

Friedman, T. L. (2005). *The world is flat: A brief history of the twenty-first century.* Farrar, Straus, and Giroux.

Gilley, B. (2004). *China's democratic future: How it will happen and where it will lead.* Columbia University Press.

Gertz, B. (2000). *The China threat: How the People's Republic targets America.* Regency.

Global Citizen. (2020). *More information on the WTO.* https://www.citizen.org/article/more-information-on-the-world-trade-organization-wto

Hacker, J., & Pierson, P. (2019). Plutocrats with pitchforks: The distinctive politics of right-wing populism in the United States [Manuscript]. https://www.law.berkeley.edu/wp-content/uploads/2019/09/Hacker_Pierson_APSA_2019.pdf

Halper, S. (2010). *The Beijing consensus: How China's authoritarian model will dominate the twenty-first century.* Basic Books.

Hartnett, S. J. (2011). Google and the "twisted cyber spy" affair: U.S.–China communication in an age of globalization. *Quarterly Journal of Speech, 97,* 411–34.

Hartnett, S. J. (2021). *A world of turmoil: The United States, China, and Taiwan in the long cold war.* Michigan State University Press.

Hartnett, S. J., & Stengrim, L. (2006). *Globalization and empire: The U.S. invasion of Iraq, free markets, and the twilight of democracy.* University of Alabama Press.

Hemphill, C. S., & Weiser, P. J. (2017). Beyond Brooke Group: Bringing reality to the law of predatory pricing. *Yale LJ, 127,* 2048.

Hoyng, R., & Chong, G. (Eds.). (2022). *Critiquing communication innovation: New media in a multipolar world.* Michigan State University Press.

Hufbauer, G. (2013). A misguided fix on solar panels? *Peterson Institute of International Economics.* https://www.piie.com/experts/peterson-perspectives/misguided-fix-solar-panels

Irwin, D. A. (2020). *Free trade under fire.* Princeton University Press.

Jacques, M. (2009). *When China rules the world.* Penguin.

Jia, L., & Nieborg, D. (2022). Analyzing Chinese platform power: Infrastructure, finance, and geopolitics. In R. Hoyng & G. Chong, *Critiquing communication innovation: New media in a multipolar world* (pp. 1–28). Michigan State University Press.

Kennedy, S. (2020, July 27). Washington's China policy has lost its Wei. *CSIS Briefs.* https://www.csis.org/analysis/washingtons-china-policy-has-lost-its-wei

Krekel, B., Bakos, G., & Barnett, C. (2009). *Capability of the People's Republic of China to conduct cyber warfare and computer network exploitation.* U.S.–China Economic and Security Review Commission. https://nsarchive2.gwu.edu/NSAEBB/NSAEBB424/docs/Cyber-030.pdf

Krugman, P. (1997, March 21). In praise of cheap labor. Slate. https://slate.com/business/1997/03/in-praise-of-cheap-labor.html

Krugman, P. (2020). *Arguing with zombies: Economics, politics, and the fight for a better future.* W. W. Norton.

Krugman, P., & Venables, A. J. (1995). Globalization and the inequality of nations. *The Quarterly Journal of Economics, 110*(4), 857–80.

Lau, L. J., Qian, Y., & Roland, G. (2000). Reform without losers: An interpretation of China's dual-track approach to transition. *Journal of Political Economy, 108*(1), 120–43.

Lee, T., & Varas, J. (2020, September 16). The total cost of Trump's tariffs. *American Action Forum.* https://www.americanactionforum.org/research/the-total-cost-of-trumps-new-tariffs

Lei, W. (2019). The story of reform in Xiaogang Village. *China Plus.* http://chinaplus.cri.cn/mychina/life/35/20190627/309120.html

Li, M., Balistreri, E. J., & Zhang, W. (2020). The US–China trade war: Tariff data and general equilibrium analysis. *Journal of Asian Economics, 69,* 101216.

Lieberthal, K., & Wang, J. (2012). *Addressing U.S.–China strategic distrust.* Brookings Institution.

Liu, T., & Woo, W. T. (2018). Understanding the US-China trade war. *China Economic Journal, 11*(3), 319–40.

Mann, J. (2007). *The China fantasy: Why capitalism will not bring democracy to China.* Penguin.

Milanovic, B. (2016). *Global inequality: A new approach for the age of globalization.* Harvard University Press.

Miles, T. (2019, June 17). China pulls WTO suit over claim to be a market economy. *Reuters.* https://www.reuters.com/article/us-usa-china-wto-eu/china-pulls-wto-suit-over-claim-to-be-a-market-economy-idUSKCN1TI10A

Nathan, A., Diamond, L., & Plattner, M. (Ed.). (2013). *Will China democratize?* Johns Hopkins University Press.

Navarro, P., & Autry, G. (2011). *Death by China: Confronting the dragon—A global call to action.* Pearson Prentice Hall.

Osnos, E. (2015). *Age of ambition: Chasing fortune, truth, and faith in the new China.* Farrar, Straus, and Giroux.

Palmer, D. (2020, October 10). Why Trump lost his battle against the trade deficit. *Politico.* https://www.politico.com/news/2020/10/06/trump-trade-deficit-426805

Pei, M. (2008). *China's trapped transition: The limits of developmental autocracy.* Harvard University Press.

Pence, M. (2018, October 4). *Remarks by Vice President Pence on the administration's policy toward China.* The White House. https://www.whitehouse.gov/briefings-statements/remarks-vice-president-pence-administrations-policy-toward-china/

Perlez, J. (2018, October 5). Pence's China speech seen as portent of "New Cold War." *New York Times.* https://www.nytimes.com/2018/10/05/world/asia/pence-china-speech-cold-war.html

Pritchett, L. (1997). Divergence, big time. *Journal of Economic Perspectives, 11*(3), 3–17.

Public Citizen. (2020). *More information on the World Trade Organization.* https://www.citizen.org/article/more-information-on-the-world-trade-organization-wto/

Reinhart, C. M., & Rogoff, K. S. (2009). *This time is different: Eight centuries of financial folly.* Princeton University Press.

Rodrik, D. (2008). The real exchange rate and economic growth. *Brookings Papers on Economic Activity, 2008*(2), 365–412.

Rodrik, D. (2013). Unconditional convergence in manufacturing. *The Quarterly Journal of Economics, 128*(1), 165–204.

Rodrik, D. (2017). *Straight talk on trade: Ideas for a sane world economy.* Princeton University Press.

Rodrik, D. (2020, July). *Why does globalization fuel populism? Economics, culture, and the rise of right-wing populism* (no. 27526) [Working paper]. National Bureau of Economic Research. https://doi.org/10.3386/w27526

Rogin, J. (2018, October 5). Pence: It's up to China to avoid a Cold War. *Washington Post.* https://www.washingtonpost.com/news/josh-rogin/wp/2018/11/13/

pence-its-up-to-china-to-avoid-a-cold-war/

Russo, F. (2019). Politics in the boardroom: The role of Chinese Communist Party committees. *The Diplomat.* https://thediplomat.com/2019/12/politics-in-the-boardroom-the-role-of-chinese-communist-party-committees/

Stern, M. (2016, November 16). Report from the field: The rust belt's blues turn it red. *American Prospect.* https://prospect.org/power/report-field-rust-belt-s-blues-turn-red/

Stiglitz., J. (2002). Globalization and its discontents. Norton.

Storesletten, K., & Zilibotti, F. (2014). China's great convergence and beyond. *Annual Review of Economics, 6*(1), 333–62.

Taylor, A. (2018, April 13). A timeline of Trump's complicated relationship with the TPP. *Washington Post.* https://www.washingtonpost.com/news/worldviews/wp/2018/04/13/a-timeline-of-trumps-complicated-relationship-with-the-tpp/

Trump, D. (2017). *The inaugural address.* The White House. https://www.whitehouse.gov/briefings-statements/the-inaugural-address/

Wan, J., & Reckard, B. (2020). Huawei and the 2019 cybersecurity crisis: Sino–US conflict in the age of convergence. In P. Dodge (Ed.), *Communications convergence in contemporary China: International perspectives on politics, platforms, and participation* (pp. 97–126). Michigan State University Press.

Whalen, J. (2019, June 23). Huawei digs in for a long battle with the U.S. *Washington Post.* https://www.washingtonpost.com/business/2019/06/23/huawei-digs-long-battle-with-us/

WTO (2020a). A unique contribution. *Understanding the WTO: Settling disputes.* World Trade Organization. https://www.wto.org/english/thewto_e/whatis_e/tif_e/disp1_e.htm

Wu, J. (2005). *Understanding and interpreting Chinese economic reform.* Thomson/South-Western.

Wu, M. (2016). The 'China, Inc.' challenge to global trade governance. Harvard International Law Journal, 57(2), 261–324. http://www.law.harvard.edu/studorgs/ilj/

Wübbeke, J., Meissner, M., Zenglein, M. J., Ives, J., & Conrad, B. (2016). Made in China 2025. *Mercator Institute for China Studies. Papers on China, 2,* 74.

Yan, Y. (2002). Managed globalization: State power and cultural transition in China. In P. L. Berger & S. P. Huntington (Eds.), *Many globalizations: Cultural diversity in the contemporary world* (pp. 19–47), Oxford University Press.

Yang, G., & Wei, W. (Eds.). (2021). *Engaging Social Media in China: Platforms, Publics, and Production.* Michigan State University Press.

Zhan, S. (2017). Hukou reform and land politics in China: Rise of a tripartite alliance. *The China Journal, 78*(1), 25–49.

Zilibotti, F. (2017). Growing and slowing down like China. *Journal of the European Economic Association, 15*(5), 943–88.

China's Foreign Direct Investment Expansion

News Coverage of U.S.–China Economic and Security Review
Commission Reports

Hamilton Bean

Trade and investment are the twin pillars of economic growth. When China joined the World Trade Organization (WTO) in 2001, it opened the door not only to the increased exchange of goods and services among countries (trade) but also to capital provided to businesses in one country by investors located in another country (investment). At the beginning of the U.S.–China trade war in 2018, bilateral trade stood at $737 billion, while bilateral investment (stock) in the prior year totaled $147 billion (Office of the United States Trade Representative, 2019). Although trade is the focus of the current dispute, this chapter demonstrates that to adequately understand the role of journalism in the U.S.–China *trade* war, analysts must devote equal attention to institutional and media discourses of *investment*, especially China's foreign direct investment (FDI) in the United States.

According to the U.S. Bureau of Economic Analysis, U.S. FDI in China grew to $120 billion in 2019, with the sharpest growth in the past six years, while Chinese FDI in the United States grew from nearly none in 2008 (the earliest date available) to $60 billion in 2019, with the highest growth in 2013–16. U.S. FDI in China is double Chinese FDI in America. These figures show that FDI has steadily increased in both countries—with plateaus attributable to the September 2001 terrorist attacks, the 2008 U.S. economic recession, and the

Trump administration's policies—but these figures also mask major tension. According to the Congressional Research Service (Schwarzenberg, 2019), U.S. investors persistently claim that China's FDI restrictions severely limit growth opportunities for U.S. firms in China, and U.S. policymakers have long voiced concern over investments by China's government-backed entities in the United States, largely because China targets U.S. industries and technologies critical to future economic development and national security. Therefore, this chapter scrutinizes both U.S. institutional discourse and media coverage of China's FDI expansion, illustrating how the media indexing hypothesis, i.e., the "media conveyor belt" (Baum & Potter, 2008), helps to account for U.S.–China conflict and trade war rhetoric. Simply put, China's FDI expansion has consistently generated U.S. media calls for U.S. government agencies to confront China's "unfair" investment practices, while *China Daily* journalists and commentators have attempted to contain and downplay those calls—a rhetorical pattern consistent with broader U.S.–China political discourse (Hartnett, 2011). Indeed, as this chapter argues, public deliberation about China's FDI in the United States tends not to mirror nuanced economic reasoning but to mimic larger political narratives, many of which—as seen in the annual Reports of the U.S.–China Economic and Security Review Commission (known as the U.S.–China Security Review Commission until 2003)—are wrapped in longstanding anti-China sentiments.

To support this thesis, the chapter first summarizes the sixteen annual reports produced by the U.S.–China Economic and Security Review Commission between 2002 and 2018. It then presents an analysis of both U.S. newspapers and *China Daily's* coverage of those reports and related commentary. This analysis adds to our understanding of war and peace journalism (Ha et al., 2020) and Baum and Potter's (2008) foreign policy market equilibrium model. This chapter offers a rhetorical approach, identifying foundational tensions and themes in the antecedents of the recent trade war. The analysis reveals an entrenched rhetorical pattern in U.S.–China political discourse, highlighting the improbability of achieving mutual understanding, cooperation, and peace in the absence of a shared "reimagining" of the U.S.–China relationship (Hartnett et al., 2017).

Commentators often cite China's accession to the WTO on December 11, 2001, as the catalyst of the recent U.S.–China trade war (Blustein, 2019). Intense political struggle in the United States marked China's accession, as both Democratic and Republican proponents described it as a means of enriching both countries in the short term, while promoting the longer-term development of the rule of law and democratic governance in China. As President Bill Clinton declared in a March 9, 2000, speech,

> Supporting China's entry into the WTO . . . is about more than our economic interests; it is clearly in our larger national interest. It represents the most significant opportunity that we have had to create positive change in China since the 1970s, when President Nixon first went there, and later in the decade when President Carter normalized relations. I am working as hard as I can to convince Congress and the American people to seize this opportunity. (para. 7)

Democratic and Republican opponents of China's WTO accession, however, emphasized China's poor track record of human rights, the 1989 Tiananmen Square massacre, and China's perceived threat to U.S. economic and security interests. U.S. Trade Representative Robert Lighthizer warned in an April 18, 1999, *New York Times* op-ed that the United States would one day "regret" backing China's ambitions:

> The Clinton Administration may not see the link between China's actions in various areas, but you can be sure that the Chinese do. After all, China is neither a free market nor a democratic country. Its leaders view economics the same way they view defense, foreign policy or human rights. It is a means of expanding the power of the state and maintaining control of its population. (para. 11–12)

While those who promoted official "engagement" with China vied with antagonists who resisted the Clinton administration's initiatives throughout the 1990s, Chinese leaders depicted WTO accession as strengthening China's economic growth, thereby bolstering the legitimacy of the Chinese Communist Party (CCP). President Jiang Zemin remarked in a September 8, 1999, press conference:

> Firstly, the WTO will not be comprehensive without the entry of China, the largest developing country in the world, since it is an international organization. Secondly, China can only join the WTO as a developing country. Thirdly, there should be a balance between China's rights and duties for its entry into the organization. (para. 4)

These conflicts reached a turning point in 2000, when, in order for China to gain WTO membership, the United States government had to agree to forgo an annual waiver (one granted to China since the 1980s) that allowed the country to maintain its "free trade" status with the United States regardless of China's human rights record. President Clinton worked to grant permanent normal trade relations (PNTR) to China. Nevertheless, in the waiver's place, U.S. lawmakers created two new entities to serve similar oversight functions. The first entity, the Congressional-Executive Commission on China (CECC) was created on October 10, 2000, to focus on China's human rights practices (the CECC's work lays outside the scope of this chapter). The second entity, the U.S.–China Economic and Security Review Commission, created on October 30, 2000, has played a pivotal role in constructing the "China threat" narrative among U.S. audiences. By China threat, I refer to U.S. officials' fears—both real and imagined—that China's rising economic fortunes will come at the expense of America's economic power, that China's political model will become an attractive alternative to democracy, and that the United States and China are inevitably headed toward armed conflict (Mahbubani, 2019).

Because it is the epicenter of the "China threat" narrative, and because it was founded specifically in response to China's economic growth, this chapter focuses on the U.S.–China Economic and Security Review Commission's annual reports and associated media coverage. The following sections describe the work of the U.S.–China Economic and Security Review Commission, explain how that work is depicted in selected U.S. and Chinese media coverage, and discuss the implications of that coverage for understanding war and peace journalism and Baum and Potter's (2008) foreign policy market equilibrium model. The analysis demonstrates that both American and Chinese responses to these reports tend to exacerbate tensions between the two nations, hence fueling the kinds of misunderstandings and stereotypes that have given rise to "trade war" rhetoric.

The U.S.–China Economic and Security Review Commission: Constructing the China Threat

The U.S.–China Economic and Security Review Commission's mandate is to "monitor, investigate, and submit to Congress an annual report on the national security implications of the bilateral and economic relationship between the United States and the People's Republic of China . . . and to provide recommendations, where appropriate, to Congress for legislative and administration action" (U.S.–China Economic and Security Review Commission, 2019). The commission has produced sixteen annual reports so far (between 2002 and 2018). The leadership of the U.S. House of Representatives and Senate appoint the twelve commissioners to serve two-year terms. The commissioners, who usually hail from business, government, nongovernmental, and academic institutions, typically (but not always) display a "hawkish" stance toward China irrespective of political affiliation. The commissioners select a chairman and vice chairman from their membership. An executive director and ten staff members support the commission's work. In order to produce its annual reports (which generally exceed three hundred pages), the commission holds hearings, conducts research, and engages in fact-finding missions, all of which rely on subject matter experts internal and external to the commission.

The structure of the commission's sixteen annual reports has varied little since 2002. Each report begins with a formal "transmittal letter" to congress, followed by an executive summary and introductory sections. Multiple chapters and subsections follow, which address issues related to trade and investment, security, China's international affairs, and technology. The views of the commissioners sometimes follow the reports' conclusions, along with multiple appendices addressing institutional structures and processes, background information, and sources. The reports are also presented with secret information in a "classified" format (examples were unobtainable for this discussion). The law that created the commission was amended in 2003, codifying the topics to be covered: proliferation, economic reforms, energy, U.S. capital markets, corporate reporting, regional economic and security impacts, U.S.–China bilateral programs, WTO compliance, and media control (U.S.–China Economic and Security Review Commission, 2019).

As a result of their prescribed format, the annual reports exhibit a remarkable level of consistency. The commission's first report in 2002 listed the key themes and recommendations: achieving a better understanding of China's perceptions of the United States; requiring U.S. companies to report their investments in and technology transfers to China; making full use of WTO rules and safeguards; ensuring that U.S. sources of capital do not fund China's proliferation activities; countering China's foreign and defense policies in ways that promote U.S. interests; monitoring the U.S. defense industry's dependency on Chinese imports; and subverting China's attempts to obtain sensitive U.S. military technology (U.S.–China Security Review Commission, 2002). Versions of these themes are present sixteen years later in the commission's 2018 report (the latest report obtainable for this chapter), with the commission's top ten recommendations focusing on (items in italics were new in 2018): discovering vulnerabilities vis-à-vis U.S.–China information and communications technology collaborations and supply chains; holding China accountable to WTO rules; *identifying Chinese media products aimed at U.S. audiences*; directing U.S. defense and intelligence agencies to scrutinize *the security implications of the Belt and Road Initiative (BRI)*; countering *CCP propaganda*; and evolving Chinese defense structures (U.S.–China Economic and Security Review Commission, 2018). Thus, the latest commission report demonstrates increasing U.S. concern regarding China's propaganda and media efforts, rather than trade issues.

Nevertheless, the commission's 2018 report (released in November, several months into the U.S.–China trade war) led with a summary of "trade enforcement actions" against China, which were among the earliest shots fired in the dispute. The commission argued, "The Trump Administration's trade policies target Chinese technology transfer requirements and insufficient intellectual property protections, the growing U.S. trade deficit, and national security risks posed by an overreliance on steel and aluminum imports, among other factors" (U.S.–China Economic and Security Review Commission, 2018, pp. 1–2). Framing China as an unfair and untrustworthy trading partner, the commission consistently underlined its key message: "The Chinese government continues to resist—and in some cases reverse progress on—many promised reforms of China's state-led economic model" (p. 29). Despite acknowledging China's retaliatory moves in response to U.S. actions, the term "trade war" was never mentioned within the body of the report (a handful of citations included it).

None of the commission's reports contain systematic, detailed discussion of whether and how prior years' recommendations have been addressed by the U.S. government, nor do the reports contain sections addressing how China itself has responded (if at all) to the noted concerns. This means that each year's report feels disconnected from the prior reports and therefore fails to provide readers with any sense of historical change, political evolution, or the possibility of improvement in U.S.–China relations. Moreover, for an institution created in response to China's accession to the WTO, a remarkable proportion of the commission's annual reports focus not on the exchange of goods and services, but on investment or other issues. For example, the commission's first annual report in 2002 stressed the need to better monitor and control bilateral investment flows. The report stated that an estimated 90 percent of Chinese investment in the United States was to acquire ownership of U.S. companies, while 90 percent of U.S. investment in China was to expand operations, thereby transforming China into an export platform that (as detailed by Beckman & Hartnett in this volume) has hastened the decline of the U.S. manufacturing sector. The 2002 report also emphasized that Chinese technology transfer policies and practices were not in compliance with WTO rules. The U.S. Trade Representative's 2002 "Report to Congress on China's WTO Compliance" stated:

> China [has] implemented its commitment to greater transparency in the adoption and operation of new laws and regulations unevenly at best. [. . .] the Administration found China's overall effort to be plagued by uncertainty and a lack of uniformity. [. . .] the lack of effective IPR [intellectual property rights] enforcement remained a major challenge. [. . .] compliance problems involve entrenched domestic Chinese interests that may be seeking to minimize their exposure to foreign competition. (pp. 3–5)

To secure access to the Chinese market, U.S. corporations had assented to both formal and informal technology transfer agreements, as well as financed valuable research and development centers across China. Chinese students and scholars in the United States, in turn, were accused of facilitating China's acquisition of sensitive U.S. technology. The commission's 2002 report depicted China as the overwhelming beneficiary of U.S. investment and know-how at the expense of U.S. workers and national security. Pre-WTO accession images of increased U.S.–China trade and investment leading to a shared rise in living standards, improved quality of life, and strong ties and governance in both countries had already been replaced in 2002 with images of a U.S. sell out, i.e., an American workforce obligated to accept fewer opportunities, lower pay, and reduced benefits in order to advance the global competitiveness of U.S. corporations in the face of China's rise. We can therefore see that since at least 2002, the United States has taken notice of China's rapid climb up the technological innovation ladder and expressed clear institutional concerns over China's influence in global markets and security arenas.

Importantly, the announcement of China's Belt and Road Initiative (BRI) in 2013 aimed to export China's economic and political model to countries around the world under the guise of development-related FDI. The commission's 2015 report expressed concern that BRI signaled a new level of Chinese diplomacy and outbound investment (U.S.–China Economic and Security Review Commission, 2015). By 2018, the commission had hardened its conclusions, stating, "BRI could pose a significant challenge for U.S. interests and values because it may enable China to export its model of authoritarian governance and encourages and validates authoritarian actors abroad" (p. 259). In response, in 2018, the United States overhauled and consolidated its own development finance institutions in order to better compete with China (Zengerle, 2018). In its 2018 report, the commission continued to emphasize investment issues, noting that BRI-related investments in coal power could contribute to poor environmental standards in developing countries. Increased agricultural investments had also targeted areas on China's periphery in order to lessen import dependence on the United States. Yet, bilateral U.S.–China investment issues remained at the heart of the report.

The commission's 2018 report noted that Chinese FDI in the United States in the previous eighteen months had dropped a whopping 92 percent due to controls on capital outflows and uncertainty regarding the increased U.S. institutional scrutiny of Chinese investment. The report did not characterize this drop as either a success or failure but alluded to the slowdown as a potential improvement vis-à-vis U.S. national security. Specifically, the Committee on Foreign Investment in the United States (CFIUS), which the Trump administration expanded in 2018 to intensify its oversight efforts, had so far blocked $5.8 billion in Chinese investments in sectors deemed too sensitive to U.S. competitiveness and national security. Nevertheless, venture capital investments from China had accelerated, presumably seeking to further fuel China's increasing technological development (CFIUS plans to scrutinize venture capital investments in the future). While Chinese investment (excluding venture capital) in the United States had plummeted, U.S. investment in China had increased due to the liberalizing of restrictions in industries including banking, automobiles, and agriculture. Despite these reversals, the commission noted that U.S. efforts to prevent Chinese regulators and companies from pressuring foreign counterparts to transfer proprietary technology or intellectual property (IP) had been unsuccessful. It was, however, China's "large-scale investment in next-generation defense technologies" (p. 11) that caused the most alarm, threatening "the U.S. military's technological superiority" (p. 11). The commission convincingly argued that China's weapons systems development from these investments could "seriously erode historical U.S. advantages in networked, precision strike warfare during a potential Indo-Pacific conflict" (p. 11). Clearly, in the commission's view, investment issues paralleled trade as a principal driver of the China threat (to repeat, a threat both real and perceived).

In summary, assessment of the national security implications of U.S.–China trade since China's WTO accession has permitted the U.S.–China Economic and Security Review Commission to extend its scrutiny to broad political, economic, technological, and cultural domains. The sixteen annual reports from 2002 to 2018 have consistently emphasized differences and divisions between China and the United States, asserting that the negative implications of U.S.–China trade are real, dire, and imminent. A roughly equal number of the reports' pages have been devoted to U.S.–China investment flows rather than to U.S.–China bilateral trade, underscoring the need for current trade war stakeholders to understand the FDI dynamics at work. The next section describes and explains selected media coverage of the work of the U.S.–China Economic and Security Review Commission in relation to the FDI dynamics noted above.

How Media Coverage of the U.S.–China Economic and Security Review Commission Conveys and Parlays the China Threat

A July 7, 2019, Nexis Uni and Google News search of the largest U.S. newspapers (by circulation) for the phrase "U.S.-China Economic and Security Review Commission" from 2000 to 2019 provided the material for this analysis: the *New York Times* (international edition) revealed sixty-seven articles, the *Washington Post* revealed seventy-five results, *USA Today* provided ten, the *Los Angeles Times* offered thirty-nine, and the *Wall Street Journal* revealed eighty-eight entries. By contrast, *China Daily* (established in 1981) returned 102 articles. *Global Times* is China's other leading English-language newspaper, with an English version established in 2009. Its commission-related content mostly mirrored *China Daily*'s content and therefore did not warrant separate analysis (the author cannot read Chinese; therefore, only English-language sources were used for this study). The volume of *China Daily* articles suggests that the CCP has not ignored the commission's work; rather it has attempted to "parlay" the commission's work, expecting that *China Daily* coverage of the commission could somehow transform it into a valuable foil for China.

Analysis of the entire corpus proceeded along two lines. First, it ascertained whether the U.S.–China Economic and Security Review Commission is invoked to support an overall war frame, a mixed frame, or whether any particular frame could be identified at all. It can be presumed that U.S. journalists citing material produced by the U.S.–China Economic and Security Review Commission would rarely invoke a peace frame because the commission's outputs are not peace oriented. Therefore, this analysis describes how U.S. media coverage usually (but not always) serves as a "conveyor belt" in reporting what the U.S.–China Economic and Security Review Commission wants the public to know. By contrast, *China Daily* journalists and commentators often aim to counter the war frame, or invert it, in order to improve China's international image or depict China as a victim of U.S. ignorance and belligerence.

Conveying the China Threat in U.S. Newspapers

Across the U.S. corpus, prominent themes in the coverage of the U.S.–China Economic and Security Review Commission include trade, espionage, cybersecurity, military affairs, telecommunications, science and technology, and media censorship. Yet, approximately half of the U.S. newspaper coverage of the commission relates to investment issues, rather than strictly the exchange of goods and services (trade). Exemplary *New York Times* headlines include, "How Lenovo Lost in U.S. after 'Security' Card was Played" (2006), "Goldman Sachs's China Deal Prompts Questions About Country's U.S. Investment" (2017), and "White House Looks to Use Emergency Law to Halt Chinese Investment" (2018). Headlines from the *Washington Post, USA Today, Los Angeles Times*, and the *Wall Street Journal* echo the investment theme, with examples including, respectively, "U.S. May Scrutinize IBM's China Deal" (2005), "Smithfield CEO Defends Merger" (2013), "Intel to Build Big Chip Plant in China" (2007), and "GE Deal Gives China's Haier Long-Sought Overseas Foothold" (2016). Such coverage tends to use the U.S.–China Economic and Security Review Commission's work in support of the perceived need to intensify U.S. scrutiny of China's FDI flows.

For example, in reporting on the 2007 Chinese acquisition of a U.S. maker of computer disk drives, the *New York Times* conveyed the commission's China threat discourse: "'This is clearly a critical component of a computer system and the purchase by the Chinese or other nations merits a full review to determine what our risks are,' said Michael Wessell, a commissioner of the U.S.–China Economic and Security Review Commission, a group that monitors the national security implications of trade with China for Congress" (Markoff, 2007, para. 17). Likewise, in eyeing China's acquisition of U.S. pork producer Smithfield Foods in 2013, the *New York Times* cited the commission's Daniel Slane, "Mr. Slane said that the fact that Shuanghui [the Chinese firm] was effectively controlled by the Chinese government meant that it presented a national security threat to the United States. The top executive at Shuanghui 'is a high-ranking member of the Chinese Communist

Party,' Mr. Slane said, and he was appointed to that job by the [Communist] party" (Wyatt, 2013, para. 16–17). The *New York Times'* coverage of the commission tends to follow this pattern of citing the commission as a source of expertise, as illustrated in a 2018 article discussing the White House's efforts to halt Chinese investment:

> A 2017 report from the U.S.-China Economic and Security Review Commission, a group created by Congress to monitor relations between the countries, said Chinese investment in the United States had been strategically focused on information and communications technology, agriculture and biotechnology. This presents potential risks to American national and economic security, said the report, which noted that American companies lacked 'reciprocal' treatment in China and that they had to disclose valuable technological information to gain access to the Chinese market. (Swanson & Rappeport, 2018, para. 12)

Whether such media coverage of Chinese FDI should be considered appropriate or overwrought can only be determined retrospectively; that is, if China increasingly behaves as the emerging hegemon that some commentators fear, then such media coverage will later be deemed prescient. However, if China's rise follows a peaceful and cooperative course, then such coverage will likely be judged as supporting an overblown China threat narrative. Along these lines, most of the articles in the U.S. corpus have straightforwardly cited the commission's work in support of a China threat narrative, but a few article writers have challenged it. For example, in coverage of an innocuous academic paper from a Chinese researcher that sparked reactionary fears of a Chinese cyberattack on the U.S. power grid, the *New York Times* reported in 2010, "It [the controversy] shows [an] atmosphere already charged with hostility between the United States and China over cybersecurity" (Markoff & Barboza, 2010, para. 18). The journalists claimed that China threat discourse was having subtle but important impacts, "The difference between Mr. Wang's [the Chinese academic] explanation and Mr. Wortzel's [vice chairman of the commission] conclusion is of more than academic interest," they noted (para. 18), implying that China hawks were distorting ambiguous events to fit the commission's China threat narrative. In a related example, a 2005 article concerning the potential Chinese acquisition of the energy company Unocal cited the commission's William Reinsch, "What we're seeing in Washington shows the hysteria about China" (Lohr, 2005, para. 12). Unocal was later sold to Chevron, rather than China's CNOCC Ltd.

Moving beyond the largest U.S. newspapers for a moment illustrates the extensive coverage of the commission's work. For example, a Nexis Uni search in the three months following the November release of the commission's 2018 report revealed 309 articles in outlets ranging from trade publications (e.g., *Inside Cyber Security*) to international news services (e.g., Yerepouni Daily News). Much of this reporting underscored the investment-oriented aspects of the dispute. As one headline declared, "It's not a Trade War with China. It's a Tech War" (Morell & Kris, 2018). Noted counter-examples aside, U.S. newspapers invoking the commission's work have mostly provided a steady flow of journalism that reflects and reinforces the China threat discourse and current trade-war rhetoric. Chinese officials have also invoked the commission, but for different purposes, as the next section explains.

Parlaying the China Threat in *China Daily*

China Daily is China's largest English-language publication, with a global circulation of 900,000. It is widely seen as a propaganda arm of the CCP (Lim & Bergin, 2018). In 2018, the U.S. Department of Justice ordered that the outlet register under the Foreign Agents Registration Act (FARA). In addition to its online and print publications, *China Daily* places supplements in U.S. newspapers that are designed to look like regular news articles but actually promote China's interests (many countries routinely engage in this practice). These supplements include labels that the materials are distributed by *China Daily*; nevertheless, President Donald Trump hyperbolically claimed in 2018 that a *China Daily* supplement that ran in *Des Moines (IA) Register* was evidence of China's "interference" in U.S. elections (Eller, 2018). Trump's bluster aside, the fact that *China Daily* and other party-supported outlets can advertise freely in the United States, while U.S. media are blocked from so acting in China, indicates the lack of reciprocity between the two nations.

Even though *China Daily* news and commentary concerning the U.S.–China Economic and Security Review Commission is aimed at non-Chinese audiences, it helps to illustrate how Chinese media attempts to parlay the commission's work into a valuable foil for the CCP. In broad terms, *China Daily*'s coverage of the commission can be divided into the topics of Hong Kong, trade, education, media, defense, cybersecurity (including espionage), and technology—themes that largely mirror the U.S. newspaper coverage. As expected, a large proportion of the *China Daily* coverage, perhaps slightly more than fifty percent, focuses on refuting the security threat claims concerning Chinese investment in the United States. Headlines such as "Experts Against US Review of China Investment Deals" (2016; news report), "Investment Protectionism a New US Weapon" (2017; opinion), and "Chinese FDI No Threat to US" (2017; news report) typify China's defensiveness and attempts to counteract the commission's alarmist rhetoric. Seldom do *China Daily*'s headlines attack the commission directly, with "USCC Report on China Truthless, Prejudicial" (2010; news report) being a notable exception. Nearly all of *China Daily*'s coverage of the commission can be categorized as involving either a peace frame or a war frame, with wielders of the "win-win" peace frame crafting headlines such as "US, China Energy Coop Benefits Both" (2006; news report), "Chinese Investment in US: A Stabilizer for Bilateral Ties" (2017; opinion), and "Sino-US Military Engagement, Cooperation" (2015; news report). Such overtly peace-oriented headlines are absent from the U.S. corpus, but they can also be viewed with some suspicion. The CCP's "win-win" rhetoric has been deployed with blithe unilateralism in response to all manner of international conflicts. Its aim is to sooth audiences rather than address concerns. Instead of peace journalism, the win-win frame can be seen as war journalism with a "façade of harmony" (Dodge, 2017).

China Daily writers who employ a war frame, by contrast, attempt to parlay statements and reports critical of China into arguments that depict the United States as habitually and unfairly targeting China, seeking to undermine its economic growth and sovereignty. Headlines in this vein include "Foreign Meddling Threatens Rule of Law" (2019; opinion), "US Spying Activities Are out of Control" (2013; opinion), and "Tripartite Axis Would Fail" (2004; a reference to U.S.–Japan–Taiwan; opinion). The parlay strategy works rhetorically, in both the war frame and peace frame, because it is embedded within China's broader rhetoric of "traumatized nationalism" (Hartnett, 2011). This rhetoric "combines the wounds of that nation's history as a colonial victim with a new chest-thumping bravado" (p. 413). Among traumatized nationalism's principal tropes are U.S. "error," "hypocrisy," and "propaganda." Hartnett (2011) explained how these three tropes work in a causal chain:

> [S]tep 1 shows the US as a factory of factual error; step 2 then demonstrates how American thinking is so factually wrong because it is driven by a series of self-contradictions that amount to a national disease of hypocrisy; step 3 then argues that the combination of error and hypocrisy can be explained by the propaganda needs of the US Empire, which strives to blanket the world with lies. (p. 426)

Examples abound of *China Daily*'s attempts to parlay the commission's outputs into valuable inputs for China's traumatized nationalism counterattack strategy. For example, in an April 17, 2018, opinion piece concerning the commission's recommendation to require Chinese media companies operating in the United States to register as foreign agents, one expert declared that "the US should abandon its prejudices against China and properly evaluate China's public diplomacy and cultural exchange programs" ("Attack on Confucius Institutes Motivated," para. 9). Presumably, "proper" evaluation meant avoiding the error of "prejudice" (step 1) stemming from U.S. officials' "Cold-War mentality and double standard" (step 2; para, 6). Since those hypocritical officials were now in control, the writer lamented, the "anti-China hawks [were] giving the bugle call for battle" (step 3, para. 6).

While the Commission often reports on (and *China Daily* responds to) issues seemingly far removed from trade and investment (e.g., Hong Kong protests and international media practices), economic issues are, in fact, frequently addressed. For example, an August 23, 2018, unsigned *China Daily* editorial, "US Will Aggravate Self-Inflicted Wounds by Persisting with Tariffs," argued that the Trump administration's "misperception" (step 1, para. 4) was due to the president's contradictory stance that "protection will lead to great prosperity and strength" (step 2, para. 10), which the commission's own reporting had debunked by showing recent declines in U.S. exports. The U.S. administration's actions could therefore only be interpreted as an effort to "ultimately block all Chinese imports to the US and discourage US companies from outsourcing operations to Chinese territory—as part of a strategy in the bigger geostrategic rivalry the Trump administration envisions" (step 3, para. 5). Yet, even *China Daily*'s coverage of the commission that deploys the tropes of traumatized nationalism can invoke peace (or rather the "win-win" frame), as when the writers of the op-ed maintained, "If the two sides sort out some of the issues that have emerged, there is no reason why they cannot both continue to benefit from the trade" (para. 12).

Returning to the peace frame more directly, *China Daily* news reports and commentaries deploying it parlay the commission's criticisms of China into calls for cooperation and mutual benefit. These writers generally cite the commission as a voice of U.S. antagonism toward China, but there are instances where the writers cherry-pick parts of the commission's reports and public statements to support their arguments. For example, we can see this tactic in "US, China Energy Coop Benefits Both," where the unnamed author cites Katharine Fredriksen's testimony before the commission. Fredriksen, a principal deputy assistant secretary of Energy, stated,

"While there are notable difference in our approaches, cooperation between our two countries will promote greater energy security in our respective countries, as well as in the world" (2006, para. 3). Yet, the commission cites Fredriksen's comments differently in its own 2006 annual report, highlighting China's "aggressive energy initiatives" (p. 99). Similarly, in "Sino-US Military Engagement, Cooperation," *China Daily* U.S. staff writers Jerome Sibayan and Michael Marra (2015) optimistically noted that a delegation led by the Chinese Academy of Military Science productively interacted with commission representatives during a 2014 panel at the U.S. Army War College. However, the commission has consistently warned of Chinese military expansionism.

In sum, U.S. newspaper coverage (news reports and opinion columns) of the commission have been largely supportive of the commission's conclusions (with notable exceptions) and suspicious of China, while *China Daily*'s coverage (news reports and opinion columns) of the commission evidences the tropes of traumatized nationalism, with occasional flickers of a peace frame (or "pseudo" peace frame, depending on one's suspicions of China) visible. The chapter next turns to the implications of this coverage.

Implications for War and Peace Journalism and the Foreign Policy Market Equilibrium Model

Peace journalism gives voice to all sides, exposes lies and untruths, focuses on common people, and aims to find shared solutions and promote peace initiatives (Ha et al., 2020). War journalism, by contrast, escalates conflict by focusing on violence, serves as a propaganda tool, sides with elites, and aims at achieving "victory" for one's own country. While couched in seemingly neutral technocratic jargon, the U.S.–China Economic and Security Review Commission's annual reports provide ample ammunition for the authors of war journalism and offer relatively few resources for those who promote peace. The themes of the commission's annual reports reveal—as might be expected—that images of peace between the United States and China are almost totally absent. U.S.–China relations are portrayed as a zero-sum game: China's gain is the United States' loss. In fact, where peace is discussed, it is typically in reference to the CCP's use of peace rhetoric in efforts to conceal its alleged "coordinated, long-term effort to transform China into a dominant global power" (U.S.–China Economic and Security Review Commission, 2018, p. 25).

Chinese investment in even the most mundane industries sparks reactionary concerns among some U.S. stakeholders—with hog farming (U.S.–China Economic and Security Review Commission, 2013), manure management (Wyatt, 2013), and even Canadian retirement homes (Wong, 2017) deemed U.S. national security and technology transfer threats. The commission has thus served as a powerful generator and amplifier of China threat discourse, which top U.S. newspapers have done little to question. U.S. reporting of the Chinese government's denials of the commission's allegations (such as industrial espionage) is far from peace journalism. Neither is it peace journalism to report on U.S. corporate complicity in downplaying security breaches for fear of spooking investors, or asserting that U.S. partnerships with Chinese firms are "commercial" in nature. Reporting Chinese government denials and/or U.S. complicity merely reinforces the perpetrator/victim image—it does not promote peace.

While the commission's annual reports are not news reports and thus cannot be considered "war journalism," they clearly exhibit many of the same characteristics: few experts and stakeholders who have briefed the commission (lists are provided in the annual reports) hail from Chinese organizations or possess Chinese surnames, thereby omitting voices from all sides. These experts and stakeholders overwhelming represent elite organizations and interests, rather than ordinary citizens. Significantly, key figures in the current U.S.–China trade war, including U.S. Trade Representative Robert Lighthizer, have testified before the commission. The annual reports do not advance shared solutions nor promote peace initiatives. In 2002, William A. Reinsch, the only commissioner to dissent from the inaugural report's conclusions, was perhaps prescient when he bluntly stated, "by consistently seeing the glass half empty rather than half full, the Report . . . adds to the level of paranoia about China in this country, and contains recommendations that could make that paranoia a self-fulfilling prophecy" (2002, p. 206). Indeed, since 2002, the commission's reports have been cited in innumerable articles (far beyond the newspapers surveyed herein) that have had little to do with trade and/or investment but much to do with amplifying China threat discourse. Despite claims of bipartisan agreement, there is no consensus among U.S. lawmakers or China scholars about whether China threat discourse is justified or not (Bush & Hass, 2019). My own opinion is that such discourse is overwrought: China and the United States will inevitably confront major differences in values and objectives, but the shared goals of peace and prosperity can continue to undergird bilateral and multilateral cooperation.

Regarding the foreign policy market equilibrium hypothesis, the hypothesis maintains that mass media plays a "critical role . . . in shaping the public's attitudes about, and influence on, foreign policy" (Baum & Potter, 2008, p. 39). Because this analysis did not scrutinize how publics actually respond (or not) to media coverage of the commission, it could only focus on whether or not the media "conveyer belt" metaphor held true. As Baum and Potter note, "The indexing hypothesis ["conveyer belt"] has proven durable in part because media do frequently transmit elite messages with largely intact frames" (p. 50). Analysis of the U.S. corpus lends support for the indexing hypothesis (with some notable exceptions). *China Daily's* coverage, however, shows how commentators sympathetic to the CCP's point of view attempt to parlay the commission's China threat discourse. It may be, as Baum and Potter claim, that "the media's framing of elite rhetoric has an independent causal effect on public perceptions of conflict characteristics" (p. 40), but that causal effect could not be assessed here (subsequent chapters take up this question in relation to other media forms and contexts). This chapter has instead examined how China's FDI expansion has exacerbated conflicts with the United States, with the U.S.–China Economic and Security Review Commission being a primary agent in documenting and amplifying these conflicts. While most prior commission reports have been studied mostly by experts and media commentators working in international relations, we can expect that the mounting "casualties" of the trade war (U.S. farmers, exporters, consumers, etc.) will spur increased reporting on the commission's work in the future (as either an ally or adversary).

Importantly, Baum and Potter's hypothesis focuses on the interrelationships among three groups: publics, decisionmakers, and mass media. This analysis suggests that the role of *institutional* actors in the marketplace, such as the commission or related entities, is not yet well theorized in the hypothesis. The commission is not equivalent to "decisionmakers," as it has no policymaking authority. However, the commission is led by former policymakers (with a handful of current lawmakers also appointed). Those who brief the commission also typically hold decision-making positions in business, government, and nongovernmental and academic institutions. The commission also supplies its reports directly to decisionmakers in Congress and other members of the U.S. government. For example, in defending congressional scrutiny of Lenovo's acquisition of IBM's personal computer division in 2005, Representative Frank Wolf (R-VA) told reporters that concerns about the U.S. State Department's use of Lenovo computers had been brought to his attention by two members of the commission. "They deserve the credit for this," Wolf remarked (Lohr, 2006, para. 12). In this way, the commission can be associated with the decisionmakers' portion of Baum and Potter's triad. As scholars have argued, however, the work of quasi-institutional actors, such as the commission, the Defense Science Board, or the Intelligence and National Security Alliance, needs increased public scrutiny (Hartnett & Goodale 2008). How commercial interests slyly gain voice and influence in policymaking arenas must be better understood.

The commission also relies, in part, on media coverage of China as both an input in its reporting process and as a means of amplifying the commission's voice among decisionmakers and publics. The commission is certainly least associated with the "publics" despite being briefed (and sometimes headed) by leaders of organizations that claim to represent the public interest, i.e., the American Federation of Labor and Congress of Industrial Organizations (AFL–CIO), the National Corn Growers Association, and Sasakawa Peace Foundation, among others. Commentary from representatives of these organizations generally supports the "competitive" view of U.S.–China relations. I therefore argue that institutions such as the commission constitute a shadowy fourth actor whose role in the foreign policy marketplace needs to be better understood and managed. Indeed, the meanings of security are routinely created, maintained, or transformed in crucial institutional settings (Bean & Rice, 2019). Institutional actors can be immensely creative at crafting selective interpretations of texts (e.g., media reports) that, when subsequently inscribed in other authoritative texts (e.g., laws), serve to *perform* (i.e., embed, extend, and reify) actions that, previously, they had merely documented (Cooren, 2004). Analysts must therefore be attuned to the ways that institutional actors seek to "securitize" areas of U.S.–China investment, moving those investments from the mundane to the extraordinary. Such moves can be powerful discursive ammunition for war journalism. The ways these moves are performed in media reporting is subtle, however, requiring careful analysis by those committed to moving the U.S. and China past their mutual recriminations. The chapters in this volume are a much-needed contribution in understanding how media organizations and publics reinforce or resist such rhetorical slights of hand.

Conclusions

This analysis was limited to speakers in institutional and traditional media settings and did not engage how audiences actually make sense of (i.e., ignore, assent to, or resist) their discourse. The analysis nevertheless revealed fear and anxiety on both sides, with the U.S.–China Economic and Security Review Commission, and most U.S. journalists, asserting that China's FDI expansion has eroded U.S. power and bolstered the CCP's influence. *China Daily* commentators, by contrast, have argued that U.S. error, hypocrisy, and dominance have aimed to thwart China's rise. Each side displays frustration and anxiety that they cannot adequately control the other. While a handful of *China Daily* voices expressed visions of cooperation, both sides would do well in the future to better promote the shared desires of common people to live in secure, prosperous, and harmonious societies. Journalists and commentators have played a crucial role in promoting or impeding this frustration and anxiety, and they will continue to do so. Therefore, better ascertaining the media's role vis-à-vis U.S.–China relations is essential if stakeholders are to develop interventions that avoid a future confrontation between these two powerful countries.

Finally, on a personal note, on September 21, 2018, as an early round of trade war tariffs were being announced in both China and the United States, I led a class of University of Colorado Denver / International College Beijing students to the Asian Infrastructure Investment Bank (AIIB) in Beijing. There, we met with AIIB officials to discuss the mission of the new institution, its operations, and internal and external communication. The AIIB is not without criticism, but visiting the first multilateral development bank headquartered in China with my students underscored what is possible when people from different countries collaboratively work together to solve shared economic and social problems. The trade war that began in 2018 marks a significant culmination (and perhaps structural reconfiguration) of the ongoing conflict between the United States and China in the economic arena, but our visit to the AIIB suggested to me that the current trajectory of U.S.–China relations is not inevitable. A different path could be taken. Toward this end, the subsequent chapters analyze how mainstream journalists and social media users have covered this conflict and their influence on public opinion, as well as the impact of both on U.S.–China relations.

REFERENCES

Baum, M. A., & Potter, P. B. (2008). The relationships between mass media, public opinion, and foreign policy: Toward a theoretical synthesis. *Annual Review of Political Science, 11*, 39–65.

Bean, H., & Rice, R. M. (2019). Organizational communication and security. In B. C. Taylor & H. Bean (Eds.), *The handbook of communication and security* (pp. 136–52). Routledge.

Blustein, P. (2019). *Schism: China, America, and the fracturing of the global trading system.* Centre for International Governance Innovation.

Bush, R. C., & Hass, R. (2019, March 4). The China debate is here to stay. *Order from chaos.* Brookings Institution. https://www.brookings.edu/blog/order-from-chaos/2019/03/04/the-china-debate-is-here-to-stay/

Clinton, W. J. (2000, March 9). *Full speech of Clinton's speech on China trade bill.* Institute for Agriculture and Trade. https://www.iatp.org/sites/default/files/Full_Text_of_Clintons_Speech_on_China_Trade_Bi.htm

Cooren, F. (2004, May 1). Textual agency: How texts do things in organizational settings. *Organization, 11*(3), 373–93. https://doi.org/10.1177%2F1350508404041998

Dodge, P. S.-W. (2017). Imagining dissent: Contesting the façade of harmony through art and the internet in China. In S. J. Hartnett, L. Keränen, & D. Conley (Eds.), *Imagining China: Rhetorics of nationalism in the age of globalization* (pp. 311–338). Michigan State University Press.

Eller, D. (2018, September 28). Citing ad in *Des Moines Register*, Trump accuses China of meddling in U.S. elections. *Des Moines Register.* https://www.desmoinesregister.com/story/news/politics/2018/09/26/donald-trump-des-moines-register-ad-attack-china-meddling-united-nations-president-election/1434194002/

Ha, L., Yang, Y., Ray, R., Matanji, F., Chen, P., Guo, K., & Lyu, N. (2020). How US and Chinese media cover the US–China trade conflict: A case study of war and peace journalism practice and the foreign policy equilibrium hypothesis. *Negotiation and Conflict Management Research.* https://doi.org/10.1111/ncmr.1218

Hartnett, S. J. (2011, October 6). Google and the "twisted cyber spy" affair: US–Chinese communication in an age of globalization. *Quarterly Journal of Speech, 97*, 411–34.

Hartnett, S. J., & Goodale, G. (2008). Debating 'the means of apocalypse': The Defense Science Board, the military–industrial complex, and the production of imperial propaganda. In D. M. Timmerman & T. F. McDorman (Eds.), *Rhetoric and democracy: Pedagogical and political practices* (pp. 181–224). Michigan State University Press.

Hartnett, S. J., Keränen, L. B., & Conley, D. (Eds.). (2017). *Imagining China: Rhetorics of nationalism in an age of globalization.* Michigan State University Press.

Li, H. (2018, April 17). Attack on Confucius Institutes motivated. *China Daily.* http://global.chinadaily.com.cn/a/201804/17/WS5ad52d10a3105cdcf65189a5.html

Lighthizer, R. E., (1999, April 18). A deal we'd be likely to regret. *New York Times.*

Lim, L., & Bergin, J. (2018, December 7). Inside China's audacious global propaganda campaign. *The Guardian.*

Lohr, S. (2005, July 6). The big tug of war over Unocal. *New York Times.*

Mahbubani, K. (2019, February). What China threat? How the United States and China can avoid war. *Harpers.* https://harpers.org/archive/2019/02/what-china-threat/

Markoff, J. (2007, August 24). Chinese seek to buy a U.S. maker of disk drives. *New York Times.*

Markoff, J., & Barboza, D. (2010, March 20). Academic paper in China sets off alarms in U.S. *New York Times.*

Morell, M., & Kris, D. (2018, December 14). It's not a trade war with China: It's a tech war. *Washington Post.*

Office of the United States Trade Representative. (2019). *The People's Republic of China.* https://ustr.gov/countries-regions/china-mongolia-taiwan/peoples-republic-china

Schwarzenberg, A. B. (2019, August 28). U.S.-China investment ties: Overview and issues for congress. *Congressional Research Service.* https://crsreports.congress.gov/product/pdf/IF/IF11283/2

Swanson, A., & Rappeport, A. (2018, March 28). White House looks to use emergency law to halt Chinese investment. *New York Times.*

Sibayan, J., & Marra, M. (2015, April 22). Sino-US military engagement, cooperation. *China Daily.* http://www.chinadaily.com.cn/kindle/2015-04/22/content_20507470.htm

US, China energy coop benefits both. (2006, August 5). *China Daily.* https://www.chinadaily.com.cn/china/2006-08/05/content_657781.htm

U.S.-China Economic and Security Review Commission. (2019). *Charter.* https://www.uscc.gov/charter

U.S.-China Economic and Security Review Commission. (2018). *Report to Congress.* https://www.uscc.gov/annual-report/2018-annual-report-congress

U.S.-China Economic and Security Review Commission. (2015). *Report to Congress.* https://www.uscc.gov/annual-report/2015-annual-report-congress

U.S.-China Economic and Security Review Commission. (2013). *Report to Congress.* https://www.uscc.gov/annual-report/2013-annual-report-congress

U.S.-China Economic and Security Review Commission. (2006). *Report to Congress.* https://www.uscc.gov/annual-report/2006-annual-report-congress

U.S.-China Security Review Commission. (2002). *Report to Congress.* https://www.uscc.gov/annual-report/2002-annual-report-congress

U.S. Trade Representative (2002). *Report to congress on China's WTO compliance.* Council on Foreign Relations. https://www.cfr.org/content/publications/attachments/SPRing0315.09-thru-15.13.pdf

US will aggravate self-inflicted wounds by persisting with tariffs. (2018, August 23). *China*

Daily. http://www.chinadaily.com.cn/a/201808/23/WS5b7ec34ba310add14f387770.html

Wong, K. A. (2017, July 11). Canadian nursing home deal spurs questions about Chinese money. *New York Times*.

Wyatt, E. (2013, July 10). Senators question Chinese takeover of Smithfield. *New York Times*.

Zemin, J. (1999, September 8). *President Jiang Zemin on China's access to WTO*. Embassy of the People's Republic of China in the United States of America. http://www.china-embassy. org/eng/zt/wto/t36909.htm

Zengerle, P. (2018, October 4). Congress, eying China, votes to overhaul development finance. *Reuters*. https://www.reuters.com/article/us-usa-congress-development/congress-eying-china-votes-to-overhaul-development-finance-idUSKCN1MD2HJ

National Images as Integrated Schemas

How Americans and Chinese Think about Each Other and
the U.S.–China Trade War

Lars Willnat, Shuo Tang, Jian Shi, and Ning Zhan

Most of the research on how the media influence perceptions of foreign nations has focused on two theories to explain the relationship between exposure to news about international affairs and public opinion about foreign nations. *Agenda-setting* asks how people learn about the importance of global issues from the media, which might influence the issues they consider important when thinking about foreign countries (see McCombs & Shaw, 1972; McCombs, 2005), while *framing* asks how news consumers are guided by the media to see a foreign nation from a particular frame of reference, which might alter the way people perceive that nation (see Goffman, 1974; Entman, 1993).

While the media might affect how the public thinks about other countries by presenting them with international news, people's perceptions of foreign nations are also influenced by their pre-existing beliefs and stereotypes (see Cuddy et al., 2009; Dovidio et al., 2010). Most Americans, for example, are likely to hold stereotypical views about nations such as China or Russia; not necessarily because U.S. news media outlets cover these nations in stereotypical ways, but because their perceptions of these nations are influenced by deeply rooted beliefs that often date back to the Cold War era and beyond.

The surveys were funded by the John Ben Snow Foundation and Syracuse University.

Moreover, attitudes toward foreign nations are influenced by personal background factors, such as personal experiences with foreigners, visits to other countries, and openness to foreign cultures in general. These personal factors likely interact with national images to help form the more general attitudes people hold toward foreign nations. Agenda-setting and framing therefore work alongside stereotypes and personal experiences to enable news consumers to form opinions about international affairs.

Relations between China and the United States offer an ideal test case for analyzing how such national images interact with news exposure to affect perceptions of foreign affairs. Most Chinese and Americans have not visited the other country (UN World Tourism Organization, 2019) but have likely encountered numerous images of the other nation through the news and entertainment media in their home countries. While long-term exposure to such mediated images should contribute to relatively stable perceptions of China and the United States, news coverage of the other country's political and economic affairs might affect people's more ephemeral attitudes and feelings toward the other nation.

The present study aims to analyze how these pre-existing beliefs and personal factors interact with news exposure to influence the ways American and Chinese people think about each other. Grounded in international image theory (Herrmann & Fischerkeller, 1995; Herrmann, 2013), we argue that individuals maintain general images of foreign nations and that these national images, which interact with news exposure, shape their perceptions of foreign policy issues. Moreover, we argue that national images can be conceptualized as mental schemas that are built on people's stereotypical perceptions of nations and other predispositions, such as patriotism or more accepting attitudes toward different cultures and values.

The data for our analysis come from two national online surveys conducted in the United States and China in early 2019. The surveys, which are based on identical questionnaires to allow for comparative analysis, explore whether national images of the United States and China are associated with media exposure and perceptions of the U.S.–China trade war among the American and Chinese public. The goal of this comparative analysis is to validate the components of national images in two very different political and cultural systems and contribute to a more precise conceptualization of national images. This, in turn, should help us better understand how foreign affairs coverage might affect U.S.–China relations in general and how it influenced public opinion about the trade war in particular.

The Concept of National Images

Conceptualizations of national images vary significantly across disciplines, including public relations, cross-national finance and business, and international politics (Kang & Yang, 2010; Nye Jr., 2008; Wang, 2006). In media studies, analyses of national images often rely on cognitive (what we know about a nation) and affective (how we feel about a nation) components to measure this concept. However, national images are never monolithic and are often constructed within complex and even contradictory social and cultural contexts, meaning they can be multilayered, contested, and conceived in opposition to the image of one's own nation (Hartnett et al., 2017). Moreover, national images function as important guidelines for understanding international affairs. As Castano, Bonacossa, and Gries (2016) noted, national images "serve an information-reduction function and enrich our understanding of our bilateral relationships. They may simplify our views of the world, but they do so by adding interpretative elements that were not there in the first place" (p. 353). As we see in Beckman and Hartnett and Bean in this volume, in the case of the U.S.–China trade war, this "information-reduction function" means many Americans hold feelings about the trade war that are not informed by sophisticated understandings of international relations or economics. In this case, prevalent "national images" are deeply emotional but not necessarily informed by economic reasoning.

These findings support Boulding's (1959) argument that national images help simplify a complex international environment. Based on Asch's (1952) earlier work on Gestalt psychology, he reasoned that national images primarily consist of three elements: a nation's geographic space, its perceived hostility or friendliness, and its perceived strength or weakness. Boulding maintained that these dimensions could be used to predict the actions of people who rely on such national images in their decision-making processes (Herrmann, 2013).

Later studies (Karlins et al., 1969; Peabody, 1985) conceptualized national images as stereotypes (e.g., ally or enemy) that individuals maintain about other countries to help them simplify the world, even in the absence of much knowledge about international affairs (Castano et al., 2016). Stereotypes are commonly defined as "a socially shared set of beliefs about traits that are characteristic of members of a social category" (Greenwald & Banaji, 1995, p. 14). For this study, we define national stereotypes as "stored beliefs about characteristics of a specific country that are socially shared" (Herz & Diamantopoulos, 2013, p. 402). Although there has been little empirical work on the origins of national stereotypes, most are formed either through direct experience with the relevant national groups or indirectly through education or the media (Schneider, 2005).

Herrmann and Fischerkeller's (1995) international image theory extended this viewpoint of national images as stereotypes by arguing that national images operate as cognitive simplification devices (schemas) that allow people to make sense of the international environment. According to Herrmann (2013, p. 11), national images are "clusters of knowledge" that help people shape their interpretations of new information and replace information that people are missing. In other words, national images allow people to process and judge information about international affairs, which would otherwise require a deeper understanding of how the world operates.

Following previous studies based on international image theory (Herrmann & Fischerkeller, 1995; Herrmann, 2013), we propose that national images consist mostly of pre-existing stereotypes or mental schemas that not only help people understand international affairs but also influence their attitudes toward related foreign affairs issues (Castano et al., 2016). Nisbet et al. (2004), for example, found that predispositions toward the United States in predominantly Muslim countries acted as "perceptual screens" that allowed individuals to process news content in ways that confirmed their existing anti-American attitudes.

While perceptions of other nations likely are based on simple heuristics such as "enemy" or "friend" (Cottam, 1999; Herrmann, 1985, 1986; Hurwitz & Peffley, 1990; Silverstein, 1989), stereotypes of people from other nations are more complex because they represent shared beliefs about the personal attributes of "others" with unfamiliar customs, cultures, or habits (Leyens et al., 1992). Recent studies have confirmed stereotypical perceptions of Chinese and Americans that contain both positive and negative attributes (Ruble & Zhang, 2013; Zhang, 2015; Zhu, 2016). Moreover, studies conducted in Mexico, Thailand, and Taiwan found stereotypes of Americans that were mainly attributed to how domestic and U.S. television programs portray Americans (Tan et al., 1986; Tan & Suarchavarat, 1988). Similarly, Willnat et al. (1997) found associations between foreign TV consumption and stereotypical perceptions of Americans in Hong Kong and mainland China. Overall, these findings suggest that stereotypes of nations and people are closely linked to, and are influenced by, exposure to domestic and foreign media.

Because national images have traditionally been conceptualized as consisting of cognitive and affective components (Boulding, 1959; Fiske et al., 2002), our national image model includes an explicitly emotional measure of feelings toward people of other nations. It is reasonable to assume that attitudes toward a nation are influenced at least partly by how the people of that nation are perceived from the outside. Thus, Americans who hold positive perceptions of the Chinese should also think more positively about China, even if they do not necessarily agree with China's domestic or foreign policies. The same should be true for Chinese who hold positive views of Americans.

Moreover, we assume that national images are linked with general knowledge about other countries and their people acquired over a person's lifetime. According to previous studies, the news media's reporting of foreign affairs significantly influences the communication process of knowing about other nations (Kunczik, 2002) and, subsequently, influences public opinion toward these nations (Albritton & Manheim, 1985; Manheim & Albritton, 1983; Perry, 1985, 1987). Thus, people's images of foreign nations likely incorporate knowledge that differs depending on how much they have learned about these nations in the past.

Connecting Personal Traits with National Images

International research conducted by the Pew Research Center (Poushter, 2020; Silver et al., 2019) found that younger people across most nations surveyed tend to have more positive views of the United States or China. Such favorable perceptions might be due to the fact that younger people tend to be less burdened by historical baggage and more open-minded about the effects of globalization. Fung et al. (2018) argue that national images are influenced by the interactions of people's news exposure and personal traits, such as patriotism or personal experiences with a country. Based on survey interviews with Chinese respondents who were asked about their perceptions of the United States in 2007, the authors suggest that media exposure and personal traits influence mostly the cognitive components of the national image that the respondents held about the United States. Likewise, we assume that national images are shaped by personal traits such as general openness toward foreign cultures and personal experiences with people from other nations. In this study, we analyze the potential effects of four personal traits on the formation of national images: cosmopolitanism, patriotism, cultural affinity, and personal experiences with foreign nations.

Due to rapid globalization over the past few decades, cosmopolitanism has become an important predisposition for understanding attitudes and behaviors toward other nations and their peoples (Leung et al., 2015). The literature contains several different conceptualizations of cosmopolitanism, such as cultural openness measured by the eagerness to learn from and engage with cultures (Cleveland et al., 2009; Skrbis et al., 2004), the tendency among individuals to see themselves as global citizens rather than citizens of a specific nation (Riefler & Diamantopoulos, 2009), and advocating international relationships and respecting cultural diversity (Leung et al., 2015). The notion that cosmopolitanism is associated with people's perceptions of other nations is supported by studies that found correlations between cosmopolitanism and more positive perceptions of foreign products (Cleveland et al., 2009; Jin et al., 2015). Owing to the likelihood that cosmopolitanism strongly influences how people view other nations, we included this concept in our model as an essential personal trait.

The way people feel about their own nation also should influence how they think about other nations. Several studies have found that feelings of patriotism can shape people's attitudes toward other countries by defining the other nation as different from one's own (Fung et al., 2018; Gries et al., 2011; Hurwitz & Peffley, 1990; Lay & Torney-Purta, 2007; Sinkkonen, 2013). Because patriotism is likely to influence an individual's perceptions of another nation, especially those that are perceived as adversaries or competitors, we also included the concept of patriotism as a personal trait in our model.

Studies on international relations also found that political similarities (Nincic & Russett, 1979) and "strategic affinity" (or common interests) between nations can significantly reduce the likelihood of conflict between them (Maoz et al., 2006). Similarly, the related concept of "cultural affinity" can positively influence consumers' perceptions of products from other nations (e.g., Oberecker & Diamantopoulos, 2011). While cultural affinity has not been linked directly to national images in previous studies, it likely influences people's thoughts and feelings about other nations. For example, individuals might be more likely to treat nations with which they believe they share common values as friends or allies. We therefore consider cultural affinity a personal trait in our model.

Finally, while stereotypes or a lack of knowledge about other nations might distort outsiders' perceptions of these nations, visiting a foreign country or meeting people from other countries should make people more familiar with these nations. Such intergroup contact has been found to reduce prejudice between members of traditionally opposed ethnic groups (Ata et al., 2009; Barlow et al., 2012) and to decrease intergroup anxiety and prejudice toward outgroup members (Pettigrew &

Tropp, 2006; Techakesari et al., 2015). Consequently, we added personal experiences with China or the United States as a personal trait in our model.

Perceptions of National Images and the U.S.–China Trade War

Based on the above discussion, we propose that people's image of another nation is built on mental schema that mostly consist of a combination of deeply rooted stereotypes about the other nation and its people, general feelings of like or dislike toward the people of the other nation, and previously acquired knowledge about the other nation. Furthermore, we propose that personal traits, such as cosmopolitanism, patriotism, cultural affinity, and personal experiences with other nations influence these national images or schemas.

In addition, exposure to international news should add to what people already know about a nation. Previous studies found that more exposure to foreign news is associated with an increase in people's knowledge about foreign affairs (Korzenny et al., 1987; McNelly & Izcaray, 1986). Moreover, even though foreign news is often negative and focused on conflict (e.g., Galtung & Ruge, 1965; Gozenbach et al., 1992), people exposed to more news are likely to have a more nuanced understanding of foreign affairs than those who consume less news. Thus, exposure to international news should lead to more informed perceptions of other nations and make audiences more immune to negative foreign news coverage because of their ability to process information more critically (Perry, 1989). Consequently, we argue that national image, personal traits, and news exposure will significantly influence a nation's perceived favorability.

Given the growing economic tensions between the United States and China over the past decade, public perceptions of favorability toward the other nation should significantly influence people's attitudes toward the U.S.–China trade war. For example, Americans who have favorable views of China should be more concerned about the negative consequences of the trade war for bilateral relations between the two nations than those who have less favorable views. They should also worry that greater trade tariffs could increase consumer costs, job losses, and reduce personal income—consequences that have been extensively covered by the media of both nations (Lian, 2018; Swanson & Tankersley, 2019). In addition, individuals with more exposure to news about the trade war should be more likely to reject additional trade tariffs because they have a better understanding of the fact that trade tariffs usually hurt domestic economies and lead to higher consumer prices. We therefore argue that individuals exposed to more news about the trade war, and who are more concerned about its negative effects, will be less likely to believe that tariffs are an effective approach to win the U.S.–China trade war.

In short, this study tests to what extent national images, personal traits, and media exposure are associated with how Americans and Chinese perceive the U.S.–China trade war. If their perceptions of the trade war are indeed associated with their national images of "the other," Americans and Chinese might be less likely to assess the trade war's consequences rationally, relying instead on heuristic shortcuts (Tversky & Kahneman, 1974) linked to their national images.

Methods

Data for this study come from two national online surveys conducted in May (United States) and July (China) of 2019, with national samples of 1,250 American adults and 1,311 Chinese adults, respectively. The respondents in both countries were recruited by Qualtrics, a professional survey organization that provides access to representative online panels. Both samples were formed based on quotas for age and gender by following the latest available census data. The cooperation rate was 93 percent in the United States and 90 percent in China. The questionnaire was initially written in English, translated into Chinese by a bilingual media scholar, and then double-checked by two Chinese graduate students familiar with public opinion research.

The American sample comprised 51 percent females and 49 percent males with a median age of thirty-nine years. Most respondents were either high school (20.4 percent) or college graduates (27.6 percent) with a median yearly income of $50,000–$55,000. The respondents were reasonably representative of race (72 percent Caucasian, 14.6 percent African American, 4.3 percent Asian) and political affiliation (25.2 percent Republicans, 34 percent Democrats, 31.7 percent Independents). While the overall sample compared favorably to the 2010 U.S. Census data, respondents were slightly older, more educated, and racially less diverse than the U.S. population. However, a comparison of our sample with representative samples used by the Pew Research Center in 2019 revealed only minor differences between the demographic characteristics of the two samples. Therefore, we are fairly confident that the sample is representative of the U.S. population.

The Chinese sample consisted of 49 percent females and 51 percent males with a median age of thirty-six years, including respondents from all provinces, autonomous regions, and municipalities (excluding Hong Kong and Macau). Most respondents (71.9 percent) had degrees from vocational schools or above, lived in urban areas (88.1 percent), and had median monthly incomes of RMB 6,000–8,000. Compared to a 2019 national sample of Chinese internet users by the China Internet Network Information Center (CNNIC, 2019), our sample contained respondents slightly more likely to be female, older, urban, and better educated.

Variables

Media Exposure. In the United States, exposure to traditional news media was assessed by asking respondents about the number of days in the past week on which they watched national TV news, read printed national newspapers, and used news websites. They were also asked how frequently they watched Fox News and MSNBC. In China, respondents were asked about the number of days in the past week on which they watched TV news, read a printed daily newspaper, and used news websites.

Social Media Use. The use of social media was measured by asking respondents how many days in the past week they used social media sites (U.S.: Facebook, Twitter, Instagram, YouTube, Reddit, Snapchat; China: WeChat, QQ, Weibo, TikTok, Baidu Tieba). Responses to these items were combined in a *social media use* index (U.S.: $M = 3.38$, $SD = 1.97$, $\alpha = .80$; China: $M = 4.93$, $SD = 1.58$, $\alpha = .73$).

Measures of National Images

Stereotypes. Stereotypes of China were measured using a five-point semantic differential scale that presented respondents with ten dichotomous descriptions of China, including items such as "rich/poor cultural heritage" or "strong/weak economy." The scale items were derived from previous research on stereotypes (Zhang, 2015), which we then pretested in a pilot study of 374 respondents on Mechanical Turk. Based on this pilot study, we selected the ten most relevant descriptions for the final scale. Responses to these ten items were then combined in a *China stereotype* index ($M = 3.49$, $SD = .77$, $\alpha = .82$). Stereotypes of the United

States were measured with the same items that were used to assess stereotypes of China, except for "communist/capitalist" and "sells copycat/original products." Responses to these eight items were combined in a *U.S. stereotype* index (M = 3.93, SD = .61, α = .70).

Stereotypes of Chinese were measured using a five-point semantic differential scale that presented respondents with ten dichotomous descriptions of Chinese, including items such as "lazy/hardworking" or "educated/uneducated." The ten items were selected from a pool of forty descriptions (Terracciano & McCrae, 2007) through the Mechanical Turk pilot study mentioned above. Responses to these ten items were combined in a *Chinese stereotype* index (M = 3.72, SD = .81, α = .86). Stereotypes of Americans were measured with the same five-point semantic differential scale that presented the respondents with ten dichotomous descriptions of Americans, including items such as "open-minded/closed-minded" or "shy/bold." Similar to the procedure used to identify stereotypes of Chinese, the ten descriptions of Americans were selected through a pilot study of 127 Chinese college students. Responses to these ten items were combined in an *American stereotype* index (M = 4.04, SD = .66, α = .71).

Feelings. To assess how respondents felt toward "the other," they were asked to rate their feelings toward the American/Chinese people on a 101-point temperature scale (0 = cold, 100 = warm) (U.S.: M = 62.7, SD = 25.14; China: M = 58.5, SD = 23.82).

Knowledge. General knowledge about China was measured with six questions that asked respondents, for example, to name the capital of China or identify China's political system. Similarly, general knowledge of the United States was measured with five questions that asked respondents, for example, to name the United States' capital or identify President Trump's political party. The answers to these questions were added into a *knowledge index* for each country ranging from 0 (ill-informed) to 1 (well-informed) (U.S.: M = .37, SD = .25; China: M = .71, SD = .25).

Measures of Personal Traits

Cosmopolitanism. General openness toward foreign influences was assessed by asking the respondents how much they agreed (1 = strongly disagree, 5 = strongly agree) with five statements developed by Cleveland and Laroche (2007): "I like to observe people of other cultures, to see what I can learn from them"; "I am interested in learning more about people who live in other countries"; "I enjoy being with people from other countries to learn about their unique views and approaches"; "I enjoy exchanging ideas with people from other cultures or countries"; and "I find people from other cultures stimulating." Agreement with each of the statements were combined in a *cosmopolitanism* index (U.S.: $M = 4.01$, $SD = .82$, $\alpha = .92$; China: $M = 3.90$, $SD = .60$, $\alpha = .86$).

Patriotism. Respondents' patriotism was measured by asking them how much they agreed (1 = strongly disagree, 5 = strongly agree) with three statements: "It is important to have been born in the U.S./China to be truly American/Chinese"; "I feel attached to a shared Chinese/American identity"; and "I'm proud to be a Chinese/American citizen." The responses were combined in a *patriotism* index (U.S.: $M = 3.73$, $SD = .92$, $\alpha = .70$; China: $M = 4.39$, $SD = .74$, $\alpha = .86$).

Cultural Affinity. Perceptions of cultural affinity between Americans and Chinese were measured by asking respondents about the extent to which they thought that people in the United States shared similar values with people in China (1 = no extent, 4 = great extent).

Personal Experiences. To gauge the level of interaction with Chinese/American people, the respondents were asked whether they had ever met a person from China/the U.S., have friends or relatives who are American/Chinese, know anyone currently living or working in the U.S/China, have ever traveled to the U.S./China, or are interested in visiting the U.S./China. The answers were added into a *personal interaction index* (U.S.: $M = 2.09$, $SD = 1.41$, $\alpha = .66$; China: $M = 2.46$, $SD = 1.61$, $\alpha = .71$).

Other Measures

Overall Favorability. To assess respondents' overall perceptions of China and the United States, they were asked how favorably (= 4) or unfavorably (= 1) they view the U.S./China (U.S.: $M = 3.25$, $SD = 1.12$; China: $M = 3.05$, $SD = 1.07$).

Perceptions of the U.S.–China Trade War. A series of four questions were asked to measure respondents' perceptions of specific aspects of the U.S.–China trade war: "How strongly do you support or oppose the policy of raising tariffs on products imported from the U.S./China?" (1 = strongly oppose, 5 = strongly support); "How concerned are you about the trade war between the United States and China?" (1 = not concerned at all, 5 = very concerned); "Will the trade war with the U.S./China be good or bad for your personal finances/for the U.S. economy, or will it have no impact?" (1 = bad, 2 = will have no impact, 3 = good).

Demographics. Both surveys included standard demographic control variables for assessing the respondents' gender, age, education, political party affiliation (Democrat and Republican in the United States, Communist party member in China), place of residence (urban, suburban, and rural), and income.

Findings

The first part of our analysis focuses on how Americans and Chinese think about each other's nation and people. Overall, the findings indicate that Americans and Chinese share similar levels of favorability toward the other nation. About four in ten Americans (38.9 percent) and Chinese (36.7 percent) reported very or at least somewhat favorable attitudes toward the other nation. Despite these similarities in the perceived favorability of the other nation, how Americans and Chinese viewed each other as "people" differed significantly. While a majority (56.4 percent) of Americans held favorable views toward the Chinese, less than half (42.5 percent) of the Chinese viewed Americans as favorable.

In addition to asking respondents about their overall feelings toward the other nation and its people, we measured their stereotypical perceptions of each other. While Americans thought of China mostly as a country with a "rich cultural heritage" and "advanced science and technology," many of them also saw it as "authoritarian." The Chinese people were mostly seen as "hardworking," "disciplined," "motivated," and "family-oriented." Similarly, the Chinese thought of the United States as having "advanced science and technology," a "powerful military," and as a country that is "rich" and "modern." The top traits that characterized Americans, according to our Chinese respondents, were "bold," "ambitions," "free," and "open-minded."

While these perceptions of "the other" are important, our analysis focuses on the *strength* of national stereotypes rather than their particular content. In other words, we are mostly interested in how deeply ingrained these stereotypes are in people's minds. Overall, the findings indicate that Chinese ($M = 3.93$) not only held stronger stereotypes of the United States compared to how Americans ($M = 3.49$) thought about China but also perceived Americans ($M = 4.04$) in more stereotypical ways compared to how Americans saw the Chinese ($M = 3.72$). Thus, national stereotypes were more prevalent among Chinese citizens. As indicated in other chapters herein, this finding suggests that the more controlled media ecosystem in China, as compared to America, likely produces a narrower band of responses to international affairs, albeit with stronger and more coherent feelings about them. In short, most Americans' stereotypes about China fall all over the political map and are not strongly held, while most Chinese stereotypes about America fall within a narrower band of perspectives but are more firmly held.

Perception of the U.S.–China Trade War

As expected, the majority of Americans (86.3 percent) believed that trade with China is very or at least somewhat important to the United States' economy. Similarly, most Chinese (82.9 percent) recognized the importance of trade with the United States. More than six in ten Americans (63.3 percent) also reported that they were concerned about the U.S.–China trade war. These worries were even more pronounced in China, where more than eight in ten respondents (82.4 percent) were concerned about the economic dispute between the two nations.

The obvious concerns about the trade war among respondents in both nations likely reflected their fear that this economic dispute could harm their respective national economies. However, Americans were significantly less concerned about this possibility than the Chinese. While slightly less than half of the Americans (47.1 percent) were concerned about the negative impact of the trade war on the U.S. economy, more than seven in ten Chinese (72.3 percent) were worried that the trade war could negatively affect their domestic economy. Similarly, more Chinese (47.1 percent) than Americans (36.8 percent) were worried that the trade war could affect their finances negatively.

In light of these concerns, it is somewhat surprising that a substantial number of respondents in each nation supported the idea of increasing the existing trade tariffs. Nearly half of the Americans (45.8 percent), for example, agreed with President Trump's policy to increase the current tariffs on Chinese imports, while only about one-third (29.2 percent) opposed further tariff hikes. Similarly, almost six in ten of the Chinese (58.4 percent) supported the idea of increasing the tariffs on U.S. imports, while only 18.8 percent opposed such an increase. While support for the tariffs in the United States correlated closely with partisan backing for President Trump, the strong support for additional trade tariffs on U.S. imports among Chinese citizens can be explained by the fact that the Chinese media framed the trade war as an attack on China and the counter-tariffs as a tit-for-tat against a foreign aggressor (Wei & Kubota, 2019). Therefore, it is reasonable to assume that Chinese citizens viewed the additional tariffs on U.S. imports as a necessary and justified reaction to the tariffs imposed on Chinese goods by the United States.

Predictors of Favorability toward the United States and China

To test whether the components of a national image are associated with the perceived favorability of a nation, we developed a hierarchical regression model to predict the respondents' overall favorability toward the other nation with four sets of related variables. The model included demographics background factors such as sex, age, and education (Block 1); measures of traditional and social media usage (Block 2); personal traits, including cosmopolitanism, patriotism, cultural affinity, and personal experiences (Block 3); and components of respondents' national images, including stereotypes of a nation and its people, feelings toward Chinese/ Americans, and knowledge about a nation (Block 4).

As table 1 shows, all four variable blocks are significantly associated with how favorably American and Chinese respondents viewed the other nation. Among Americans, younger, more conservative men who had higher incomes and lived in urban areas had more favorable attitudes toward China. Among Chinese, by contrast, younger women with higher income levels had the most positive attitudes toward the United States.

News exposure turned out to be a relatively strong predictor of how Americans saw China but much less so for how Chinese thought about the United States. Americans who read newspapers more regularly, were more exposed to MSNBC, and used social media more frequently tended to have more positive perceptions of China. More frequent use of news websites, by contrast, was associated with somewhat less favorable perceptions of China. Among Chinese, reading newspapers was positively associated with perceptions of the United States, while watching TV news correlated with more negative views. Of course, these differences in media exposure are partly due to the fact that U.S. media consumers have access to very different media outlets than Chinese audiences.

Personal traits also were strong predictors of how favorably Americans and Chinese viewed the other nation. Respondents with higher levels of cosmopolitanism, cultural affinity, and more direct personal experiences with China or the United States generally perceived the other nation more favorably. Interestingly,

TABLE 1. Predictors of Overall Favorability toward China and the United States

	PERCEPTIONS OF CHINA AMONG AMERICANS	PERCEPTIONS OF THE U.S. AMONG CHINESE
DEMOGRAPHICS		
Female	−.10**	.08**
Age	−.16***	−.08**
Education	.01	.06
Republican/Communist	.09**	.07*
Urban resident	.12***	.04
Income	.11**	.12***
ΔR^2 (in %)	8.3***	5.1***
MEDIA EXPOSURE		
Newspapers	.25***	.12**
National TV	.01	−.07*
Fox News	.05	—
MSNBC	.12***	—
Online news	−.12***	.04
Social media	.22***	−.03
ΔR^2 (in %)	16.3***	1.0*
PERSONAL TRAITS		
Cosmopolitanism	.12***	.19***
Patriotism	.07**	−.29***
Experience with China/U.S.	.20***	.17***
Cultural affinity	.32***	.35***
ΔR^2 (in %)	17.4***	29.9***
IMAGE OF CHINA/U.S.		
Stereotypes of China/U.S.	−.01	.09**
Stereotypes of Chinese/Americans	−.02	−.14***
Feelings toward Chinese/Americans	.20***	.54***
Knowledge about China/U.S.	−.12***	−.04*
ΔR^2 (in %)	4.0***	18.6***
Total R^2 (in %)	46.1***	54.5***
Total N	1,207	1,241

Note: Cell entries represent standardized regression coefficients. *$p < .05$, **$p < .01$, ***$p < .001$

Americans with a stronger sense of patriotism were more likely to have favorable views of China, while more patriotic Chinese reported more negative views of the United States.

As predicted, the components of national images were associated with the perceived favorability of nations, albeit not consistently. While stereotypes of China and its people did not predict more favorable attitudes toward China among Americans, more positive feelings toward the Chinese people were significantly associated with more favorable views of China. On the other hand, Americans who knew more about China felt less favorable toward this nation.

Among Chinese, stronger stereotypes of the United States were associated with more positive perceptions of the United States, while stronger stereotypes of Americans and more knowledge of the United States were associated with more negative perceptions. As expected, Chinese with more positive feelings toward Americans perceived the United States more favorably.

Overall, media exposure, personal traits related to national images, and the components of national images contributed significantly to people's perceived favorability of a nation. The fact that news exposure played a more important role for Americans was surprising, but likely due to the fact that news stories about the trade war fed into Americans' fear of being outpaced by China's fast-growing economy. Consequently, such stories might have resonated more among American than Chinese audiences. This conclusion is supported by the finding that, among Chinese, the perceived favorability of the United States was mostly influenced by personal traits and stereotypical perceptions of the United States.

Predictors of Support for Additional Trade Tariffs

The final analysis focuses on the predictors of respondents' support for additional trade tariffs. To this end, we developed a hierarchical regression model to predict how strongly respondents support hikes in trade tariffs on goods imported from the other nation. As in the earlier model, which tested predictors of the perceived favorability of nations, this model considered the respondents' demographic background factors (Block 1), measures of traditional and social media usage (Block 2), personal traits (Block 3), and components of national images (Block 4). An additional fifth block included predictors that test people's perceived favorability of the other nation (the dependent variable in the earlier regressions), their concerns about the negative effects of the trade war on their finances and the economy (combined in one variable), and their concerns about the effects of the trade war on their nation.

As shown in table 2, all five regression blocks are significantly associated with support for tariffs in both nations. In general, support for additional trade tariffs was driven more by demographics among the American rather than the Chinese respondents. In the United States, conservative men with higher income levels living in urban areas were the most supportive of additional trade tariffs. In China, by contrast, only older respondents were slightly more supportive of additional trade tariffs.

Based on the assumption that Americans and Chinese learn about the trade war from the news media, we expected significant associations between the respondents' news exposure and their perceptions of the trade war. Overall, the findings indicate that exposure to news was a more powerful predictor of support for tariffs in the United States than in China. While exposure to Fox News and social media was associated with more support for tariffs among Americans, exposure to news websites correlated with more support for tariffs among Chinese. Meanwhile, Americans who watched more news on MSNBC were less supportive of the additional tariffs.

The findings also indicate a strong association between partisanship, media exposure, and support for the tariffs among more politically conservative Americans: Republicans with more exposure to Fox News were significantly more supportive of additional tariffs than more liberal Americans. Thus, conservative Americans not only supported the U.S. administration's tariff policy but also were likely to do so when exposed to the Trump-aligned Fox News.

While personal traits such as cosmopolitanism and personal experiences were not significantly associated with people's attitudes toward the trade war, higher levels of cultural affinity surprisingly were associated with stronger support for additional trade tariffs among Americans. More in line with expectations, higher levels of patriotism correlated with more support for additional trade tariffs in both nations. Thus, patriotism played a critical role in how American and Chinese citizens perceived the trade war. However, given that patriotic Americans had more favorable perceptions of China, whereas patriotic Chinese saw the United States more negatively, the connection between patriotism and trade tariffs might have been driven by different processes in each nation. Patriotic Americans likely supported Trump's trade policies because they were perceived as protecting the U.S.

TABLE 2. Predictors of Support for Additional Trade Tariffs

	SUPPORT FOR TRADE TARIFFS AMONG AMERICANS	SUPPORT FOR TRADE TARIFFS AMONG CHINESE
DEMOGRAPHICS		
Female	−.06*	.03
Age	−.03	.09**
Education	−.03	.01
Republican/Communist	.37***	.03
Urban resident	.08**	−.05
Income	.10**	−.01
ΔR^2 (in %)	17.9***	1.3*
MEDIA EXPOSURE		
Newspapers	.06	−.03
National TV	.02	.02
Fox News	.33***	—
MSNBC	−.12***	—
Online news	−.02	.09**
Social media	.10**	.03
ΔR^2 (in %)	11.0***	1.1**

economy from unfair trade practices. Thus, it appears that Americans separated their overall views of China from their perceptions of the economic dispute between the two nations. On the other hand, Chinese patriots probably saw additional trade tariffs as a "payback" for the United States' attempts to force economic concessions from China. If that was the case, such views might have affected their perceptions of the United States as a whole.

The various components of national image showed significant, albeit inconsistent, associations with respondents' support for trade tariffs. Among Americans, more knowledge about China and stronger stereotypes of the Chinese were associated with less support for additional tariffs. Among Chinese, stronger stereotypes of the United States and more positive feelings toward Americans were associated with less support for additional tariffs among the Chinese respondents, while stronger stereotypes of Americans were associated with more support.

As expected, perceptions of the trade war significantly influenced the

TABLE 2 (continued)

	SUPPORT FOR TRADE TARIFFS AMONG AMERICANS	SUPPORT FOR TRADE TARIFFS AMONG CHINESE
PERSONAL TRAITS		
Cosmopolitanism	−.03	−.03
Patriotism	.23***	.28***
Experience with China/U.S.	.02	−.05
Cultural affinity	.11***	−.03
ΔR^2 (in %)	4.8***	7.4***
IMAGE OF CHINA/U.S.		
Stereotypes of China/U.S.	−.01	−.10**
Stereotypes of Chinese/Americans	−.09**	.08*
Feelings towards Chinese/Americans	−.04	−.16***
Knowledge about China/U.S.	−.05*	.01
ΔR^2 (in %)	1.3***	2.2***
PERCEPTIONS OF THE OTHER & TRADE WAR		
Favorability toward China/U.S.	−.02	−.09*
Concern about trade war	−.03	.12***
Perceptions of trade war's negative impact	−.34***	−.12***
ΔR^2 (in %)	8.1***	2.3***
Total R^2 (in %)	43.1***	14.3***
Total N	1,203	1,237

Note: Cell entries represent standardized regression coefficients. *$p < .05$, **$p < .01$, ***$p < .001$

respondents' level of support for additional trade tariffs. As expected, Americans and Chinese who thought that the trade war could negatively affect their domestic economies or their own financial situations were les supportive of increased trade barriers. In addition, Chinese who were more concerned about the trade war favored additional tariffs.

At the same time, greater favorability of the other nation was only marginally associated with public support of the trade war. While Chinese who saw the United States more favorably were less supportive of additional trade tariffs, Americans did not exhibit such a relationship. Thus, it appears that the overall favorability of a nation might be an insufficient predictor of foreign policy attitudes—at least among Americans.

Conclusions

This study sheds new light on how people perceive other nations and foreign affairs issues by relying on pre-existing national images as mental schemas. The findings suggest that the cognitive and affective components of national image contributed significantly to the perceived favorability of China and the United States. Stereotypes of the United States and its people, for example, were found to be associated with how favorably Chinese viewed the United States. Cultural affinity and positive feelings toward the "other" people correlated with more favorable perceptions of the other nation among Chinese and Americans.

While these associations were relatively strong and uniform in direction, especially for the affective components of national image, it is noteworthy that stereotypical perceptions of China and the Chinese people were not associated with how favorably Americans viewed China as a nation. Instead, Americans with more knowledge about China tended to view China more negatively. Thus, while perceptions of the other nation were driven primarily by affective components of national image (such as feelings toward the "other" people), cognitive components of national image (stereotypes and knowledge) appear to have more distinct effects on overall favorability of a nation. This could be related to the fact that stereotypical perceptions of the "other" nation and its people were significantly stronger among Chinese respondents than Americans, possibly reflecting widespread exposure to U.S. news and entertainment products in China.

Our findings also confirmed that national image and media exposure interact to influence people's favorability toward other nations and related foreign affairs issues. Americans with more frequent exposure to newspapers, television news, and social media tended to see China positively, while exposure to news websites correlated with more negative perceptions. Among Chinese, however, only greater consumption of newspapers showed weak associations with more favorable views of the United States. These weak associations between media exposure and favorability toward the United States in China might be explained by the fact that Chinese views of the United States are more closely linked with stereotypical perceptions of the United States and Americans—and therefore are more difficult to be shaped through short-term news exposure. Among Americans, on the other hand, weaker stereotypical perceptions of China and its people might have been more easily overwritten by exposure to current news about China. Overall, though, it is clear that national images generally have a more significant impact than the news media on how Americans and Chinese think about each other.

In contrast to the diverse associations found for the components of national image, personal traits showed fairly consistent associations with favorability toward the other nation. Both Americans and Chinese with higher levels of cosmopolitanism, cultural affinity, and more personal experiences tended to report more favorable perceptions of the other nation. Patriotism, on the other hand, was associated with more favorable perceptions of China among Americans and with more negative views of the United States among the Chinese. This difference might be due to how patriotism is cultivated in each country. In China, patriotism is often linked with state-led nationalism (Zhao, 1998) and anti-Western sentiment, which frame Western nations as a threat to China (Xu, 1998). In contrast, in the United States, patriotism is often defined as an attachment to shared cultural and political values (Nathanson, 1993), such as the American flag, the Constitution, or Independence Day celebrations. It therefore does not necessarily reflect hostility toward other nations.

While national image and personal traits were associated with the perceived favorability of the other nation, more favorable perceptions of the other nation were associated with less support for the U.S.–China trade war only among Chinese citizens. Thus, it appears that general feelings of favorability toward a nation do not necessarily affect the way people think about foreign policy issues.

Our findings also indicate that the components of national image were associated with support for additional trade tariffs in both nations—but not all of these relationships were consistent with our expectations. Among Americans, for example, stronger (and more positive) stereotypes of Chinese correlated with less support for additional tariffs, while higher levels of cultural affinity correlated with *more* support.

Finally, the results show that national image, personal traits, and media exposure are uniquely associated with support for additional trade tariffs in both samples, suggesting a direct rather than indirect (through favorability) effect of these variables on foreign policy perceptions. Americans, especially more conservative respondents with higher levels of patriotism and exposure to the pro-Trump Fox News, were more supportive of additional trade tariffs. These findings, of course, are related to the fact that conservative Americans are likely strong supporters of President Trump, and by extension, supporters of his trade policies. Among Chinese, mostly older respondents with higher levels of patriotism and more exposure to online news showed greater support for additional trade tariffs.

The fact that Americans who felt culturally connected with the Chinese were more supportive of additional trade tariffs is puzzling, especially because cultural affinity correlated with more positive perceptions of China and the Chinese people. However, cultural affinity is slightly more pronounced among Republicans and more patriotic Americans, which could lead to interactions that explain the positive correlation between cultural affinity and support for additional trade tariffs. Among Chinese, the components of national image correlated in more expected ways: both stronger stereotypes of the United States and more positive feelings toward this nation were associated with less support for additional tariffs.

In conclusion, this comparative study shows that national images significantly influence the way we think about other nations. The U.S.–China trade war, which has been framed as a confrontation between two economic superpowers that are highly codependent, provides a fitting example of how national images can interact with news media consumption to shape the public's understanding of foreign affairs in a complex world. Future studies should explore how these national images are affected by an increasingly partisan news media and a steady decline in foreign news reporting.

REFERENCES

Asch, S. (1952). *Social psychology.* Prentice-Hall.

Albritton, R. B., & Manheim, J. B. (1985). Public relations efforts for the third world: Images in the news. *Journal of Communication, 35*(1), 43–59.

Ata, A., Bastian, B., & Lusher, D. (2009). Intergroup contact in context: The mediating role of social norms and group-based perceptions on the contact-prejudice link. *International Journal of Intercultural Relations, 33*(6), 498–506.

Barlow, F. K., Paolini, S., Pedersen, A., Hornsey, M. J., Radke, H. R. M., Harwood, J., Rubin, M., & Sibley, C. G. (2012). The contact caveat: Negative contact predicts increased prejudice more than positive contact predicts reduced prejudice. *Personality and Social Psychology Bulletin, 38*(12), 1629–43.

Boulding, K. E. (1959). National images and international systems. *Journal of Conflict Resolution, 3*(2), 120–31.

Castano, E., Bonacossa, A., & Gries, P. (2016). National images as integrated schemas:

Subliminal primes of image attributes shape foreign policy preferences. *Political Psychology, 37*(3), 351–66.

Cleveland, M., & Laroche, M. (2007). Acculturation to the global consumer culture: Scale development and research paradigm. *Journal of Business Research, 60*(3), 249–59.

Cleveland, M., Laroche, M., & Papadopoulos, N. (2009). Cosmopolitanism, consumer ethnocentrism, and materialism: An eight-country study of antecedents and outcomes. *Journal of International Marketing, 17*(1), 116–46.

Cottam, M. L. (1999). The enemy image. In American Psychological Association (Eds.), *Encyclopedia of Psychology*. Cambridge University Press.

Cuddy, A. J. C., Fiske, S. T., Kwan, V. S. Y., Glick, P., Demoulin, S., Leyens, J. P., & Ziegler, R. (2009). Stereotype content model across cultures: Towards universal similarities and some differences. *British Journal of Social Psychology, 48*, 1–33.

CNNIC (China Internet Network Information Center). (2019). *44th China statistical report on internet development*. http://www.cnnic.cn/hlwfzyj/hlwxzbg/hlwtjbg/201908/P020190830356787490958.pdf

Dovidio, J. F., Hewstone, M., Glick, P., & Esses, V. M. (2010). Prejudice, stereotyping and discrimination: Theoretical and empirical overview. In J. F. Dovidio, M. Hewstone, P. Glick, & V. M. Esses (Eds.), *The SAGE Handbook of Prejudice, Stereotyping and Discrimination* (pp. 3–29). https://doi.org/10.4135/9781446200919.n1

Entman, R. M. (1993). Framing: Toward clarification of a fractured paradigm. *Journal of Communication, 43*(4), 51–58.

Fiske, S., Cuddy, A., Glick, P., & Xu, J. (2002). A model of (often mixed) stereotype content: Competence and warmth respectively follow from perceived status and competition. *Journal of Personality and Social Psychology, 82*(6), 878–902.

Fung, T. K., Yan, W., & Akin, H. (2018). In the eye of the beholder: How news media exposure and audience schema affect the image of the United States among the Chinese public. *International Journal of Public Opinion Research, 30*(3), 443–72.

Goffman, E. (1974). *Frame analysis: An essay on the organization of experience*. Harvard University Press.

Gozenbach, W. J., Arant, M. D., & Stevenson, R. L. (1992). The world of US network television news: Eighteen years of international and foreign news coverage. *Gazette, 50*, 53–72.

Greenwald, A. G., & Banaji, M. R. (1995). Implicit social cognition: Attitudes, self-esteem, and stereotypes. *Psychological Review, 102*(1), 4–27.

Gries, P. H., Zhang, Q., Crowson, H. M., & Cai, H. (2011). Patriotism, nationalism and China's US policy: Structures and consequences of Chinese national identity. *China Quarterly, 205*, 1–17.

Hartnett, S., Keränen, L., & Conley, D. (2017). A gathering storm or a new chapter? In S. Hartnett, L. Keränen, & D. Conley (Eds.), *Imagining China: Rhetorics of nationalism in an age of globalization* (pp. ix–xlv). Michigan State University Press.

Herrmann, R. K. (1985). *Perceptions and behavior in Soviet foreign policy.* University of Pittsburgh Press.

Herrmann, R. K. (1986). The power of perceptions in foreign-policy decision making: Do views of the Soviet Union determine the policy choices of American leaders? *American Journal of Political Science, 30,* 841–75.

Herrmann, R. K. (2013). Perceptions and image theory in international relations. In L. Huddy, D. O. Sears, & J. S. Levy (Eds.), *The Oxford handbook of political psychology* (pp. 334–63). Oxford University Press.

Herrmann, R. K., & Fischerkeller, M. P. (1995). Beyond the enemy image and spiral model: Cognitive–strategic research after the cold war. *International Organization, 49*(3), 415–50.

Herz, F., & Diamantopoulos, A. (2013). Activation of country stereotypes: Automaticity, consonance, and impact. *Journal of the Academy of Marketing Science, 41*(4):400–417.

Hurwitz, J., & Peffley, M. (1990). Public images of the Soviet Union: The impact on foreign policy attitudes. *The Journal of Politics, 52*(1), 3–28.

Jin, Z., Lynch, R., Attia, S., Chansarkar, B., Gülsoy, T., Lapoule, P., & Purani, K. (2015). The relationship between consumer ethnocentrism, cosmopolitanism and product country image among younger generation consumers: The moderating role of country development status. *International Business Review, 24*(3), 380–93.

Kang, M., & Yang, S.-U. (2010). Comparing effects of country reputation and the overall corporate reputations of a country on international consumers' product attitudes and purchase intentions. *Corporate Reputation Review, 13*(1), 52–62.

Karlins, M., Coffman, T. L., & Walters, G. (1969). On the fading of social stereotypes: Studies in three generations of college students. *Journal of Personality and Social Psychology, 13*(1), 1–16.

Korzenny, F., Del Toro, W., & Gaudino, J. (1987). International news media exposure, knowledge, and attitudes. *Journal of Broadcasting & Electronic Media, 31*(1), 73–87.

Kunczik, M. (2002). Globalisation: News media, images of nations and the flow of international capital with special reference to the role of rating agencies. *Journal of International Communication, 8*(1), 39–79.

Lay, J. C., & Torney-Purta, J. (2007). Patriotism and political participation among Russian and American adolescents. https://www.researchgate.net/publication/228424688_Patriotism_and_political_participation_among_Russian_and_American_adolescents

Leung, A. K. Y., Koh, K., & Tam, K. P. (2015). Being environmentally responsible: Cosmopolitan orientation predicts pro-environmental behaviors. *Journal of Environmental Psychology, 43,* 79–94.

Leyens, J. P., Yzerbyt, V. Y., & Schadron, G. (1992). The social judgeability approach to stereotypes. *European Review of Social Psychology, 3*(1), 91–120.

Lian, J. (2018). 中美贸易战会给我们带来多大影响？[What is the impact of the China–US trade war on us?] *Qiu Shi.* http://www.qstheory.cn/2018-08/13/c_1123261331.htm

Manheim, J. B., & Albritton, R. B. (1983). Changing national images: International public relations and media agenda setting. *American Political Science Review, 78*(3), 641–57.

Maoz, Z., Kuperman, R. D., Terris, L., & Talmud, I. (2006). Structural equivalence and international conflict: A social networks analysis. *Journal of Conflict Resolution, 50*(5), 664–89.

McCombs, M., & Shaw, D. (1972). The agenda-setting function of mass media. *Public Opinion Quarterly, 36*(2), 176–87.

McCombs, M. (2005). A look at agenda-setting: Past, present and future. *Journalism Studies, 6*(4), 543–57.

McNelly, J. T., & Izcaray, F. (1986). International news exposure and images of nations. *Journalism Quarterly, 63*(3), 546–53.

Nathanson, S. (1993). *Patriotism, morality, and peace.* Rowman & Littlefield.

Nisbet, E. C., Nisbet, M. C., Scheufele, D. A., & Shanahan, J. E. (2004). Public diplomacy, television news, and Muslim opinion. *Harvard International Journal of Press/Politics, 9,* 11–37.

Nincic, M., & Russett, B. (1979). The effect of similarity and interest on attitudes toward foreign countries. *Public Opinion Quarterly, 43*(1), 68–78.

Nye Jr., J. S. (2008). Public diplomacy and soft power. *Annals of the American Academy of Political and Social Science, 616*(1), 94–109.

Oberecker, E. M., & Diamantopoulos, A. (2011). Consumers' emotional bonds with foreign countries: Does consumer affinity affect behavioral intentions? *Journal of International Marketing, 19*(2), 45–72.

Peabody, D. (1985). *National characteristics.* Cambridge University Press.

Perry, D. K. (1985). The mass media and inference about other nations. *Communication Research, 12*(4), 595–614.

Perry, D. K. (1987). The image gap: How international news affects perceptions of nations. *Journalism Quarterly, 64*(2–3), 416–33.

Perry, D. K. (1989). Assessing the import of media-related effects: Some contextualist considerations. *World Communication, 21,* 69–82.

Pettigrew, T. F., & Tropp, L. R. (2006). A meta-analytic test of intergroup contact theory. *Journal of Personality and Social Psychology, 90*(5), 751–83.

Poushter, J. (2020, January 8). How people around the world see the U.S. and Donald Trump in 10 charts. *Pew Research Center.* https://www.pewresearch.org/fact-tank/2020/01/08/how-people-around-the-world-see-the-u-s-and-donald-trump-in-10-charts/

Riefler, P., & Diamantopoulos, A. (2009). Consumer cosmopolitanism: Review and replication of the CYMYC scale. *Journal of Business Research, 62*(4), 407–19.

Ruble, R. A., & Zhang, Y. B. (2013). Stereotypes of Chinese international students held by Americans. *International Journal of Intercultural Relations, 37*(2), 202–211.

Schneider, D. (2005). *The psychology of stereotyping.* Guilford Press.

Silver, L. Y., Devlin, K., Huang, C. (2019, December 5). People around the globe are divided in their opinions of China. *Pew Research Center.* https://www.pewresearch.org/fact-tank/2019/12/05/people-around-the-globe-are-divided-in-their-opinions-of-china/

Silverstein, B. (1989). Enemy images. The psychology of U.S. attitudes and cognitions regarding the Soviet Union. *American Psychologist, 44*, 903–13.

Sinkkonen, E. (2013). Nationalism, patriotism and foreign policy attitudes among Chinese university students. *China Quarterly, 216*, 1045–63.

Skrbis, Z., Kendall, G., & Woodward, I. (2004). Locating cosmopolitanism: Between humanist ideal and grounded social category. *Theory, Culture & Society, 21*(6), 115–36.

Swanson, A., & Tankersley, J. (2019, July 15). Tariffs on China don't cover the costs of Trump's trade war. *New York Times.*

Techakesari, P., Barlow, F. K., Hornsey, M. J., Sung, B., Thai, M., & Chak, J. L. Y. (2015). An investigation of positive and negative contact as predictors of intergroup attitudes in the United States, Hong Kong, and Thailand. *Journal of Cross-Cultural Psychology, 46*(3), 454–68.

Terracciano, A., & McCrae, R. R. (2007). Perceptions of Americans and the Iraq invasion: Implications for understanding national character stereotypes. *Journal of Cross-Cultural Psychology, 38*(6), 695–710.

Tan, A., Li, S., & Simpson, C. (1986). American TV and social stereotypes of Americans in Taiwan and Mexico. *Journalism Quarterly, 63*(4), 809–14.

Tan, A., & Suarchavarat, K. (1988). American TV and social stereotypes of Americans in Thailand. *Journalism Quarterly, 65*(3), 648–54.

Tversky, A., & Kahneman, D. (1974). Judgment under uncertainty: Heuristics and biases. *Science, 185*(4157), 1124–31.

UN World Tourism Organization. (2019). *Yearbook of tourism statistics: Data 2013–2017; 2019 Edition.* https://www.unwto.org/global/publication/yearbook-tourism-statistics-data-2013-2017-2019-edition

Walkey, F., & Chung, R. (1996). An examination of stereotypes of Chinese and Europeans held by some New Zealand secondary school pupils. *Journal of Cross-Cultural Psychology*, *27*(3), 283–92.

Wang, J. (2006). Managing national reputation and international relations in the global era: Public diplomacy revisited. *Public Relations Review*, *32*(2), 91–96.

Wei, L., & Kubota, Y. (2018, June 25). China's Xi tells CEOs he'll strike back at U.S. *Wall Street Journal*.

Willnat, L., He, Z., & Hao, X. (1997). Foreign media exposure and perceptions of Americans in Hong Kong, Shenzhen, and Singapore. *Journalism and Mass Communication Quarterly*, *74*(4), 738–56.

Xu, G. (1998, May 1). Anti-American nationalism in China since 1989. *China Report, 34*(2), 179–198. https://doi.org/10.1177/000944559803400202

Zhang, L. L. (2015). Stereotypes of Chinese by American college students: Media use and perceived realism. *International Journal of Communication, 9*, 1–20.

Zhao, S. (1998). A state-led nationalism: The patriotic education campaign in post-Tiananmen China. *Communist and Post-Communist Studies, 31*, 287–302.

Zhu, L. (2016). A comparative look at Chinese and American stereotypes. *Journal of Intercultural Communication, 42*(1), 1–15.

PART 2

Media Coverage of the Trade War in the United States

U.S. Television News Coverage of the Trade War

Partisan vs. Nonpartisan Media

Rik Ray and Yanqin Lu

The trade war between the United States and China has been framed in multiple ways by the news media, ranging from a political to an economic confrontation (Bradsher & Myers, 2018; Wang, 2018). Approaching the trade war from a political standpoint can provide meaningful insights into how the U.S. news media presents foreign policy issues. The current media environment in the United States has become increasingly fragmented, and many individuals, enclosed in echo chambers, seek like-minded information from partisan media (Stroud, 2008). Such exposure to partisan news content increases the extent of opinion polarization (Levendusky, 2013a; Warner, 2018) and erodes support for bipartisan compromise with the other party (Levendusky, 2013b). Previous studies on media bias in political issues have primarily focused on electoral events (Entman, 2010; Morris, 2007; Niven, 2001), international conflicts, and wars (Dickson, 1994; Luther & Miller, 2005; Vallone et al., 1985). In this chapter, we extend the literature by exploring how U.S. television news media presented the U.S.–China trade war.

According to a Pew survey conducted in 2016 (Doherty et al., 2016), the economy was the most important issue among American voters during the 2016 U.S. presidential election, with 84 percent of registered voters indicating this issue would influence their voting decision. Reducing the trade deficit with China was one of the key campaign planks of Republican candidate Donald Trump (Corasaniti et al., 2016). He argued that "China, and many others, are taking advantage of U.S. with our terrible trade pacts" (Trump, 2016). He also accused China of unfair trade practices, including intellectual property theft and the provision of excessive government subsidies. Because of such claims, the 2016 U.S. presidential election campaign was marked by populist rhetoric, anti-elitism, and pro-nationalist sentiments (Oliver & Rahn, 2016), in turn triggering increased levels of polarization and partisanship in the news media's coverage of Trump and his policies. Despite the growing popularity of social media and news websites as news sources, television remains the most popular medium for consuming news in the United States, with 47 percent of the public preferring to watch the news rather than reading newspapers (Mitchell, 2018).

However, there are differences in the political news coverage of broadcast and cable news networks, with cable news often blurring the boundaries between hard and soft news (Coe et al., 2008). For example, Fox News frequently exhibits a partisan bias, favoring Republican views on policy issues, while MSNBC tends to favor Democratic viewpoints. Broadcast networks, such as ABC and PBS, usually adhere to professional journalistic norms of objective and balanced reporting, while CNN increasingly moves from reporting the news to offering left-leaning opinions. While Ha et al., in "Comparing U.S. and Chinese Media Coverage of the U.S.–China Trade War" in this volume, provide a more comprehensive comparison of the media coverage of the U.S.–China trade war, this chapter solely focuses on how the major national broadcast and cable news outlets in the United States covered this topic. The data suggests that much, but not all, of the admittedly limited range of U.S. news representations studied here depicting President Trump's "trade war" tend to rely upon what media scholars call a "provocation narrative." The biased sources addressed herein drive this narrative with a pro-Trump and anti-China sentiment, yet our analysis suggests that even the nonpartisan and mainstream media sources analyzed herein tend to fuel the fires of distrust and misperception, turning the "trade war" into yet one more moment of U.S.–China miscommunication.

Professional Journalism and Partisanship in U.S. Television News Media

The modern ideals of nonpartisan and objective journalism started gaining popularity in the twentieth century when the tension between commercial interests and the partisan leanings of the press increased due to consolidation and declining competition in the industry (McChesney, 2003; Pickard, 2019). In the 1940s, a wide coalition of legislators, citizens, and journalists tried to align the profession with its public service aspect by establishing the Hutchins Commission. Despite resistance from some of the commercial press and broadcasters, "the Hutchins Commission did encourage greater reflexivity in the news media, which became further internalized within American journalism's professional norms" (Pickard, 2015). Until its repeal in 1987, the Fairness Doctrine required licensed television and radio stations to provide balanced coverage on issues of public importance.

However, the relaxation of media ownership restrictions in the 1980s has led again to increased consolidation in the U.S. media industry, with five companies controlling more than 90 percent of the U.S. media market (Rapp & Jenkins, 2018). The five companies are AT&T, Comcast, Disney, 21st Century Fox (now Fox Corporation, following Disney's partial acquisition in 2019), and ViacomCBS. Precisely as originally feared by the proponents of the Hutchins Commission, American media was devolving back into a series of interlocked monopolies, hence compromising the quality and range of news available to consumers. At the same time, by repealing the Fairness Doctrine, the U.S. Congress enabled Fox News and other cable news networks to fuel increased partisanship by producing opinionated political news coverage that consistently violates professional journalistic norms (Coe et al., 2008). Gans (2007) distinguished between journalistic news produced by professional journalists and everyday news that refers to other forms of informational content shared by common people among their family, friends, and coworkers. Professional journalists adopt a formal approach to news gathering and sharing, focusing on reporting about issues of salience to society. Such coverage relies on the objective reporting of facts, not on opinions, rumors, and speculation. Schudson (2001) contends these norms help practitioners to carve out a cohesive identity for the profession and to pass on shared values to future generations of journalists. According to Gans (2004), professional journalism practices in the 1960s and 1970s were consistent with the political reformist ideals that characterized the Progressive Era from the late nineteenth to early twentieth centuries, when professional journalism was oriented toward public service and the common good. However, this understanding of political news reporting may not always be consistent with actual practices. Indeed, many practitioners routinely engage in exploratory and investigative political journalism, where they take a stance on issues and advocate for social changes (Schudson, 2007). In partisan cable news networks, such advocacy has become more pronounced, meaning political news is presented as a blend of news, views, and entertainment.

U.S. foreign policy often shapes the narrative of the U.S. news coverage of international events (Gans, 2004). Coverage of international conflicts involving the United States, for example, is often framed from the perspective of the president's actions toward confronting foreign enemies (Kaplan, 2003). This phenomenon is pertinent to the discussion of American news media's coverage of foreign affairs in general, including the U.S.–China trade war. However, in light of the changes in news production practices and consumption habits due to the increasing convergence of media platforms, there have been calls to reassess the norms of news values (Harcupp & O'Neill, 2016) and the role of journalism in society (Deuze, 2005; Singer, 2007). Within this larger historical context, the 2016 U.S. presidential election marked a significant turning-point in evolving notions of partisan bias and, hence, the lack of objectivity of major broadcasters. President Trump's rhetoric against CNN, ABC, NBC, the *New York Times*, and other legacy news media further polarized the media environment. The president often referred to these outlets as reporting "fake news," which was declared Word of the Year in 2017 by the American Dialect Society (American Dialect Society, 2018). In doing so, Trump escalated the adversarial relationship between politicians and the news media (Meeks, 2020) to a point where conventional wisdom of partisan bias and objectivity in political news reporting was shattered. Given the complexity of Trump's relationship with the media and the lack of more recent empirical investigation of political partisanship in U.S. television news coverage, our analysis sheds additional light on the political biases of major U.S. television news outlets. Moreover, our analysis of this new age of partisan and biased news coverage adds fresh insights to our understanding of how the U.S.–China relationship has been, to large extent, poisoned by these partisan media outlets.

Evaluating Television News Coverage of the U.S.–China Trade Conflict

Several approaches to the modeling and measurement of media bias have shown that bias can result from either the consumers' selective exposure to a news outlet or the source of news. Consumers with distinct ideological orientations are more likely to seek news that confirms their own beliefs (Mullainathan & Shleifer, 2005). As a result, partisan news outlets tend to skew their reporting to cater to their consumers' preconceived notions (Gentzkow & Shapiro, 2006). By contrast, Besley and Prat (2006) suggest that the government plays a significant role in controlling how media outlets report certain political issues. Groeling (2013) identified two broad categories of choices made by news professionals that promote partisan coverage of issues: selection bias and presentation bias. Selection bias refers to the disproportionate sampling of the news stories that favor one narrative over the other, leading to unbalanced coverage. Presentation bias can usually be examined through content analyses focusing on aspects such as sources, framing, and tone.

We performed a content analysis to examine the partisanship and bias in the coverage of the U.S.–China trade war by U.S. broadcast and cable news channels. To cover the entire political-ideological spectrum from conservative to liberal, we selected television news outlets that have been previously identified in the literature as representative of those positions. Fox News was selected as the representative of conservative, pro-Trump partisan news outlets (Yglesias, 2018). ABC News was selected as the representative of centrist and neutral commercial broadcast news because it had the highest ratings in 2018 (Battaglio, 2018), alongside the public broadcaster PBS. Considering CNN's unfavorable coverage of Trump and his policies, and its mostly liberal audience, we grouped CNN with MSNBC to represent the liberal end of the political spectrum (Pew Research Center, 2014).

To collect the television news content, we used Nexis Uni to access the transcripts of the newscasts. We used the keywords "China" and "trade" to search for all relevant news stories published between January 1 and December 31, 2018. We selected only the *Special Report with Bret Baier* on Fox News and *The Beat with Ari Melber* on MSNBC, which are the primetime evening newscasts. CNN.com is one of the most popular online news sites, and it maintains a strong social media presence. While CNN is a global TV news broadcaster, its online audience is larger than its TV audience, and Facebook is its most important social media platform (Boland, 2018; CNN, 2017). Consequently, we examined the online version of its news articles featured on its Facebook page rather than the TV broadcasts. We used Facebook's search function to identify the relevant news articles from CNN using the keywords "China" and "trade."

We decided to include all the relevant news articles that we could identify in the database. With this approach, the news coverage of the five news outlets yielded a total of 221 articles. Among the five TV channels analyzed in this study, Fox News covered the U.S.–China trade war most frequently ($N = 75$), followed by CNN ($N = 48$), PBS ($N = 42$), ABC News ($N = 38$), and MSNBC ($N = 18$). The articles were coded by three graduate students and a faculty member of Bowling Green State University. Several training sessions were conducted to ensure that all coders understood the coding scheme and reached acceptable intercoder reliability. An additional coder double-coded 10 percent of the news articles to compute the intercoder reliability, and an average coder agreement of 74.3 percent was achieved across the coded variables used in our analysis.

Measures

Number of Sources. Common approaches to assess the ideological bias of news outlets include the analysis of the news sources, use of language, gatekeeping, and journalistic attitudes (Covert & Wasburn, 2007). The number of sources used in a news story can provide a general idea of the relative importance afforded to the story and the commitment toward balanced coverage. To determine how comprehensively the issue was covered, we counted the number of sources used in each news story and compared them across the outlets.

Diversity of News Sources. The diversity of news sources is an important factor for determining the balance of a news story. We measured this variable by summing the presence of different types of sources in a news story, including government, consultants and think tanks, academics and universities, agriculture, retail and trade, manufacturing, non-university education, the general public, and "other" sources. The presence of each category of source was coded as 1.

Presence of Multiple Frames. A hallmark of professional journalism practice is fair and unbiased reporting. It is achieved by presenting multiple sides of a story. By providing a voice to all parties, news media can present audiences with facts that can be interpreted without value judgments. News framing pertains to the way news is presented and how it is communicated to the public (Entman, 1993).

Moreover, news framing allows for complex constructs to be simplified for the general public's comprehension (Scheufele & Tewksbury, 2007). A biased report is unlikely to exhibit the presence of competing frames in the story. It will try to push one narrative over the others based on the outlet's ideological orientation. Although news stories often contain multiple frames, they might have an additive rather than a neutralizing function. In such cases, news coverage of the trade war is unlikely to be neutral. For our analysis, we coded each news story for the presence (= 1) or absence (= 0) of competing frames.

Provocation Narratives. According to Boudana and Segev (2017a), a provocation narrative is a deliberate effort to frame news stories in a manner that represents the opposite party in poor light. Moreover, they found that China is frequently portrayed negatively by media outlets in the United States and other Western nations. In the context of international news coverage, a provocation narrative can be understood as a mechanism for shifting the blame of initiating a conflict and/or justifying violent responses (Boudana & Segev, 2017b). Thus, each news story was coded for the presence (= 1) or absence (= 0) of a provocation narrative that sought to blame either China or Trump, hence discrediting their positions in the eyes of the target audience.

Support for Trade Tariffs. The U.S.–China trade war involves the two largest economies in the world, making it an important foreign policy issue. However, the deeply polarized political rhetoric surrounding the issue in the United States renders it a domestic political issue as well. To determine support for tariffs in a news story, we computed a summated scale of four dichotomous items indicating the presence of a specific narrative in the news story. The presence of the items "protectionism is needed or justified" and "the tariff is the best move to solve the trade deficit" were coded 1 for each item. The presence of the items "the trade war is hurting the U.S." and "Trump is heading in the wrong direction" was coded -1 for each item.

Attribution of Responsibility. The responsibility frame in a news story is concerned with the presentation of an issue that places the responsibility for the occurrence of the issue on a particular individual, government, or group (Semetko & Valkenburg, 2000). We analyze how the different news outlets attributed the responsibility for the trade deficit to the United States and China. Professional journalism norms suggest that neutral media outlets will either refrain from attributing the responsibility to just one country or simply not include a responsibility frame in the story to ensure balanced and objective coverage of the issue. However, the coverage of international political conflicts might be shaped by a partisan media outlet's disposition toward the incumbent government's policies. Accordingly, the responsibility frame was coded to determine whether a news story attributed responsibility for the trade war to the United States, China, or both nations, or whether it made no reference to responsibility.

Findings: Partisan vs. Nonpartisan Media

We first compared the norms of professional journalism between partisan (Fox News, CNN, MSNBC) and nonpartisan media (PBS, ABC News). Our findings indicated that the partisan media coverage ($M = 4.21$, $SD = 1.89$) of the U.S.–China trade war featured more sources than the nonpartisan media coverage ($M = 2.66$, $SD = 1.61$, $t(186) = 6.42$, $p < .001$). However, the variety of sources in the partisan media coverage ($M = 1.73$, $SD = 1.04$) was not significantly different from that in the nonpartisan media coverage ($M = 1.80$, $SD = .93$, $t(219) = .50$, $p = .62$). Both partisan and nonpartisan media primarily relied on government officials (partisan: 81.6 percent; nonpartisan: 87.5 percent) and think-tank consultants (partisan: 31.2 percent; nonpartisan: 47.5 percent). Indeed, studies have consistently found that political elites are the major sources in the news coverage of international affairs (Bennett, 1990; Zaller, 1994).

As shown in figure 1, partisan media outlets were more likely to interview people in the retailing and manufacturing sectors strongly affected by the trade war. At the same time, nonpartisan news channels tended to present the voice of the general public. This difference may be explained by the fact that the partisan media outlets examined in this chapter are 24/7 cable news networks. Compared with broadcast news channels, cable news outlets focus on news revenues and, thus, have more resources at their disposal to interview sources from different sectors (Pew Research Center, 2019). Moreover, by interviewing people from the retailing and manufacturing sectors, cable news outlets can cater to their audiences, who are often more affluent and interested in the economic implications of the news topic (Public Opinion Strategies, 2019).

As expected, the nonpartisan media outlets were more likely to use multiple frames to cover the trade war between the United States and China ($\chi^2 = 14.58$, $df = 1$, $p < .001$). Of the news stories published by nonpartisan media outlets, 65 percent covered the trade war with multiple frames. By contrast, only 38.3 percent of the stories published by partisan media outlets featured multiple frames. The lack of multiple frames in the partisan media's coverage suggests that they presented one-sided perspectives based on their partisan leanings. While such a journalistic practice could be considered biased, it is likely to attract more audiences who favor the outlet's political leaning.

Compared with the nonpartisan media outlets, the partisan news networks were more likely to adopt a provocation narrative in their coverage of the trade war ($\chi^2 = 12.71$, $df = 1$, $p < .001$). While only 13.8 percent of the news stories published by the nonpartisan media outlets adopted a provocative narrative, 36.2 percent of the news stories published by the partisan media outlets used a narrative that accused a party in a manner to discredit its position among the outlet's audience.

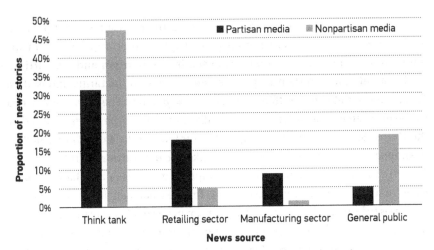

FIGURE 1. Distribution of Sources among Partisan and Nonpartisan Media Outlets

One major accusation in the partisan media outlets' coverage of the U.S.–China trade war was that many of China's trade practices violate free-market norms, such as intellectual property protection and protectionist policies. For example, in a newscast on December 5, 2018, a Fox News correspondent discussed the lack of headway in negotiating "China's intellectual property theft, forced technology transfer, protectionist tariffs, ownership rules, and cyber hacking" (Baier, 2018).

In another Fox newscast, broadcast on August 3, 2018, the host turned the audience's attention to a video clip of the National Economic Council director, Larry Kudlow, who argued that "China better take President Trump's efforts to solve the unfair and illegal trade, and their tariff problem, their lack of reciprocity, their technology stealing, their I.P. theft, they better take President Trump seriously." A regular Fox News guest, Charles Lane then speculated that China's refusal to concede before the midterm elections was "to encourage political backlash against this president's trade policy, and (China is) going to see if that works. And if the president and his party take reverses in the fall election, I think it is going to make the Chinese feel vindicated that he was less popular than he seemed, and vice versa" (Baier, 2018). Although Lane's analysis was a fair assessment of China's intention, when considered in the context of Fox's overall position on the issue, such comments serve to reinforce the provocation narrative. Such provocation narratives in the coverage are likely to discredit China and the Chinese government among the audience (Boudana & Segev, 2017a).

Next, we explored the differences between the partisan and nonpartisan media in terms of whether their coverage supported or opposed the tariffs imposed on China. The positions espoused by the partisan and nonpartisan media outlets through their respective news stories on the tariffs imposed on China were significantly different, $t(217) = 5.74$, $p < .001$. The stories published by the partisan media outlets were more likely to support the tariffs imposed by the United States on China ($M = .46$, $SD = 1.15$), while the stories published by the nonpartisan media outlets were more likely to oppose these tariffs ($M = -.26$, $SD = .71$). In addition, the partisan and nonpartisan media outlets had diverging views in terms of the country responsible for the trade deficit between the two countries ($\chi^2 = 10.24$, $df = 2$, $p < .01$). The partisan media tended to blame China (56.6 percent) for the trade deficit, while most nonpartisan media outlets attributed the responsibility to both countries (63.6 percent). In general, the nonpartisan media's coverage was more balanced because it included both support of and opposition to the tariffs and discussed both countries' responsibilities for the trade deficit.

In sum, the nonpartisan media outlets followed the code of professional journalism by adopting multiple frames and avoiding the provocative narrative in their coverage of the U.S.–China trade war. By contrast, the partisan media outlets did not feature multiple frames and frequently adopted the provocative narrative in their coverage of the issue. Moreover, they were more likely to support the tariffs imposed on China and blame China for the trade deficit. The following section explores whether the subversion of professional journalistic practices by the partisan media outlets should be attributed to pro-Democrat and pro-Republican media.

Pro-Democrat vs. Pro-Republican Media

Next, we focused on the coverage of the trade war by the media outlets that are liberal-leaning or critical of Trump (CNN, MSNBC) and those that are conservative-leaning (Fox News). In terms of the number of sources used in the coverage of the U.S.–China trade war, there were no significant differences between the more conservative Fox News ($M = 4.11$, $SD = 1.91$) and the more liberal CNN and MSNBC ($M = 4.32$, $SD = 1.87$, $t(139) = .66$, $p = .51$). Similarly, the coverage of Fox News ($M = 1.63$, $SD = 1.04$) and CNN/MSNBC ($M = 1.85$, $SD = 1.04$) did not show any significant differences in terms of the variety of sources. However, as shown in figure 2, Fox News predominantly relied on government officials (88 percent), while CNN and

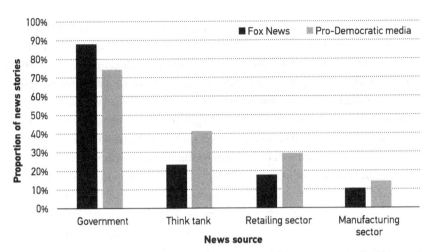

FIGURE 2. Distribution of Sources among Pro-Republican and Pro-Democrat Media Outlets

MSNBC media relied more on think tanks, consultants, and individuals in the retailing and manufacturing sectors.

Contrary to our expectations, Fox News was more likely to use multiple frames in their coverage of the U.S.–China trade war than CNN and MSNBC (χ^2 = 59.82, df = 1, p < .001). Most of the Fox News coverage (68 percent) presented multiple frames, while only a few stories (4.5 percent) published by CNN and MSNBC covered the trade war with multiple perspectives. This discrepancy may be attributed to a more comprehensive and sustained coverage of the issue by Fox News than any other media outlet. The trade war was used as a cue to discuss the domestic economic implications of Trump's policies. For example, following Larry Kudlow's statement on the August 3 newscast, a panel discussion was initiated among other guests. They discussed various perspectives (e.g., tariffs hurting U.S. consumers and businesses, approval for President Trump's hardline approach from the business community, and China's intentional delay in making concessions) of the trade war in terms of how these perspectives could affect Republican candidates in the midterm elections (Baier, 2018).

Moreover, the findings indicate that Fox News adopted more provocation narratives in its coverage of the trade war than CNN and MSNBC (χ^2 = 14.58, df = 1, p < .001). While provocation narratives were used in 19.7 percent of the stories published by CNN and MSNBC, they were used in more than half of the articles (50.7 percent) published by Fox News, wherein China was accused of intentionally violating Western business norms. As mentioned earlier, such provocation narratives prevent the audience from processing the news rationally and considering alternative responsibilities (Boudana & Segev, 2017b). For example, a newscast in November 2018 discussed the increasing tensions between the United States and China over trade, highlighting the position of both President Trump and President Xi on the issue. However, the follow-up discussion and comments from other guests on the show were sharply critical of China, accusing it of economic espionage and calling it "the biggest national security threat long-term this country will ever face (*sic*)" (Emanuel, 2018). In another instance, Fox News correspondent Kenneth Corke claimed that China "has intentionally targeted industries and crops in the Midwest with higher fees in retaliation for new U.S. tariffs" (Emanuel, 2018). Such accusatory statements and speculations about China's motives are visible throughout their trade war coverage. Thus, even though Fox News used multiple frames in its coverage of the trade war, viewers likely were influenced by those overwhelmingly negative comments on China.

Furthermore, we found that in its stories, the position of Fox News on the tariffs imposed on China was significantly different from those of CNN and MSNBC. Fox News was more likely to support the tariffs imposed on China ($M = .97$, $SD = .96$), while CNN and MSNBC adopted a slightly opposing view toward the tariffs ($M = -.12$, $SD = 1.07$, $t(138) = 6.35$, $p < .001$). However, the opposition stories by CNN and MSNBC can be attributed to their disagreement with the Trump administration's policy standpoint and not on the issue overall. As discussed earlier, this indicates that all media outlets acknowledged the existence of a trade imbalance between China and the United States. In a December 2018 newscast, MSNBC host Ari Melber took aim at Trump by saying, "He had said that that deal with China was closed, then said he was quote, a tariff man and threatened to bring the hammer down on China." Melber then proceeded to invite author Tony Schwartz to elaborate on his opinion of the "trade confusion" being about "something larger which is Donald Trump's failure as a leader" (Melber, 2018).

Finally, our findings indicate that Fox News discussed the responsibility for the trade deficit differently than CNN and MSNBC ($\chi^2 = 20.99$, $df = 2$, $p < .001$). More than half of the stories published by CNN and MSNBC (51.9 percent) attributed the responsibility to both countries, while almost three-quarters of the stories published by Fox News (73.5 percent) blamed China for the trade deficit. Interestingly, MSNBC's coverage of the trade war was rather cursory and only served to contextualize its criticism of Trump's failure as a political leader. In contrast, CNN's coverage was more objective and usually focused on the implications of the tariffs and their roles in escalating the trade war.

Conclusions

While most of our findings align with the past literature on the wide range of ideological leanings and partisan biases of some U.S. television news media, it is interesting to note how such biases are manifested in the coverage of an international policy issue, especially one as fraught with emotion and nationalism as the U.S.–China "trade war." We began this chapter by noting that the objectivity norm has been a hallmark of American journalism for more than a century, yet this chapter demonstrates how tackling the demands of generating profits while engaging in fair and objective journalism, all while facing a communication insurgency from social media, has become a precarious balancing act. President Trump's relentless war on the mainstream media has accelerated these questions, leaving many American news consumers teetering between outlets whose objectivity, political leanings, or outright bias seem to change each day. Nonetheless, media scholars have argued that, even in the face of these evolutions in our shared media ecosystem, it is possible to provide objective coverage of an issue by including multiple frames in a news story. Yet, as Budak et al. (2016) noted, it is also possible to advocate a certain ideological position without "explicitly favor(ing) a political party"—which is precisely what we found in this analysis. As we have shown, Fox News featured multiple frames in their coverage of the trade war, yet correspondents, guests, and hosts often pushed provocation narratives that discredited China's position while promoting Trump's apparent success in negotiating the trade deficit. Thus, the multiple frames complemented rather than neutralized each other, in turn fueling a stronger sense of bias.

The partisan leanings of Fox News, MSNBC, and CNN played an important role in determining the amount of news coverage each outlet devoted to the trade war as well as their choice of news sources. But partisanship alone does not fully explain why Fox News paid so much more attention to the trade war than other media outlets. Considering the limitations of our study, we can only speculate that Fox News utilized the issue to keep Trump and the Republican party in the news cycle before the midterm elections while consolidating its conservative audience base. Providing wider coverage of the trade war built a narrative that painted a more favorable picture of the implications of the tariffs and Trump's protectionist policies. On the other hand, CNN's approach may have been informed by professional journalistic norms, which led to more balanced and less partisan coverage of the trade war. We speculate that the ambivalence of CNN and other broadcast networks regarding the impact of the trade tariffs, when considered alongside the barrage of biased reporting from FOX, might have undermined the U.S. public's ability to understand the negative impact of the trade war on the global economy. Thus, we are left wondering if U.S. television news outlets are too partisan or not partisan enough. Given the polarized political climate and the fragmented news media ecosystem, future research should focus on resolving this dilemma of reconciling journalistic objectivity with the normative ideals of the press.

This chapter's findings have further implications for Americans' attitudes toward China and the United States' domestic politics. Given that Fox News is viewed and trusted by a majority of Republicans (Jurkowitz & Mitchell, 2020), conceivably, its accusation that China engages in unfair trade practices will continue to play a critical role in shaping Republicans' attitudes toward China. According to a recent Pew report (Silver et al., 2019), Republicans are more likely than Democrats to hold an unfavorable opinion of China and consider China the most threatening country to the United States. Such negative opinions of China may have helped the Trump administration secure more support for its hardline approach amid the trade dispute between the two countries. In addition, by relying on the U.S. government's sources to justify the Trump administration's tariff policy, Fox News may have taken advantage of this issue to help the president rally public support among his fellow Republicans.

Nevertheless, it is worth noting that both the nonpartisan and the left-leaning media outlets adopted a slightly opposing view of the tariff policy. In this case, the tariff policy may have backfired on Trump in terms of his job approval ratings, especially among those affected by China's counter-tariffs (Saad, 2019). In other words, similar to many other domestic issues, the media's coverage of the trade war may have contributed to the fragmentation and polarization of public opinion in the United States. Given the limitations of our content analysis, we were unable to answer these important questions completely; however, the next chapter will explore the news media's role in shaping public opinion about the trade war in the United States.

REFERENCES

American Dialect Society. (2018, January 6). Fake news is 2017 American Dialect Society word of the year. https://www.americandialect.org/fake-news-is-2017-american-dialect-society-word-of-the-year

Baier, B. (Host). (2018, August 3). *Fox special report with Bret Baier* [Television broadcast]. Fox News Channel.

Baier, B. (Host). (2018, December 5). *Fox special report with Bret Baier* [Television broadcast]. Fox News Channel.

Battaglio, S. (2018, September 25). ABC wins the morning and evening ratings races, but network news is still losing viewers overall. *Los Angeles Times.*

Benen, S. (2018, March 8). Why Trump's latest request to China didn't make any sense. *MSNBC.* http://www.msnbc.com/rachel-maddow-show/why-trumps-latest-request-china-didnt-make-any-sense

Bennett, W. L. (1990). Toward a theory of press-state relations. *Journal of Communication, 40*(2), 103–25.

Besley, T., & Prat, A. (2006). Handcuffs for the grabbing hand? Media capture and government accountability. *American Economic Review, 96*(3), 720–36.

Bradsher, K., & Myers, S. L. (2018, October 15). Trump's trade war is rattling China's leaders. *New York Times.*

Boland, G. (October 11, 2018). The top Facebook publishers in September 2018. *Newswhip.* https://www.newswhip.com/2018/10/the-top-facebook-publishers-september/

Boudana, S., & Segev, E. (2017a). The bias of provocation narratives in international news. *International Journal of Press/Politics, 22*(3), 314–32.

Boudana, S., & Segev, E. (2017b). Theorizing provocation narratives as communication strategies. *Communication Theory, 27*(4), 329–46.

Budak, C., Goel, S., & Rao, J. M. (2016). Fair and balanced? Quantifying media bias through crowdsourced content analysis. *Public Opinion Quarterly, 80*(S1), 250–71.

Coe, K., Tewksbury, D., Bond, B. J., Drogos, K. L., Porter, R. W., Yahn, A., & Zhang, Y. (2008). Hostile news: Partisan use and perceptions of cable news programming. *Journal of Communication, 58*(2), 201–19.

CNN (2017). CNN Digital #1 in audience, video, mobile, social, and millennial reach. *CNN Digital* [Press release]. http://cnnpressroom.blogs.cnn.com/2017/09/28/cnn-digital-biggest-audience-video-mobile-social-millennial/

Corasaniti, N., Burns, A., & Appelbaum, B. (2016, June 28). Donald Trump vows to rip up trade deals and confront China. *New York Times.*

Covert, T. J. A., & Wasburn, P. C. (2007). Measuring media bias: A content analysis of *Time* and *Newsweek* coverage of domestic social issues, 1975–2000. *Social Science Quarterly, 88*(3), 690–706.

Deuze, M. (2005). Popular journalism and professional ideology: Tabloid reporters and editors speak out. *Media, Culture & Society, 27*(6), 861–82.

Dickson, S. H. (1994). Understanding media bias: The press and the U.S. invasion of Panama. *Journalism Quarterly, 71*(4), 809–19.

Doherty, C., Kiley, J., & Johnson, B. (2016). 2016 Campaign: Strong interest, widespread dissatisfaction. *Pew Research Center*. https://www.people-press.org/2016/07/07/2016-campaign-strong-interest-widespread-dissatisfaction/

Emanuel, M. (Host). (2018, July 26). *Fox special report with Bret Baier* [Television broadcast]. Fox News Channel.

Emanuel, M. (Host). (2018, November 22). *Fox Special Report with Bret Baier* [Television broadcast]. Fox News Channel.

Entman, R. M. (1993). Framing: Toward clarification of a fractured paradigm. *Journal of Communication, 43*(4), 51–58.

Entman, R. M. (2010). Media framing biases and political power: Explaining slant in news of campaign 2008. *Journalism: Theory, Practice & Criticism, 11*(4), 389–408.

Farhi, P. (2003). Everybody wins: Fox News channel and CNN are often depicted as desperate rivals locked in a death match. In fact, the cable networks aren't even playing the same game. There's no reason they both can't flourish. *American Journalism Review, 25*(3), 32–38.

Feldman, L., Maibach, E. W., Roser-Renouf, C., & Leiserowitz, A. (2012). Climate on cable: The nature and impact of global warming coverage on Fox News, CNN, and MSNBC. *International Journal of Press/Politics, 17*(1), 3–31.

Gans, H. J. (2004). *Deciding what's news: A study of CBS evening news, NBC nightly news, Newsweek, and Time*. Northwestern University Press.

Gans, H. J. (2007). Everyday news, newsworkers, and professional journalism. *Political Communication, 24*(2), 161–66.

Gentzkow, M., & Shapiro, J. M. (2006). Media bias and reputation. *Journal of Political Economy, 114*(2), 280–316.

Gil de Zúñiga, H., Correa, T., & Valenzuela, S. (2012). Selective exposure to cable news and immigration in the U.S.: The relationship between Fox News, CNN, and attitudes toward Mexican immigrants. *Journal of Broadcasting & Electronic Media, 56*(4), 597–615.

Groeling, T. (2008). Who's the fairest of them all? An empirical test for partisan bias on ABC, CBS, NBC, and Fox News. *Presidential Studies Quarterly, 38*(4), 631–57.

Groeling, T. (2013). Media bias by the numbers: Challenges and opportunities in the empirical study of partisan news. *Annual Review of Political Science, 16*, 129–51.

Groseclose, T., & Milyo, J. (2005). A measure of media bias. *Quarterly Journal of Economics, 120*(4), 1191–1237.

Harcup, T., & O'Neill, D. (2017). What is news? News values revisited (again). *Journalism Studies, 18*(12), 1470–88.

Jeong, G. H., & Quirk, P. J. (2019). Division at the water's edge: The polarization of foreign policy. *American Politics Research, 47*(1), 58–87.

Jurkowitz, M., & Mitchell, A. (2020). About one-fifth of Democrats and Republicans get political news in a kind of media bubble. *Pew Research Center.* https://www.journalism. org/2020/03/04/about-one-fifth-of-democrats-and-republicans-get-political-news-in-a-kind-of-media-bubble/

Kaplan, R. L. (2003). American journalism goes to war, 1898–2001: A manifesto on media and empire. *Media History, 9*(3), 209–19.

Krause, M. (2011). Reporting and the transformations of the journalistic field: U.S. news media, 1890–2000. *Media, Culture & Society, 33*(1), 89–104.

Levendusky, M. S. (2013a). Why do partisan media polarize viewers? *American Journal of Political Science, 57*(3), 611–23.

Levendusky, M. S. (2013b). Partisan media exposure and attitudes toward the opposition. *Political Communication, 30*(4), 565–81.

Lobosco, K. (2018, November 28). US trade deficit rises despite Trump's tariffs. *CNN Business.* https://www.cnn.com/2018/11/28/economy/trade-deficit-trump-xi/index.html

Luther, C. A., & Miller, M. M. (2005). Framing of the 2003 U.S.-Iraq war demonstrations: An analysis of news and partisan texts. *Journalism and Mass Communication Quarterly, 82*(1), 78–96.

McChesney, R. W. (2003). The problem of journalism: A political economic contribution to an explanation of the crisis in contemporary U.S. journalism. *Journalism Studies, 4*(3), 299–329.

McKerns, J. (1976). The history of American journalism: A bibliographical essay. *American Studies International, 15*(1), 17–34.

Meeks, L. (2020). Defining the enemy: How Donald Trump frames the news media. *Journalism and Mass Communication Quarterly, 97*(1), 211–234.

Melber, A. (Host). (2018, December 6). *The Beat with Ari Melber* [Television broadcast]. MSNBC.

Mitchell, A. (2018). Americans still prefer watching to reading the news: And mostly still through television. *Pew Research Center.* https://www.journalism.org/2018/12/03/ americans-still-prefer-watching-to-reading-the-news-and-mostly-still-through-television/

Morris, J. S. (2007). Slanted objectivity? Perceived media bias, cable news exposure, and political attitudes. *Social Science Quarterly, 88*(3), 707–28.

Mullainathan, S., & Shleifer, A. (2005). The market for news. *American Economic Review, 95*(4), 1031–53.

Niven, D. (2001). Bias in the news: Partisanship and negativity in media coverage of Presidents George Bush and Bill Clinton. *Harvard International Journal of Press/Politics, 6*(3), 31–46.

Oliver, J. E., & Rahn, W. M. (2016). Rise of the Trumpenvolk: Populism in the 2016 election. *The*

ANNALS of the American Academy of Political and Social Science, 667(1), 189–206.

Patterson, T. E., & Donsbagh, W. (1996). News decisions: Journalists as partisan actors. *Political Communication, 13*(4), 455–68.

Pew Research Center. (2014, October 21). Political polarization & media habits: From Fox News to Facebook, how liberals and conservatives keep up with politics. *Pew Research Center.* https://www.pewresearch.org/wp-content/uploads/sites/8/2014/10/Political-Polarization-and-Media-Habits-FINAL-REPORT-7-27-15.pdf

Pew Research Center. (2019, June 25). Cable news fact sheet. *State of the News Media 2019.* https://www.journalism.org/fact-sheet/cable-news/

Pew Research Center. (2019, July 23). Public broadcasting fact sheet. *State of the News Media 2019.* https://www.journalism.org/fact-sheet/public-broadcasting/

Pickard, V. (2015). *America's battle for media democracy: The triumph of corporate libertarianism and the future of media reform.* Cambridge University Press.

Pickard, V. (2019). *Democracy without journalism? Confronting the misinformation society.* Oxford University Press.

Public Opinion Strategies. (2019, February 1). *Who's watching? A look at the demographics of cable news channel watchers* [Report]. https://pos.org/whos-watching-a-look-at-the-demographics-of-cable-news-channel-watchers/

Quandt, W. B. (1986). The electoral cycle and the conduct of foreign policy. *Political Science Quarterly, 101*(5), 825–37.

Rapp, N., & Jenkins, A. (2018, August 1). Chart: These 6 companies control much of the U.S. media. *Fortune.* http://fortune.com/longform/media-company-ownership-consolidation/

Saad, L. (2019). Americans' views on trade in the Trump era. *Gallup blog.* https://news.gallup.com/opinion/gallup/267770/americans-views-trade-trump-era.aspx

Schake, K. (2016). Republican foreign policy after Trump. *Survival, 58*(5), 33–52.

Scheufele, D. A., & Tewksbury, D. (2007). Framing, agenda setting, and priming: The evolution of three media effects models. *Journal of Communication, 57*(1), 9–20.

Schudson, M. (2001). The objectivity norm in American journalism. *Journalism, 2*(2), 149–70.

Schudson, M. (2007). The concept of politics in contemporary U.S. journalism. *Political Communication, 24*(2), 131–42.

Semetko, H. A., & Valkenburg, P. M. (2000). Framing European politics: A content analysis of press and television news. *Journal of Communication, 50*(2), 93–109.

Silver, L., Devlin, K., & Huang, C. (2019). U.S. views of China turn sharply negative amid trade tensions. *Pew Research Center.* https://www.pewresearch.org/global/2019/08/13/u-s-views-of-china-turn-sharply-negative-amid-trade-tensions/

Singer, J. B. (2007). Contested autonomy: Professional and popular claims on journalistic norms. *Journalism Studies, 8*(1), 79–95.

Stroud, N. J. (2008). Media use and political predispositions: Revisiting the concept of selective exposure. *Political Behavior, 30*(3), 341–66.

Stroud, N. J. (2010). Polarization and partisan selective exposure. *Journal of Communication, 60*(3), 556–76.

Trump, D.J. [@realDonaldTrump]. (2016, June 29). The @USCHAMBER must fight harder for the American worker. China, and many others, are taking advantage of U.S. with our terrible trade pacts [Tweet]. Twitter. https://web.archive.org/web/20200710202822/https://twitter.com/realdonaldtrump/status/748141420528140288

Vallone, R. P., Ross, L., & Lepper, M. R. (1985). The hostile media phenomenon: Biased perception and perceptions of media bias in coverage of the Beirut massacre. *Journal of Personality and Social Psychology, 49*(3), 577–85.

Wang, X. (2018, November 24). Is fighting talk a ploy ahead of Xi–Trump summit? *South China Morning Post.* https://www.scmp.com/week-asia/opinion/article/2174554/china-us-fighting-talk-ploy-ahead-trump-xi-summit

Warner, B. R. (2018). Modeling partisan media effects in the 2014 U.S. midterm elections. *Journalism and Mass Communication Quarterly, 95*(3), 647–69.

Weatherford, M. S. (2012). The wages of competence: Obama, the economy, and the 2010 midterm elections. *Presidential Studies Quarterly, 42*(1), 8–39.

Yglesias, M. (2018). The case for Fox News studies. *Political Communication, 35*(4), 681–83.

Zaller, J. (1994). Elite leadership of mass opinion: New evidence from the Gulf War. In W. L. Bennett and D. L. Paletz (Eds.), *Taken by storm: The media, public opinion, and U.S. foreign policy in the Gulf War* (pp. 186–209). University of Chicago Press.

How Media Use and Perceptions of Chinese Immigrants and Mainland Chinese Affect Americans' Attitudes toward the U.S.–China Trade War

Ruonan Zhang, Louisa Ha, and Nicky Chang Bi

Starting in January 2018, the U.S.–China trade war caught the attention of the media worldwide. Encapsulating a typical American complaint, Peter Navarro, director of the White House National Trade Council, explained that the tariffs were calculated to help the U.S. recoup losses incurred from the forfeiting of intellectual property to China (Guilford, 2018). While some U.S. media outlets praised this new U.S. trade policy as an effective penalty for China's intellectual property theft (e.g., Fu & Chin, 2018), China criticized the U.S. trade tariffs as triggering a strong-armed political struggle that will hurt the American economy and jeopardize America's international leadership (BBC, 2018). While the United States and China traded such barbs and scholars have addressed the media's role in covering the trade war, we offer here one of the first detailed analyses of public opinion in the United States as related to the trade war.

Past studies of public opinion on foreign policy issues mostly focus on the effects of news media usage (e.g., Baum, 2011; Robinson, 2002) and political partisanship (e.g., Cavari, 2013; Koch, 2009). Less attention has been paid to the roles of long-held attitudes and stereotypes in the formation of public opinions toward

The survey was funded by the National Social Science Fund of China (NSSFC), Project #14ZDB162.

important foreign policy issues such as the U.S.–China trade war. These factors deserve consideration because most people in the United States do not have direct experience with foreign nations. Thus, their past experiences and stereotypes are the most accessible resources for interpreting foreign relations with China. However, the portrayal of Chinese immigrants in the U.S. media is mostly negative or stereotypical, reproducing either "yellow peril" narratives or "model minority" imagery (Luther et al., 2017; Kawai, 2005; Zhang, 2010). Moreover, studies have shown that while the U.S. media often portray China's government negatively, the people of China tend to be represented fairly positively (Zhang, 2015). This dichotomy presents Americans with a confusing set of claims, as the Chinese government is often portrayed as brutal and authoritarian, while the people in China are portrayed as hard-working and law-abiding. Given this conflicting set of ideas, we argue that many Americans build their sense of U.S.–China relations, in part, by drawing upon their personal experiences with Chinese immigrants. We demonstrate in this chapter how, by merging media representations of China and personal experiences with Chinese immigrants, Americans form perceptual schemas that inform their judgment on the "trade war." Our findings suggest that Americans are confused about their feelings about China as a nation and the Chinese as a people, and that they are deeply ambivalent about the trade war.

The U.S.–China trade war started in January 2018 when U.S. President Donald Trump increased tariffs on solar panels manufactured abroad by 30 percent. These tariffs targeted China, which produces most of the solar panels sold internationally (Eckhouse et al., 2018). On March 22, 2018, the Trump administration announced plans to impose further tariffs on $50 billion worth of Chinese products (Bryan, 2018a) to reduce the trade deficit and protect the United States from intellectual property theft by China through restrictions on the export of information technology products (Office of the United States Trade Representative, 2018). The trade war intensified in July 2018, when a 25 percent tariff was imposed on $34 billion worth of Chinese products (Elis, 2018); at this point, China retaliated by imposing a 25 percent tariff on $34 billion worth of products imported from America (Bryan, 2018b). Both sides kept adding tariffs to pressure the other while pursuing trade negotiation meetings until the so-called "phase one agreement" was reached on January 15, 2020.

The U.S.–China trade war has received both support and opposition from the U.S. press (Ha et al., 2020). Some observers have argued that the trade conflict can help reduce the U.S. trade deficit (Mutikani, 2019). However, Neil Hughes (2005), a World Bank executive, argued that China should not be blamed for the trade imbalance between the United States and China. Instead, American consumers are the driving force behind the U.S. trade deficit with China because of their consistent demand for cheaper products. Others have warned that the trade war could hurt Americans with lower incomes, who depend on affordable products imported from China. Finally, although the tariffs reduced imports from China, U.S. exports to China decreased even more, which, in turn, further increased the trade deficit with China (Mutikani, 2019).

Schema and Attitudinal Transfer Theory

Schema theory proposes that people's comprehension of information is an interactive process between the media content they consume and their knowledge about the topic at hand (Carrell & Eisterhold, 1983). Consequently, people's prior knowledge, preexisting stereotypes, and biases can significantly influence how they process new information. Castano et al. (2016), for example, found that people form schemas or national images of countries, and these schemas can influence their foreign policy preferences. Moreover, the mass media might facilitate the formation of such national images, thus influencing how people from one country view people from another country (Boden, 2016). Therefore, it is reasonable to assume that people's perceptions of foreign affairs are influenced by their stereotypical perceptions—or mental schemas—of foreign nations.

Americans can form schemas about the mainland Chinese people based on their exposure to news related to China, Chinese popular culture, and Chinese cultural events. But there is another group of Chinese that likely make a strong impression on Americans: Chinese immigrants. Because of the highly diversified racial composition of the U.S. population, especially in big cities, Americans might have direct contact with Chinese immigrants in their daily lives, thus forming a schema of Chinese immigrants based on their personal experiences. Applying this schema theory to our analysis, we speculate that, when people are exposed to information about the U.S.–China trade war, they simultaneously draw upon their previously formed schemas related to China and Chinese immigrants, which, in turn, will influence their perceptions of the U.S.–China trade war.

While schema theory explains how preexisting beliefs can influence people's perceptions of current events, attitude transfer theory explains how current attitudes toward one object can be transferred to another related object through a generalization process involving involuntary or spontaneous association (Glaser et al., 2015). Consumer research, especially in brand extensions, has consistently shown that consumers transfer their feelings toward one product to other unrelated products from the same brand (Czellar, 2003; Ratliff et al., 2012). For instance, people who prefer Nike basketball shoes would also be interested in buying T-shirts and baseball caps from this particular sports brand. Likewise, intergroup research has demonstrated that positive attitudes toward one group member can be transferred to other group members. Similarly, a negative stereotype of a member of an ethnic or racial group could be transferred to other members of that group (Ratliff & Nosek, 2011). Following this logic, we can infer that people's existing attitudes toward the Chinese people could be attributed to their associations with China. A negative attitude toward the Chinese may lead to support for the tariffs to put pressure on China and the belief that the tariffs will lead to positive results for the U.S. economy. Conversely, a positive attitude toward the Chinese may lead to opposition to the tariffs because they might be perceived as undermining U.S.–China relations and the belief that the tariffs could hurt the U.S. economy. Before explaining how we collected our data to pursue this thesis, we turn below to the question of what Americans might mean when they think of someone as being "Chinese," for this is a complicated term fraught with nuance.

Differences between Mainland Chinese and Chinese Immigrants

There are two types of Chinese people Americans might encounter either in person or through the mass media: mainland Chinese living in China and Chinese immigrants in the United States. Americans may rely more on media stereotypes and occasional encounters with Chinese tourists or travel experiences in China when forming their perceptions of mainland Chinese. By contrast, Chinese immigrants who live in the United States might be encountered daily and thus might be perceived as fellow Americans. At the same time, though, immigrants could also be seen as a threat by Americans, who might perceive them as competing for jobs or social welfare benefits (Mayda, 2006; Stephan et al., 2005). Moreover, Chinese immigrants not only come from mainland China, but have diverse origins, in places such as Hong Kong, Taiwan, or other Southeast Asian countries with large Chinese minority populations such as Vietnam, Malaysia, and Singapore. These Chinese immigrants are often quite different in terms of cultural background and experiences from those moving to America from China. Hence, the way Americans perceive "Chinese" immigrants might differ significantly from perceptions of Chinese people living in China. Especially Americans who live in cities with a larger population of ethnic Chinese, such as New York and San Francisco, might have perceptions of Chinese immigrants that are more likely formed by direct experiences and, as a result, might be more pronounced and mentally accessible (Doll & Ajzen, 1992).

Consequently, Americans who hold positive perceptions of mainland Chinese people should be less supportive of the tariffs because they might see the tariffs as a form of economic warfare against the Chinese people, who are not the cause of the trade deficit problem. It is important to remember that the U.S. trade tariffs target China and not Chinese immigrants living in the United States. Nonetheless, attitudinal transfer theory teaches us to expect a messy conflation, wherein actual Chinese immigrants, mainland Chinese people, ethnic Chinese immigrants from other nations, and the government of China all collapse, in the minds of Americans, into one homogeneous mass.

The recent attacks on Asian Americans, which were triggered by President Trump's anti-China rhetoric during the COVID-19 pandemic, show how easily some people may misidentify ethnicity (Strochlic, 2020). On the other hand, schema theory suggests that if Americans have positive perceptions of Chinese immigrants, they might be more likely to transfer these positive perceptions of Chinese immigrants onto China—thus making them less supportive of trade tariffs that could undermine good relations with China.

Overall, both the schema and the attitude transfer theory suggest that perceptions of Chinese immigrants or people from China could affect Americans' support for or opposition to the trade war through schema accessibility and association. However, measuring this subtle interplay of influences is extremely complicated. In the following sections, we describe how we sought to measure the relative significance of media portrayals and personal experiences in forming explanatory schemas of the Chinese people.

Effects of News Media Consumption on Public Opinion

As a common source of information about government policy and public affairs, the news media play an important role in public opinion studies. They can create and influence the public's understanding of "reality" by setting the public agenda and framing important issues with distinct perspectives. The agenda-setting theory explains the news media's ability to influence news consumers' perceived importance of topics (Shaw, 1979). In other words, news audiences perceive an issue as more important when a news item is covered prominently by the media. Building on the agenda-setting theory, scholars have argued that the media's use of particular news frames can influence individuals' interpretations of issues or events. According to Entman (1993), framing is "to select some aspects of a perceived reality and make them more salient in a communicating text, in such a way as to promote a particular problem definition, causal interpretation, moral evaluation, and/or treatment recommendation for the item described" (p. 52). Thus, frames can affect consumers' perceived relevance of the news and influence how they think about specific news items.

Importantly in the context of the U.S.–China trade war, these news frames also can change people's perceptions and attribution of responsibility (Iyengar, 1991; Kim, 2015). Thus, audiences consuming news about the U.S.–China trade war might have been influenced by the specific frames the media adopted to describe this international conflict. Consequently, Americans' opinions about the trade war might have been either reinforced or changed depending on their preexisting attitudes and the news sources they used.

According to Archetti (2010), the reporting of international news is often shaped by national interests. However, how journalists interpret national interest and frame the trade conflict can vary depending on the media organizations they work for. For example, Ha et al.'s (2020) study on how the U.S. media presented the trade war with China shows that the conservative Fox News supported the Trump administration's trade tariffs policy. In contrast, liberal cable news networks, such as CNN and MSNBC, were more critical of the tariffs. We should therefore expect that the more partisan news people consume, the more likely they are to be influenced by the views presented by those outlets. Thus, when examining the effect of media exposure on public opinion, it is important to consider the type of news audiences consume.

Method

This study is based on a national survey of 1,049 adult Americans conducted between February 3 and February 28, 2019—a period during which the trade talks between the United States and China intensified. To ensure that the sample closely resembled the U.S. population, we implemented several procedures. First, we used sampling quotas based on the 2010 U.S. Census demographics for gender, age, and ethnicity. To ensure that we only included respondents in our sample who carefully read the questionnaire, we added an attention-check question midway through the questionnaire. Those who failed the attention-check question were excluded from the sample. We also eliminated all "speeders" who completed the survey in less than four minutes (average response time was eight minutes). Finally, we excluded all respondents who were unaware of the U.S.–China trade war ($N = 230$) from the analysis to focus our analysis on respondents who were at least somewhat aware of the trade war and its implications.

After answering questions related to their perceptions of mainland Chinese and Chinese immigrants, the respondents were asked whether their views of these two types of Chinese people have changed since the beginning of the trade war. We then eliminated those respondents from the analysis who reported that their views of mainland Chinese ($N = 92$) and Chinese immigrants ($N = 103$) had changed. This was done to ensure that we focused on respondents who had fairly stable perceptions of Chinese citizens and immigrants, thus allowing us to examine the effects of respondents' pre-existing attitudes on views of the trade war. The proportion of respondents who changed their attitudes was small (less than 15 percent), indicating that Americans held fairly stable perceptions of Chinese people. The final sample size of Americans who were both aware of the U.S.–China trade war and maintained stable perceptions of mainland Chinese and Chinese immigrants was 693. We recognize that this is a limited sample size, yet our data suggest that 85 percent of those Americans surveyed held relatively stable views of both China and the Chinese people—either living in China or immigrants in America—regardless of their media habits. As anticipated by schema theory, this finding indicates that pre-existing personal experiences with Chinese people weigh more heavily on Americans' thinking about China in general and the trade war in particular than the impact of their media consumption.

Dependent Variables

Americans' opinion of the U.S.–China trade war. The dependent variable in the study was measured with the following eight items: "Do you think the tariffs on Chinese goods will help the United States in reducing the trade deficit with China?" (1= "definitely not" to 5 = "definitely yes"); "Do you support or oppose the current U.S. government's actions during the trade conflict with China?" (1 = "strongly oppose" to 5 = "strongly support"); "Thus far, what effect do you think the U.S. trade conflict with China has had on the U.S. economy/my family's financial situation/my employer's business" (1 = "very hurtful" to 5 = "very helpful"); and "In the long term, what effect do you think the U.S.–China trade conflict will have on the U.S. economy/my family's financial situation/ my employer's business" (1 = "very hurtful" to 5 = "very helpful").

The eight items were designed to investigate respondents' (1) overall support for the U.S. trade policy toward China, (2) their perceptions of the short-term effects of the trade war on the U.S. economy, and (3) their perceptions of its long-term effects. We checked these three aspects for consistency and found them to be strongly correlated. Consequently, all eight items were combined into an index measuring *Americans' attitudes toward the trade war* (Cronbach's alpha = .93, M = 2.90, SD = .85).

Predictor Variables

Perceptions of Chinese immigrants. This construct was measured by asking the respondents how much they agreed (1= "strongly disagree" to 5 = "strongly agree") with five stereotypical statements about Chinese immigrants. The questions focused on negative and positive descriptors of Chinese immigrants, such as "most of them are hardworking," "most of them are taking advantage of U.S. social benefits," "most of them are taking away jobs from Americans," "most of them contribute to the United States with their skills and knowledge," and "most of them have good jobs."

Perceptions of mainland Chinese. This construct was measured by asking the respondents how much they agreed (1= "strongly disagree" to 5 = "strongly agree") with four stereotypical statements about mainland Chinese: "most of them are hardworking," "they are taking away jobs from Americans because of products made in China," "most of them are less educated than Americans," and "most of them have a decent standard of living."

Media exposure to news about U.S.–China trade war. To measure how respondents consumed news about the U.S.–China trade war, they were first asked whether they watched (1) broadcast network TV news, such as ABC, CBS, NBC, and PBS, (2) Fox News, (3) CNN, (4) MSNBC, (5) local TV news, (6) international TV news channels, (7) news videos on YouTube, and (8) business news channels, such as Fox Business or CNBC. To measure exposure to other news outlets, respondents were asked whether they used (1) the *New York Times*, (2) the *Wall Street Journal*, (3) *USA Today*, (4) National Public Radio (NPR), (5) online news brands (e.g., *Huffington Post* or *Buzzfeed*), and (6) local newspapers, and (7) radio news.

Control variables. We controlled for respondents' age, gender, education, income, knowledge about China (1 = "I don't know anything about China at all," 5 = "I know China very well"), previous trips to China (1 = "never been there," 4 = "been there many times"), number of Chinese friends or relatives (1 = "none," 4 = "many"), and political ideology (1 = "very conservative," 7 = "very liberal"). Political ideology was included in the analysis as a key control variable because previous studies have shown that it has a stronger influence on an individual's opinions than party affiliation (Gries, 2014). Moreover, political scientists have used the political ideologies of individuals to explain public opinion, especially on foreign policy (Carmines et al., 2012; Treier & Hillygus, 2009). A common ideological dichotomy is the conservative-liberal paradigm, with conservatives tending to be hawkish and hostile toward foreign countries and immigrants (Brooks et al., 2016).

Findings

We used the entire sample ($N = 1049$) following census distribution to measure Americans' attitudes towards mainland Chinese and Chinese immigrants. As shown in table 1, although the positive attribute of "hardworking" was similar for mainland Chinese ($M = 4.12$) and Chinese immigrants ($M = 4.13$), respondents' perceptions of mainland Chinese and Chinese immigrants differed notably. Americans primarily saw mainland Chinese as a threat to Americans' jobs ($M = 2.99$, $SD = 1.22$) rather than Chinese immigrants ($M = 2.53$, $SD = 1.22$, $t(925) = 11.73$, $p < .001$). As a result, Americans had significantly more positive perceptions of Chinese immigrants ($M = 3.75$, $SD = .71$) than of mainland Chinese ($M = 3.36$, $SD = .64$, $t(802) = 15.45$, $p < .001$).

Among those who were aware of the tariffs ($N = 693$), there were more men (55 percent) than women (45 percent). Their mean age was fifty years ($SD = 16.8$), average annual income was $45,000, mean education level was some college, knowledge level about China was moderate ($M = 2.58$, on a five-point scale ranging from low to high), and most respondents had no Chinese friends or relatives ($M = 1.43$, on a four-point scale ranging from 1 = none to 4 = many).

TABLE 1. Perception of Chinese Immigrants and Mainland Chinese

ITEMS	MEAN	SD
Chinese Immigrants (living in the United States)		
Most are hardworking.	4.13	.93
Most contribute to the U.S. with their skills and knowledge.	4.07	.90
Most are taking away jobs from Americans.*	2.53	1.24
Most have good jobs.	3.71	.86
Most are taking advantage of U.S. social benefits.*	2.67	1.23
Overall Perception of Chinese Immigrants	**3.75**	**.71**
Mainland Chinese (living in China)		
Most are hardworking.	4.12	.85
Most are less educated than Americans.*	2.65	1.18
Most are taking away jobs from Americans.*	2.99	1.22
Most have a decent standard of living.	3.06	1.13
Overall Perception of Mainland Chinese	**3.36**	**.64**

Note: N = 1,049. All items were measured on a scale ranging from 1 = strongly disagree to 5 = strongly agree.
*Reverse coded in computing the overall score.

Attitudes toward the Trade Tariffs

Americans' opinions of the U.S.–China trade war are shown in table 2. While 39.6 percent of Americans supported the U.S. government's actions during the trade conflict with China, 36.2 percent opposed them. More Americans believed that the trade war was hurting (47 percent) rather than helping (34 percent) the U.S. economy in both the short and the long term. Their opinions on whether the tariffs on Chinese goods would help the United States reduce the trade deficit with China were almost equally split. While about one-third (36.7 percent) believed that the tariffs would reduce the trade deficit, another one-third (35.9 percent) believed these tariffs would not help close the deficit. Most Americans also thought the trade war did not affect their family's financial situation (61 percent) or their employers' businesses (62 percent).

To examine whether Americans' perceptions of Chinese immigrants and mainland Chinese are associated with their attitudes toward the trade war, we performed a hierarchical regression analysis. The regression model first examined whether the respondents' demographics (age, income, gender) and other personal

TABLE 2. Americans' Views of U.S.–China Trade Tariffs

ITEMS	MEAN	SD
Do you think the tariffs on Chinese goods will help the U.S. in reducing the trade deficit with China? (1 = definitely not, 5 = definitely yes)	3.07	1.18
So far, what effect do you think the U.S. trade conflict with China has on the following: my family's financial situation?	2.91	.76
So far, what effect do you think the U.S. trade conflict with China has on the following: my employer's business?	2.91	.74
So far, what effect do you think the U.S. trade conflict with China has on the following: the U.S. economy?	2.79	1.14
In the long run, what effect do you think the U.S. trade conflict with China has on the following: my employer's business or my own business if self-employed?	2.90	.90
In the long run, what effect do you think the U.S. trade conflict with China has on the following: my family's financial situation?	2.87	.91
In the long run, what effect do you think the U.S. trade conflict with China has on the following: the U.S. economy?	2.85	1.27
Do you support or oppose the current U.S. government's action during the trade conflict with China? (1 = strongly oppose, 5 = strongly support)	2.93	1.30

Note: The analysis above only includes respondents who were aware of the trade tariffs and excludes missing responses (N = 693). The scale ranges from 1 to 5 (very hurtful = 1; no effects = 3; very helpful = 5) for items 2–7.

factors, such as knowledge about China, previous trips to China, number of Chinese friends or relatives, and political ideology, predicted their attitudes toward the trade war. As shown in table 3, while more conservative Americans (b = -.28, p < .01) held more negative attitudes toward the trade war, those who reported higher levels of knowledge about China (b = .09, p < .05) exhibited more positive attitudes. Thus, conservative Americans who said they knew more about China were the most supportive of the U.S. trade tariffs.

General Perceptions of Chinese and Attitudes toward the Trade Tariffs

Perceptions of mainland Chinese and Chinese immigrants were then added into the regression model as a second block of variables. The average composite scores of the perceptions of Chinese immigrants and mainland Chinese were used to predict the respondents' opinions of the trade war in the model. The findings indicate Americans' perceptions of Chinese people and Chinese immigrants were

TABLE 3. Hierarchical Regression Predicting Americans' Support of Trade Tariffs with Composite Perception Score

CONTROL VARIABLES	COEFFICIENTS
Age	.02
Gender	.01
Education	−.05
Income	.07
Knowledge about China	.09*
Previous trip to China	−.07
Number of Chinese friends and family	−.04
Political ideology (1= conservative, 7 = liberal)	−.28***
ΔR^2 (in %)	23.1
PERCEPTIONS OF CHINESE	
Perception of Chinese immigrants	−.15***
Perception of mainland Chinese	−.08*
ΔR^2 (in %)	4.9
NEWS MEDIA EXPOSURE	
TV NEWS SOURCES	
National TV news	−.01
Fox News	.14***
CNN	−.18***
MSNBC	−.03
Local TV news	−.04
International TV news channels	−.02
News videos on YouTube	.09*
Business news channels	.09*
OTHER NEWS SOURCES	
New York Times	.03
Wall Street Journal	−.07
USA Today	.06
Local metro newspapers	−.09*
National Public Radio	−.13**
Online news brands (HuffPost, Buzzfeed, etc.)	−.03
Local radio news	.02
ΔR^2 (in %)	9.5
Total R^2	37.5
Total N	693

Note: All coefficients are standardized. The analysis above only includes respondents who were aware of the trade tariffs ($N = 693$). *p < .05; **p < .01; ***p < .001

significantly associated with their opinions regarding the trade war. As predicted, Americans with more positive perceptions of Chinese immigrants (b= –15, p < .001) and mainland Chinese (b = –.08, p < 0.05) were less supportive of the trade war. Thus, our main hypothesis was supported.

A comparison of the strength of the relationship between Americans' perceptions of Chinese immigrants and mainland Chinese and their attitudes toward the tariffs indicates that positive perceptions of Chinese immigrants were stronger predictors than perceptions of mainland Chinese. This finding contradicts our hypothesis that perceptions of mainland Chinese should be more significantly associated with Americans' attitudes toward the trade tariffs than perceptions of Chinese immigrants.

Media Exposure, Type of News Sources, and Attitudes toward the Trade Tariffs

We added the respondents' media use for information about the trade war as predictors in this regression's third block. Among the TV news exposure measures, only cable TV news consumption significantly predicted Americans' attitudes toward the trade war. While exposure to Fox News (b = .18, p < .001) and business TV news (b = .09, p < .05) were found to be associated with more support for the trade tariffs among American audiences, use of national and local TV news was not. On the other hand, exposure to CNN (b = -.14, p < .001) correlated with less support for the trade tariffs.

Among other news sources, exposure to news on YouTube (b = .09, p < .05) predicted more support for the trade tariffs, while exposure to public radio (b = -.13, p < .01) and local newspapers (b = -.09, p < .05) correlated with less support. Exposure to national newspapers, online news, and local radio news did not show any significant relationships with Americans' support for the trade tariffs.

Individual Characteristics of Chinese and Attitudes toward the Trade Tariffs

To understand how specific perceptions of Chinese immigrants and mainland Chinese might be associated with Americans' attitudes toward the trade war, we broke down the composite perception scores into individual items. These items then served as individual predictors of Americans' support for the trade tariffs.

TABLE 4. Hierarchical Regression Predicting Americans' Support of Trade Tariffs

CONTROL VARIABLES	COEFFICIENTS
Age	.02
Gender	.03
Education	−.05
Income	.07
Knowledge about China	.09*
Previous trip to China	−.06
Number of Chinese friends and family	−.02
Political ideology (1 = conservative, 7 = liberal)	−.26***
ΔR^2 (in %)	23.1
PERCEPTION OF CHINESE IMMIGRANTS	
Most are hardworking.	−.02
Most are taking advantage of U.S. social welfare.	.12**
Most are taking away jobs.	.00
Most contribute with their skills and knowledge.	−.06
Most have good jobs.	−.01
PERCEPTION OF MAINLAND CHINESE	
Most are hardworking.	.08
Most are taking away jobs.	.11*
Most are less educated.	.11**
Most have a decent standard of living.	.04
ΔR^2 (in %)	8.3

As shown in table 4, two items related to perceptions of mainland Chinese stood out as significant predictors of more support for the trade tariffs. Americans who thought that mainland Chinese are less educated than Americans ($b = .11$, $p < .01$) and that they take away American jobs ($b = .11$, $p < .01$) were more likely to support the trade tariffs. Similarly, Americans who believed that Chinese immigrants are taking advantage of U.S. social welfare benefits ($b = .12$, $p < .001$) were more supportive of the trade tariffs.

TABLE 4 (continued)

MAIN VARIABLES	COEFFICIENTS
NEWS MEDIA EXPOSURE	
TV NEWS SOURCES	
National TV news	.02
Fox News	.14***
CNN	−.18***
MSNBC	−.03
Local TV news	−.04
International TV news channels	−.02
News videos on YouTube	.08*
Business news channels	.09*
OTHER NEWS SOURCES	
New York Times	.01
Wall Street Journal	−.07
USA Today	.05
Local metro newspapers	−.08*
National Public Radio	−.12**
Online news brands (HuffPost, Buzzfeed, etc.)	−.02
Local radio news	.01
ΔR^2 (in %)	8.9
Total R^2	41.3

Conclusions

This study examined how Americans view the U.S.–China trade war and how their media exposure and perceptions of the Chinese people might influence their attitudes toward the trade war. The findings suggest that Americans' awareness of the U.S.–China trade war was not as high as anticipated. Only 79 percent of the respondents were aware of the trade war, which might be due to the fact that television news as the main news source of Americans did not cover the trade war much (Ha et al., 2020).

The findings indicate that Americans had a split view of the U.S.–China trade war. Although a slight majority of Americans were opposed to the U.S. trade tariffs imposed on China and viewed them as harmful to the U.S. economy, a considerable number of them favored the tariffs. We also found that more than half of all Americans did not believe that the trade tariffs would affect them, which may indicate that most Americans did not understand how tariffs affect the cost of products. This attitude might also be related to the absorption of the increased cost of Chinese products imported by American companies to compete in the market so that consumers did not see a direct increase in prices (Long, 2020). Furthermore, the strong U.S. economy during the trade war offset the negative effect of increases in the prices of certain products. China's retaliatory tariffs were targeted at specific sectors, such as agriculture, which is served by only 1.3 percent of the U.S. population and was not fully reflected in the survey.

Interestingly, most Americans believed that the tariffs would harm the U.S. economy, indicating a lack of confidence in the effectiveness of Trump's trade policy. Thus, our findings clearly indicate that the majority of respondents did not support Donald Trump's tariffs and did not think they would help the American economy.

The findings also support our general proposition that Americans' perceptions of mainland Chinese and Chinese immigrants predict their support for the trade tariffs—in addition to more traditional factors such as media use and political ideology. Based on the significant relationship between Americans' views of the trade war and their overall perceptions of mainland Chinese and Chinese immigrants as predicted by schema theory, our findings also indicate an attitude transfer effect from individuals' like or dislike of Chinese immigrants and mainland Chinese to their opposition to or support for the U.S. tariffs. Thus, public opinion toward the trade war was influenced by the information audiences obtained from the media and their preexisting attitudes toward the people involved in this foreign policy issue.

As our study demonstrates, several negative stereotypical perceptions of Chinese immigrants and mainland Chinese predicted Americans' support for the tariffs. For example, Americans who believed that mainland Chinese threatened jobs in the United States were more supportive of the trade tariffs. By contrast, positive perceptions of Chinese immigrants (that they contribute skills and knowledge, have good jobs, and are hardworking) and mainland Chinese (who have a decent living standard) were not associated with Americans' attitudes toward the trade war. We therefore conclude that only specifically negative perceptions affected foreign policy support. This indicates that Americans who perceived the Chinese people as competitors either for jobs (mainland Chinese) or welfare benefits (Chinese immigrants) tend to support a hard stance against China's economic threat. However, such respondents were a clear minority among those included in this study.

We also found that Americans who reported higher levels of knowledge about China were more likely to support the trade tariffs. As indicated in Beckman and Hartnett and Bean in this volume, this relationship between more knowledge about China and support for the tariffs likely represents an emerging consensus in America: that China's economic policies after its entry into the WTO have benefitted the PRC at the expense of other international players. Alternatively, as other chapters herein argue, these views also correlate with media exposure, as much of the news coverage produced by partisan outlets has emphasized China's unfair trade practices and intellectual property theft (see Ray & Lu in this volume). Such negative coverage of China might explain why Americans who think they are knowledgeable about China tend to be supportive of the trade tariffs.

Our study also shows that business and partisan cable TV channels and news videos on YouTube were the only news sources associated with Americans' attitudes toward the trade war. Results from the hierarchical regression analysis, which controlled for respondents' political ideology, indicate that business and partisan cable TV news networks played the most important role in framing people's perceptions of the U.S.–China trade war. Specifically, respondents' exposure to the more conservative Fox News and other business channels were associated with more support for the tariffs, while exposure to the more liberal CNN and NPR correlated with less support. These associations might indicate that business and partisan media outlets play an important role in polarizing and shaping opinions on foreign policy issues. Although we did not ask specifically the types of YouTube news videos participants watched, it is likely that most respondents consumed highly opinionated news videos on YouTube that criticized China.

In conclusion, this study identified perceptions of Chinese as an important factor to be considered in predicting Americans' support for the trade tariffs on China. As we have shown, Americans who held negative and stereotypical perceptions of Chinese were *more* likely to support U.S. trade tariffs on China. In contrast, Americans who relied on more liberal news sources and did not hold negative stereotypes of the Chinese were *less* likely to support the tariffs. Consequently, our results show that Americans' perceptions of the trade war were likely influenced by more than just economic considerations. Instead, it seems that these attitudes were also driven by the fear that the Chinese people might directly compete for jobs or social welfare benefits with American workers. The finding that perceptions of Chinese immigrants were more strongly associated with Americans' view of the trade war than their perceptions of mainland Chinese only underscores the importance of a perceived threat coming from people who are a direct competitor for social welfare benefits.

Overall, this study underscores how public opinion about foreign affairs is influenced by a combination of individuals' news habits and their pre-existing personal experiences with people from other nations. Because people's knowledge about other nations or immigrants can be shaped by media coverage, it is important to consider how other nations and their people are portrayed in the media. While this chapter focused on how mainstream media outlets and personal experiences might affect American public opinion regarding the trade war, later chapters will address how legacy media and social media affect Chinese public opinion—thus offering a comprehensive view of how both nations responded to the trade war.

REFERENCES

Archetti, C. (2010). *Explaining news: National politics and journalistic cultures in global context* (1st ed.). Palgrave Macmillan.

Baum, M. A. (2011). *Soft news goes to war: Public opinion and American foreign policy in the new media age.* Princeton University Press.

BBC. (2018, September 24). China accuses US of trade bullying as new tariffs imposed. *BBC.* https://www.bbc.com/news/business-45622075

Boden, J. (2016). Mass media: Playground of stereotyping. *International Communication Gazette, 78*(1–2), 121–36.

Brooks, C., Manza, J., & Cohen, E. D. (2016). Political ideology and immigrant acceptance. *Socius, 2.* https://doi.org/10.1177/2378023116668881.

Bryan, B. (2018a, March 22). Trump just slammed China with tariffs on $50 billion worth of goods in a move that could escalate into a global trade war. *Business Insider.* https://www.businessinsider.com/trump-imposes-china-tariffs-start-trade-war-hurt-stocks-dow-futures-2018–3?utm_source=markets&utm_medium=ingest

Bryan, B. (2018b, July 06). China says Trump's tariffs 'launched the largest trade war in economic history,' vows to strike back. *Business Insider.* https://www.businessinsider.com/trump-china-trade-war-government-promises-retaliation-to-tariffs-2018–7?utm_source=markets&utm_medium=ingest

Carmines, E. G., Ensley, M. J., & Wagner, M. W. (2012). Political ideology in American politics: One, two, or none? *The Forum, 10*(3). https://doi.org/10.1515/1540–8884.1526

Carrell, P. L., & Eisterhold, J. C. (1983). Schema theory and ESL reading pedagogy. *TESOL Quarterly, 17*(4), 553–73.

Castano, E., Bonacossa, A., & Gries, P. (2016). National images as integrated schemas: Subliminal primes of image attributes shape foreign policy preferences. *Political Psychology, 37*(3), 351–66.

Cavari, A. (2013). Religious beliefs, elite polarization, and public opinion on foreign policy: The partisan gap in American public opinion toward Israel. *International Journal of Public Opinion Research, 25*(1), 1–22.

Czellar, S. (2003). Consumer attitude toward brand extensions: An integrative model and research propositions. *International Journal of Research in Marketing, 20*(1), 97–115.

Doll, J., & Ajzen, I. (1992). Accessibility and stability of predictors in the theory of planned behavior. *Journal of Personality and Social Psychology, 63*(5), 754.

Eckhouse, B., Natter, A., & Martin, C. (2018, January 22). President Donald Trump imposes 30% tariffs on solar panels. *Time.*

Entman, R. M. (1993). Framing: Toward clarification of a fractured paradigm. *Journal of Communication, 43*(4), 51–58.

Echeverria-Estrada, C., & Batalova, J. (2020, January 20). Chinese immigrants in the United States. *Migration Policy Institute.* https://www.migrationpolicy.org/article/chinese-immigrants-united-states?gclid=CjwKCAjw1cX0BRBmEiwAy9tKHvuHkEJoGZMqQC jPR_OjnDg88I9nuBB0KPQ6YxIDGvok7vrayCDLGhoC3j0QAvD_BwE#Income

Elis, N. (2018, August 08). Trump to hit China with $16B in tariffs on Aug. 23. *The Hill.* https://thehill.com/policy/finance/400791-trump-to-hit-china-with-16b-in-tariffs-on-aug-23

Fu, C. L., & Chin, C. S. (2018, September 17). China is stealing American intellectual property: Trump's tariffs are a chance to stop it. *Los Angeles Times.*

Glaser, T., Dickel, N., Liersch, B., Rees, J., Süssenbach, P., & Bohner, G. (2015). Lateral attitude change. *Personality and Social Psychology Review, 19*(3), 257–76.

Gries, P. (2014). *The politics of American foreign policy: How ideology divides liberals and conservatives over foreign affairs.* Stanford University Press.

Guilford, G. (2018, March 22). Trump's new China tariffs protect US intellectual property—but hobble innovation. *Quartz.* https://qz.com/1235332/trumps-new-china-tariffs-protect-us-intellectual-property-but-hobble-innovation/

Ha, L., Yang, Y., Ray, R., Matanji, F., Chen, P., Guo, K., & Lyu, N. (2020). How US and Chinese media cover the US–China trade conflict: A case study of war and peace journalism practice and the foreign policy equilibrium hypothesis. *Negotiation and Conflict Management Research.* https://doi.org/10.1111/ncmr.12186.

Hughes, N. C. (2005). A trade war with China? *Foreign Affairs, 1*, 94–106.

Iyengar, S. (1991). *Is anyone responsible? How television frame political issues.* University of Chicago Press.

Kawai, Y. (2005). Stereotyping Asian Americans: The dialectic of the model minority and the yellow peril. *Howard Journal of Communications, 16*(2), 109–30.

Kim, S.-H. (2015). Who is responsible for a social problem? News framing and attribution of responsibility. *Journalism and Mass Communication Quarterly, 92*(3), 554–58.

Koch, M. T. (2009). Governments, partisanship, and foreign policy: The case of dispute duration. *Journal of Peace Research, 46*(6), 799–817.

Long, H. (2020, January 17). Trump's China tariffs have not caused Americans to pay $1,000 more a year: Here's why. *Washington Post.*

Luther, C. A., Lepre, C. R., & Clark, N. (2017). *Diversity in US mass media.* Wiley.

Mayda, A. M. (2006). Who is against immigration? A cross-country investigation of individual attitudes toward immigrants. *Review of Economics and Statistics, 88*(3), 510–30.

Mitchell, A. (2018). Americans still prefer watching to reading the news–and mostly still through television. *Pew Research Center.* https://www.journalism.org/2018/12/03/americans-still-prefer-watching-to-reading-the-news-and-mostly-still-through-television/

Mutikani, L. (2019, September 4). U.S. trade deficit shrinks, gap with China remains elevated. *Reuters.* https://www.reuters.com/article/us-usa-economy-trade/u-s-trade-deficit-shrinks-gap-with-china-remains-elevated-idUSKCN1VP1NT

Navarro, P., & Autry, G. (2011). *Death by China: Confronting the dragon—a global call to action.* Prentice Hall.

Office of the United States Trade Representative. (March 22, 2018). Findings of the investigation into China's acts, policies, and practices related to technology transfer, intellectual property, and innovation under section 301 of the Trade Act of 1974. https://ustr.gov/sites/default/files/Section%20301%20FINAL.PDF

Parmar, I. (2009). Foreign policy fusion: Liberal interventionists, conservative nationalists and neoconservatives: The new alliance dominating the US foreign policy establishment. *International Politics, 46*(2–3), 177–209.

Ratliff, K. A., & Nosek, B. A. (2011). Negativity and outgroup biases in attitude formation and transfer. *Personality and Social Psychology Bulletin, 37*(12), 1692–1703.

Ratliff, K. A., Swinkels, B. A., Klerx, K., & Nosek, B. A. (2012). Does one bad apple (juice) spoil the bunch? Implicit attitudes toward one product transfer to other products by the same brand. *Psychology & Marketing, 29*(8), 531–40.

Robinson, P. (2002). *The CNN effect: The myth of news, foreign policy and intervention.* Routledge.

Shaw, E. F. (1979). Agenda-setting and mass communication theory. *Gazette, 25*(2), 96–105.

Stephan, W. G., Renfro, C. L., Esses, V. M., Stephan, C. W., & Martin, T. (2005). The effects of feeling threatened on attitudes toward immigrants. *International Journal of Intercultural Relations, 29*(1), 1–19.

Strochlic, N. (2020, September 2). America's long history of scapegoating its Asian citizens. *National Geographic.* https://www.nationalgeographic.com/history/2020/09/asian-american-racism-covid/#close

Treier, S., & Hillygus, D. S. (2009). The nature of political ideology in the contemporary electorate. *Public Opinion Quarterly, 73*(4), 679–703.

Yin, J. (2007). The clash of rights: A critical analysis of news discourse on human rights in the United States and China. *Critical Discourse Studies, 4*(1), 75–94.

Zhang, L. (2015). Stereotypes of Chinese by American college students: Media use and perceived realism. *International Journal of Communication, 9*, 1–20.

Zhang, Q. (2010). Asian Americans beyond the model minority stereotype: The nerdy and the left out. *Journal of International and Intercultural Communication, 3*(1), 20–37.

How News Media Content and Fake News about the Trade War Are Shared on Twitter

A Topic Modeling and Content Analysis

Louisa Ha, Rik Ray, Frankline Matanji, and Yang Yang

Social media has created a world where people are always connected and have an open and free space for interaction. Through social information networks, social media users can now share information and endorse information shared by other users (Marwick & Boyd, 2011), thus playing an important role in forming public opinion (Kushin & Yamamoto, 2010). Politicians also take advantage of social media platforms such as Twitter to promote themselves and rally support. For example, U.S. President Donald Trump credited Twitter for providing him with an open forum to reach out to his supporters and "fight back" against "unfair" media coverage (Keith, 2016). Twitter cofounder Evan Williams called Trump a "master of Twitter" owing to his frequent and skillful use of this platform (O'Sullivan, 2019). However, after Twitter labeled Trump's tweets on mail-in ballots as false information by asking users to fact check his tweet (Dwoskin, 2020), Trump fought back and issued an executive order on "preventing online censorship" (Executive Office of the President, 2020). Thus, even though Trump benefitted enormously from Twitter as a tool to reach his many followers, the order noted that "Online platforms are engaging in selective censorship that is harming our national discourse" (Executive Office of the President, 2020, para. 7). Trump's account was permanently suspended by Twitter on January 8, 2021, for inciting violence after the insurrection at the U.S. Capitol building in Washington, D.C. (Twitter, 2021, January 8). During the trade war, Trump used Twitter heavily as the platform to promote his trade war, while social media users used it to share news and opinion about the trade war and China.

This chapter compares the differences in topics between the tweets posted by social media users and internet bots during the U.S.–China trade war. Our study shows how news media content, fake news, and conspiracy theories can spread on social media. Specifically, we examine how Twitter was used to share media content and fake news with the public in the United States during the U.S.–China trade dispute; identify the characteristics of popular tweets by analyzing how embedded links, images, and videos were used in these tweets; and discuss how these elements affected engagement with the tweets. We also explore Twitter users' actions and how their vested interests and backgrounds affected their postings on the trade war.

Social Media and International Conflict

About seven in ten (71 percent) social media users in the United States frequently get their news from Facebook or Twitter (Shearer & Matsa, 2018). On Facebook, users must be "friends" to access others' personal posts. However, Twitter is an open microblogging platform where anyone can browse and view tweets without following any specific user. Twitter was created in 2006 to connect friends and to provide a platform for personal interactions. That role changed in 2009 when its universal prompt changed from "what are you doing?" to "what is happening?" (Seib, 2012). This shift in Twitter's main function transformed it into a platform where people can share information and stay informed. Twitter upended traditional information dissemination and diplomatic relations mechanisms, such as press conferences and mainstream news coverage, by facilitating direct posting and sharing information and opinions in 140 characters (now 280 characters) to millions of active Twitter users worldwide.

Twitter usage statistics indicate that the number of active users has increased, reaching 199 million daily active users worldwide by the first quarter of 2021 (Twitter, 2021, April). A total of 1.3 billion accounts have been created, but 44 percent of these accounts never posted a tweet. In 2018, Twitter had 67 million active users per month in the United States. Eighty percent of these active users accessed the site via mobile devices, and a typical Twitter account had 707 followers on average (Smith, 2020). Twitter is now used as a tool for disseminating information, and it has become far easier than before for audiences to influence and be influenced by others. Journalists make up about 25 percent of verified accounts (Morrison, 2015), indicating that Twitter has become an essential platform for media professionals to disseminate news and information.

As Seib (2012) notes, we live in the era of rapid-reaction diplomacy thanks to social media platforms. Eighty-three percent of the world's leaders have a Twitter account (The Digital Policy Council, 2016). Twitter has facilitated real-time diplomacy, allowing political leaders to announce policies on Twitter or reach each other online. For example, Cockburn (2017) discussed how President Trump's hostile tweets toward Iran stoked sectarian conflicts in the Middle East because his tweets represented direct and public comments from the U.S. president. Twitter users in the Middle East were able to see Trump's derogatory remarks without mediation through news reports. Similarly, Šimunjak and Caliandro (2019) analyze how Trump conducted diplomacy on social media and how the rest of the world engaged in diplomatic exchanges with him. The authors conclude that Trump disrupted traditional diplomatic codes of conduct by expressing his personal opinions on his Twitter account.

President Trump had 71.8 million Twitter followers in 2018. During the U.S.–China trade war, his tweets were among the most retweeted tweets of all trade-war-related tweets analyzed in this chapter. The most retweeted tweet was Trump's hinting at a possible trade war on May 15, 2018: "Trade negotiations are continuing with China. They have been making hundreds of billions of dollars a year from the United States for many years. Stay tuned!" This particular tweet was retweeted more than 12,400 times and received close to 69,800 likes at the time of data collection.

Twitter users' ideology and political participation have become a hot topic for communication researchers. Many scholars and policymakers are viewing the platform as an agent of political change, ranging from the Russian use of cyber warfare and misinformation, Trump's presidential campaign and his presidency, to the Arab Spring revolution that played an important political role in the Middle East and North Africa (Seib, 2012; Zeitzoff, 2017).

Twitter is often seen as a "liberation technology" because it enables citizens to report news, expose wrongdoing, interact with each other, and communicate during political protests (Diamond, 2010). The technological affordances of social media (Sundar, 2008), such as the ease to share, comment, and reply, have enabled its users to exploit "existential bubbles" and form echo chambers of like-minded individuals who reinforce the same views (Barberá et al., 2015; Casetti & Sampietro, 2012). Moreover, Twitter makes it easy for individuals to stay in touch with breaking news through constant news updates, especially during times of crisis (Alabaster, 2013; Takahashi et al., 2015).

One feature that makes trending tweets unique is their ability to act as a news source for the public. While investigating the content and sources of popular tweets after the outbreak of diphtheria cases in Spain, Porat et al. (2019) found that almost half of the tweets posted online about diphtheria were informative messages. The remaining half of the tweets contained personal opinions expressing frustrations toward parents who refused to vaccinate their children and humor regarding antivaccination groups. Similar findings were observed in a study investigating content in online newspapers and social media during the outbreak of measles in the Netherlands (Radzikowski et al., 2016).

Twitter and Intermedia Agenda-Setting

Twitter facilitates its users to engage in news sharing through retweeting, thereby opening up an avenue for people to influence the public agenda (Benkler, 2006) and discuss issues that are brought up by the mainstream media (Hardy & Scheufele, 2005). Using the agenda-setting perspective, scholars have analyzed how the media influence each other by following each other's coverage and placing similar prominence on the news items. McCombs (2005) called this phenomenon intermedia agenda-setting. Despite research showing that Twitter activities are influenced by the mainstream media and TV audience ratings (Fábrega & Vega, 2013), Valenzuela et al.'s (2017) study of Chile's 2010 earthquake suggested that social media may have a stronger influence on television news coverage by playing an agenda-setting role during disasters and emergencies. Similarly, Kwak et al. (2010) compared Twitter's trending topics to headlines of CNN stories. They concluded that CNN was quicker than Twitter in reporting the same issue in more than half of the instances. However, they also noted that Twitter was faster than CNN in covering events such as sports and accidents. These findings indicate that social media users can set the agenda of the traditional news media by sharing stories and breaking news as they occur (Sayre et al., 2010).

Conspiracy Theory, Fake News, and Disinformation as Propaganda

In "U.S. Television News Coverage of the Trade War" in this volume, Ray and Lu analyzed how the U.S. news media framed the trade war and how partisan and broadcast media differed in providing news and information to the public. Here, we focus on Twitter as a source of conspiracy theories, disinformation, and fake news during the U.S.–China trade war. As news reports about the trade war tend to be brief and lack details of the behind-the-scenes negotiations between political leaders, audiences need to fill some information gaps themselves. This is important because the Trump administration needed to convince Americans that imposing tariffs on Chinese goods was the best way to solve the trade deficit with China. In contrast, the Chinese government needed to show its people why the U.S. tariffs were not justified and why they had to take the risk of retaliation (China State Department, 2018). Of course, both governments also did not want to lose the trade war right in front of their citizens (Erwin, 2019; Gasparino, 2019). Finally, it is important to note that the trade war also reflected the competition between China and the United States for global political and technological leadership (Cordesman, 2019; Roberts et al., 2019).

The U.S.–China trade war was the first major international trade dispute discussed on social media. The last major trade war that involved the United States and Japan occurred in the 1980s; however, social media was not available then. This time, the public, opinion leaders (influencers), political leaders, and the news media were all able to distribute information on social media. As most social media users were neither professional journalists nor obligated to abide by professional journalistic rules, they were able to disseminate all types of misinformation on Twitter, including conspiracy theories, disinformation, and fake news. This flood of digital misinformation created hostility, reinforced biases, and fed misperceptions about trade practices between China and the United States to the general public and policymakers.

Before analyzing misinformation on Twitter, it is important to understand the critical differences between conspiracy theories, disinformation, and fake news. A conspiracy theory is "an effort to explain some event or practice by reference to the machinations of powerful people, who attempt to conceal their role" (Sunstein & Vermuelle, 2009, p. 205). Disinformation is "false information intentionally created to mislead and misinform people with an agenda such as false advertising" (Fallis, 2015). Finally, fake news is "news articles that are intentionally and verifiably false, and could mislead readers" (Allcott & Gentzkow, 2017, p.213).

As Ha et al.'s (2019) review of research on misinformation and fake news pointed out, the spread of fake news on social media can increase its credibility and thus cause significant harm to the public. Moreover, fake news can be easily used as propaganda by governments and other parties who have a vested interest in manipulating the public.

Social Bots on Twitter

The need to increase information dissemination on social media has led to the creation of social bots, which are computer algorithms that interact with human beings, automatically produce content, and disseminate it on social media. Twitter estimates that 23 million active accounts were bots (Seward, 2014). A Pew study (Wojcik et al., 2018) analyzing the use of bots in the links shared in 1.2 million tweets found that suspected bots created 66 percent of tweeted links on popular news and current event websites. Bots can interact with humans, and some of them are sophisticated enough to generate believable human personas. This ability makes it difficult for filtering algorithms and social media users to spot bots on social media (Ferrara et al., 2016).

As Ferrara et al. (2016) noted, the adoption of these bots has had both negative and positive effects. For example, commercial companies have used bots to provide customer care services, thus providing a useful public service. However, some bots can be categorized as malicious entities as they have been designed for spreading unverified and misleading information to social media users (Ratkiewicz et al., 2011). These bots also exploit, manipulate, and mislead discussions on social media with information that can be categorized as spam, rumors, slander, and malware. Bots also have endangered democracy globally and influenced election outcomes (Varol et al., 2017). For example, by spreading fake news in support of or against politicians, bots may artificially inflate or diminish a political candidate's support and consequently interfere with election outcomes. For example, a report published by the *New York Times* about the 2016 U.S. presidential election acknowledged that pro-Trump bots outnumbered those used by Hillary Clinton five to one during the presidential election (Markoff, 2016). Moreover, Russia was found to have interfered in the 2016 U.S. election using bots, especially on Twitter (Swaine, 2018).

In light of Twitter's enormous potential to spread fake news and influence people's opinions about an international conflict, such as the U.S.–China trade war, this study aims to explore the type of messages posted on Twitter related to this issue. Specifically, we asked the following five research questions:

1. What are the differences in the content and posting patterns between bots and human tweets related to the U.S.–China trade war?
2. To what extent is news media content used in tweets related to the U.S.–China trade war and which news media are most used by Twitter users?
3. What are the users' views on the U.S.–China trade war, as reflected in the tweets?
4. What are the characteristics (links, images, videos) of the most popular tweets related to the U.S.–China trade war?
5. How does the use of links, images, and videos affect the engagement of tweets?

We collected 77,019 tweets during fourteen major events (see the introduction in this book for a description of each event) that marked the U.S.–China trade war between January 22 and December 6, 2018. We then selected the tweets that originated from the United States, which resulted in 27,804 tweets from 14,813 unique users. Among them, 1,193 were unique, verified user accounts with many followers (see figure 1 for the distribution of tweets for each event). We focused on the tweets of the first day of each event because they are likely to be breaking news for others to follow and set the agenda for other Twitter users on the topic. The days that generated the most tweets were July 6, when the U.S. government implemented tariffs on $34 billion of Chinese goods (5,583 tweets), and March 22, when Trump asked his U.S. trade representative to investigate possible tariffs on Chinese goods (4,353 tweets).

We analyzed the full corpus of the tweets using Latent Dirichlet Allocation (LDA) topic modeling, a machine-learning algorithm. We also performed a manual content analysis of a random subsample of 600 tweets to understand nuances such as the type of content being shared on Twitter and news engagement. To collect the tweets, we created a computer program using Python programming language that used Twitter's search functionality to gather the relevant tweets and then automatically retrieve and store each tweet's details. We used the keywords "China" and "trade" for the search query and limited the results to the fourteen specified days. The dataset was then filtered to contain only tweets from U.S. accounts.

LDA is a popular technique used to analyze large volumes of textual data. It uses unsupervised machine learning to discover common themes or topics in a

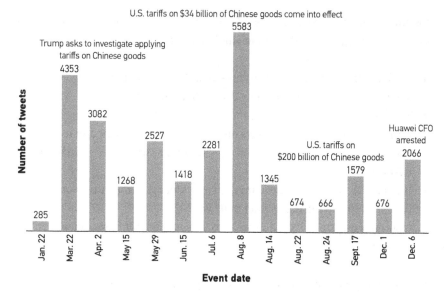

FIGURE 1. Number of Tweets on Major Events during the U.S.–China Trade War in 2018

document by estimating the probability of words appearing together. Most LDA studies either combine all tweets from a user into a document, combine tweets from a specific time interval, or use a combination of these two approaches (Guo et al., 2016). Because LDA requires large documents, we combined all the tweets from a given event into a single document, creating fourteen separate documents. Before modeling the topics, we cleaned the data by removing URLs, special characters, punctuations, numerical characters, common words, and words appearing in less than two and more than 11 documents. This cleaning was done to exclude the most and the least common words so that the model did not identify excessively redundant or obscure topics. We then categorized each word into the different parts of speech by using a natural language processing program (Loper & Bird, 2002). We trained other LDA models by using a program written in Python (Rehurek & Sojka, 2010). We tuned different parameters, such as the number of topics to be discovered and the different parts of speech. This was done to obtain an optimal model that displays interpretable patterns in words appearing in each topic. To remove unnecessary noise, we expanded the list of frequently occurring words to be excluded whenever they appeared on multiple topics.

The "discovered topics" in an LDA topic model require human interpretation to determine whether the co-occurring words indicate a common theme. After comparing models with different numbers of topics, we decided that our final model should ideally consist of five topics and should only include nouns, verbs, and adjectives from the corpus. We labeled the five topics as follows: (1) confrontation/Huawei, (2) beginning of conflict, (3) tariff/economy, (4) trade deal, and (5) punitive action/countermeasures by China. This model was applied separately to tweets from bots (automated) and non-bots (human) to compare their content (see table 1).

Tweets from Bots and Humans on the U.S.–China Trade War

Social bots have become more sophisticated in recent years, making their detection a big challenge for social media researchers. Several techniques are currently used to detect social bots, including crowdsourcing and graph- and feature-based detection (Ferrara et al., 2016). We used *Botometer*, a popular bot detection tool, to analyze our dataset of 27,804 U.S.-based tweets about the U.S.–China trade war. This program assigns each account a bot score between 0 (least likely) and 5 (most likely) based on a machine-learning algorithm that considers over 1,200 features (Davis et al., 2016). While 50 percent is generally a practical cut-off value in machine-learning algorithms, we used a higher threshold score of 3 (60 percent) to filter our dataset because we observed several legitimate accounts with scores between 2.5 and 3 during the manual content analysis coding process. This strategy resulted in 4,285 (17.4 percent) tweets being classified as those tweeted by bots.

We first used the LDA topic models to determine whether tweets by bots featured topics different from those found in regular tweets by humans. Based on the words appearing in each topic, we assigned labels to define the underlying themes (see table 1). Some of the common themes that emerged from the analysis of both types of tweets were the economic impact of the trade war, reciprocal measures from China, and constructive talks between China and the United States. The arrest of Meng Wanzhou, the chief financial officer of Huawei, was a dominant topic in human tweets.

As shown in table 1, the first topic in the human corpus also contained words that signified an escalation of the conflict, suggesting that people associated this event with increased hostility between the two countries. We found that the dominant theme for bot and human tweets was the same for two of the events under study—countermeasures from China on May 15 and the trade deal on May 20. Interestingly, the third most important topic in bot tweets was an unrelated

TABLE 1. Topic Models of Non-bot and Bot Tweets

HUMAN TWEETS

	WORDS	TOPIC LABEL
1.	Huawei, escalates, raises, truce, hits, sparks, fly, executive, arrested, hammers	confrontation + Huawei
2.	retaliates, starts, begins, launches, underway, escalates, launching, hits, begun, scale	beginning of the conflict
3.	hits, announcement, worries, Jones, drops, warns, defense, punish, closes, stiff	tariff + economy
4.	Mnuchin, treasury, progress, agrees, reached, gap, purchases, consensus, resume, abandon	trade deal
5.	ZTE, announces, launched, crackdown, escalation, Ivanka, rattling, retaliates, confusion, sows	punitive action + countermeasures from China

BOT TWEETS

	WORDS	TOPIC LABEL
1.	hits, Xi, points, raises, exports, fight, concerns, negotiations, impose, escalates	countermeasures from China
2.	moves, explains, emerging, announces, measures, tough, changing, earnings, hit, York	beginning and change + economy
3.	Huawei, truce, executive, clouding, listed, books, Amazon, article, weekend, booklovers	books (spam) + Huawei
4.	history, biggest, effect, underway, started, begins, retaliates, rattling, leaders, escalates	trade conflict
5.	Mnuchin, hold, putting, street, play, treasury, won, cut, agree, warns	trade deal

topic about books and reading. This likely indicates that some spam tweets were included in our initial dataset because of hashtag spamming (Hyun & Kim, 2016). Some words related to the trade war were observed across all the discovered topics. For example, topic 4 in the bot tweets captured various terms related to the subtopics identified in the human tweets. This problem is also found in previous studies, where LDA identified multiple issues in a single topic (Guo et al., 2016; Zhao et al., 2011).

Although the LDA algorithm assumes a mix of all topics in a document, a single topic often dominates the distribution in a given document. Among the bot tweets, countermeasures from China represented the most dominant topic for five of the fourteen events. Beginning and change + economy constituted the second most dominant topic in three events. The other three topics were dominant for two events each. Overall, the human tweets showed a more even allocation of dominant topics than the bot tweets. Confrontation + Huawei and punitive action + countermeasures from China were equally dominant in four of the fourteen events. The least common topic, beginning of the conflict, was dominant in only two events.

While topic modeling can be a useful method in categorizing large volumes of textual data, it fails to capture nuances that can be studied through content analysis. Our manual analysis of the tweets revealed that bots had some unique posting patterns. They were either more likely to tweet from the same content source using different accounts at different times or post many different tweets simultaneously. For example, @torvale1953 posted more than 72,000 tweets over its account lifetime with a bot score of 4.7/5. Another suspected bot account, @JuanMGarciaJr, tweeted only *New York Times* articles in almost every tweet about the trade war. Thus, bot tweets can amplify an issue such as the trade war by either posting many unique tweets or generating a large number of retweets.

Moreover, many bot posts supported the trade war with China, including fake tweets such as the following: "The United States wants China to give a timetable on how it will open up its markets to U.S. exports as the two countries are still 'very far apart' on resolving trade frictions, U.S."; "U.S., China tentatively agree on ending American trade deficit: White House. Can't be true. YOU PROMISED A TRADE WAR. I want the WAR. MAGA!@MorningJoe"; and "Father, please give President Trump wisdom, prudence and discernment from above to deal with China in the upcoming trade talks. Grant him tremendous success, in Jesus name Amen." These provocative bot posts indicate that Trump supporters not only supported a trade war but also proclaimed Trump as a hero for imposing trade tariffs on imported goods from China.

For our manual content analysis, we randomly selected forty tweets from each event (plus an additional forty on June 15, the day the U.S. trade tariffs were announced), resulting in a sample of 600 tweets in total. Four coders practiced with ten tweets and discussed discrepancies until they achieved acceptable agreement before coding the remaining tweets independently. The tweets were coded for originality, type of content, shared media content, and the use of video, image, and links. The first author double-coded 10 percent of the tweets to compute the intercoder reliability, which averaged 82 percent for all variables used in the analysis.

Media Content Sharing on Twitter

The news media were the primary source of information for the 600 tweets we analyzed. Overall, slightly more than half of the sources (52.6 percent) came from the news media, whereas around one-fifth listed no source at all (22.3 percent). Government sources lagged media sources, with only 9.2 percent of the tweets mentioning the government as a source. These findings indicate that users either chose to tweet their own opinions without referring to any sources or relied on media content to comment on the trade war.

Our analysis of the entire corpus of 27,804 tweets showed the even stronger visibility of the mainstream media, which was the most common source used in the tweets. Among the top ten links found in the 27,804 U.S. tweets on the trade war, all except one (Morgan Stanley's report) were media links from sources such as the *New York Times*, Fox News, the *Washington Post*, *South China Morning Post* (Hong Kong), and CNN. A *South China Morning Post*'s article titled, "China Hits Retaliation Button, Launching Tariffs as Trade War with U.S. Starts," was the fourth most shared media link. It was also the only non-U.S. media source in the analyzed tweets about the trade war.

Our content analysis of the 600 tweets found no particular news media account dominating as sources. In fact, about 32 percent of the tweets did not use any news media source. Although major U.S. news outlets such as the *New York Times* (3.3 percent), the *Washington Post* (3.4 percent), and the *Wall Street Journal* (2.8 percent) were more visible than smaller news outlets, they were not the primary sources. Instead, most tweets used various other U.S. news media sources. Overall, only 6.9 percent of the tweets incorporated links to non-U.S. media outlets.

Characteristics of Popular Tweets

We first examined the content and format of the most popular tweets on the trade war that had the highest number of average retweets and replies. Originality matters when engaging audiences on Twitter (Boehmer & Tandoc, Jr., 2015). Original tweets written by the user were the most well-received tweets based on average retweets ($M = 6.78$, $SD = 32.4$), average replies ($M = 1.26$, $SD = 5.8$), and average likes ($M = 10.63$, $SD = 49.3$). We also found that tweets with text and embedded image hyperlinks (also called "social cards") were more likely to be retweeted (M = 5.7 retweets, SD = 4.5) than text-only tweets (M = 3.2 retweets, SD = 5.3). Text-only tweets were less likely to be retweeted because they did not offer much content or interactivity for the readers. However, in our entire corpus of 27,804 tweets, embedded media content was found in only 8.7 percent of all tweets. This lack of still images and videos in our analyzed tweets might be explained by the nature of the trade war issue, which focuses more on facts and information than entertainment. Overall, these findings show that tweets with more interactive information (links to images/social cards) encourage retweets on political topics such as the trade war.

Views of the U.S.–China Trade War

Surprisingly, most analyzed tweets did not show support for or opposition to the trade war or the tariffs (79.3 percent). Among the small number of tweets that did show support or opposition, almost thrice as many users opposed (14 percent) President Trump's trade policy than those who supported it (5.7 percent). Furthermore, only 1 percent of the tweets showed mixed opinions regarding his trade policy. Those who opposed the policy were more likely to lament that the trade war is hurting the United States (21.4 percent) and that Trump is heading in the wrong direction (6.7 percent). Fewer people expressed the view that the trade war is hurting China (14.1 percent). Only 10.4 percent supported the trade tariffs as the best way to solve the conflict, and 4 percent believed that U.S. protectionism is justified. Another common view expressed in the tweets was the threat of economic competition from China (14.4 percent). Only 2.2 percent of the tweets indicated support for free trade.

Interestingly, the tweets that explicitly did or did not support the tariffs contained more positive opinions about China than what was found in the U.S. mass media (see Ray & Lu and Ha, Yang, Ray, Matanji, Chen, Guo & Lyu in this volume). In these tweets, China was often viewed as the victim of the trade dispute (12.7 percent) and economically more successful than the United States (10.9 percent). Only 6 percent of these tweets saw China as a threat to the United States' global position, and 1.7 percent concurred with the U.S. government's view that China's trade practices were unethical or unfair.

In terms of the content type depicted in the tweets, most contained information and news about the trade war as a resource (78.7 percent). Only 30 percent contained personal opinions about the trade war and issues related to the trade war, such as China's economic growth. Concerns (12.2 percent) and frustrations about the trade war (5.7 percent) and general questions about the trade war (5.7 percent) were also observed.

It should be noted that 5.2 percent of the tweets were categorized as conspiracy and misinformation. These tweets primarily attacked Trump and accused him of accepting bribes from the Chinese government during the trade war. Although such tweets were rare, they garnered many retweets. For example, the second most retweeted tweet was posted by U.S. law professor Richard Painter, who has more than 599,000 followers. Painter accused Trump of being bribed by the Chinese government, tweeting "Is China straight up bribing Donald Trump?" Similarly, the third most retweeted tweet was posted by bestselling author Kurt Eichenwald who tweeted that "China agrees to give Trump business 500 million, 72 hours later, Trump is declaring he will save jobs at a Chinese phone maker hurt by his trade sanctions. . . . ?" Because both tweets accused Trump of receiving bribes from China without providing any evidence or information about the trade dispute between the United States and China, those who read the tweets might have thought mostly about China's improper relationship with Trump instead of analyzing the tariffs' economic impact.

These examples demonstrate the so-called "multiplier effect" of tweets by prominent supporters of conspiracy theories who have thousands of followers who help spread their messages. Such conspiracy tweets also attract more eyeballs than other tweets because of their sensationalism and revelation (Konkes & Lester, 2017). Based on conservative estimates, these tweets can reach millions of people because 90 percent of the top one hundred tweets with the most likes and retweets in our sample were from accounts with over 100,000 followers. The multiplier effect can be calculated using the following formula: total potential reach = (SUM of followers of the tweeter + SUM of followers of all retweeters + further retweets of the retweeters) × percentage who read the tweet.

Taking Painter's tweet as an example, it is fairly simple to calculate the total potential reach of such conspiracy tweets: Assume that his original tweet, which was retweeted 9,655 times, was read by 50 percent of his 599,000 followers. Further, assume that each of Painter's followers had an average of 707 followers based on the national average (KickFactory, 2016), and 20 percent of these followers retweeted his tweet to their own followers. Based on these assumptions, Painter's original tweet might have been read by more than 1.67 million Twitter users: (599,000 × 50 percent) + (9,655 × 707 × 20 percent) + unknown further retweets = 1,664,717 + people.

Conclusions

This chapter illustrated that there were only minor differences in content topics between bots and human tweets regarding the U.S.–China trade war. The main difference between bots and human tweets turned out to be posting patterns. The posting pattern of bots is characterized by a vast number of tweets and odd repetitions of the same news source. Thus, even though bots might not necessarily disseminate fake news, repetition and large numbers of distributed tweets might propagate a false narrative. However, rather than blaming bots, we found that the bias and vested interests of individual influencers with large numbers of followers distorted the public discussion of the trade war through conspiracy theories that distracted the public from the facts. In fact, our data show that human users generated the most extreme content and that bots simply reproduced it. Consequently, discussions of the U.S.–China trade war on Twitter were laced with disinformation, conspiracy theories, xenophobia—and rather limited understanding of the nuances of international trade. In short, Twitter can be a machine of ugly rhetoric injecting public deliberations with toxic disinformation.

Our analysis also indicates that news media content is an important information source for tweets, as documented by the frequently included links to news media articles. However, the news sources used were quite diverse and not limited to major mainstream media, such as the *New York Times* or the *Wall Street Journal*. Nonetheless, the concentration of U.S. media sources in the tweets indicates that the domestic media's viewpoints strongly influenced U.S. tweeters. However, because most tweets contained legitimate information about the U.S.–China trade war, Twitter users who paid attention to these tweets might have acquired at least some crucial facts and information about this foreign policy dispute.

Overall, it seems fair to conclude that the portrayal of the U.S.–China trade war on Twitter was much more diverse than its coverage in the mainstream news media. Both supporters and critics of China and the United States voiced their opinions on Twitter. Unlike the U.S. news media, which relied mostly on government sources (see Ha, Yang, Ray, Matanji, Chen, Guo & Lyu in this volume), Twitter users posted diverse media sources and their own opinions. The "China threat" narrative often used by the U.S. news media was rarely found on Twitter—except for the occasional anti-China rhetoric in some prominent tweets. Instead, China was often portrayed as the victim of the trade dispute, and President Trump became a common target. Those who opposed Trump's trade policy were more likely to lament that the trade war was hurting the United States and that Trump was heading in the wrong direction with his trade policy. We also discovered that tweets about the trade war rarely used images and videos. Instead, they frequently used embedded link images that likely boosted users' engagement through shares and likes.

Twitter is a giant digital water cooler where prejudice and bias thrive. When these prejudices and biases are shared with a large number of users, they might mask the truth and stir up public unrest and political polarization (Lu et al., 2020). As our analysis indicates, people often post highly retweeted messages that are trusted and admired by many social media users. As discussed above, several influential opinion leaders propagated their prejudice and conspiracy theories regarding the trade war online. These influencers, not bots, should be the focus of studies of the source and propagation of fake news and conspiracy theories. Thus, even though most Twitter users are not journalists, they can contribute a unique form of user-generated "war journalism" to society, further escalating the conflict by sharing conspiracy theories and misinformation.

REFERENCES

Alabaster, J. (2013, March 11). Japan quake and tsunami put social networks on stage. *PC World*. https://www.pcworld.com/article/2030478/japan-quake-and-tsunami-put-social-networks-on-stage.html

Allcott, H., & Gentzkow, M. (2017). Social media and fake news in the 2016 election. *Journal of Economic Perspectives, 31*(2), 211–36.

Barberá, P., Jost, J. T., Nagler, J., Tucker, J. A., & Bonneau, R. (2015). Tweeting from left to right: Is online political communication more than an echo chamber? *Psychological Science, 26*(10), 1531–42.

Benkler, Y. (2006). *The wealth of networks: How social production transforms markets and freedom.* Yale University Press.

Boehmer, J., & Tandoc Jr., E. (2015). Why we retweet: Factors influencing intentions to share sport news on Twitter. *International Journal of Sports Communication, 8*(2), 212–32.

Casetti, F., & Sampietro, S. (2012). With eyes, with hands: The relocation of cinema into the iPhone. In P. Snickars & P. Vonderau (Eds.), *Moving data: The iPhone and the future of media* (pp. 19–32). Columbia University Press.

China State Department. (2018). White Paper on the facts about the China–US trade conflict and China's position [in Chinese]. http://news.bjx.com.cn/html/20180925/929994.shtml

Chew, C., & Eysenbach, G. (2010). Pandemics in the age of Twitter: Content analysis of tweets during the 2009 H1N1 outbreak. *PLOS One, 5*(11). https://journals.plos.org/plosone/article/file?type=printable&id=10.1371/journal.pone.0014118

Cockburn, P. (2017). Donald Trump's Twitter aggression towards Iran will deepen sectarian conflict in the Middle East. *Independent*. https://www.independent.co.uk/voices/donald-trump-iran-twitter-iraq-mosul-middle-east-instability-a7561611.html

Cordesman, A. (2019, October 1). China and the United States: Cooperation, competition, and/or conflict. *Center for Strategic and International Studies*. https://www.csis.org/analysis/china-and-united-states-cooperation-competition-andor-conflict

Davis, C. A., Varol, O., Ferrara, E., Flammini, A., & Menczer, F. (2016, April). Botornot: A system to evaluate social bots. In *Proceedings of the 25th international conference companion on world wide web* (pp. 273–274).

Diamond, L. (2010). Liberation technology. *Journal of Democracy, 21*(3), 69–83.

Digital Policy Council. (2016, January 23). World leaders on Twitter: Adoption stagnates even as follower base explodes. *PR Newswire*. https://www.prnewswire.com/news-releases/world-leaders-on-twitter—adoption-stagnates-even-as-follower-base-explodes-300208802.html

Dwoskin, E. (2020, May 27). Twitter labels Trump's tweets with a fact check for the first time. *Washington Post*.

Erwin, N. (2019, May 14). Why the U.S.–China trade war could be long and painful: No offramps. *The New York Times*.

Executive Office of the President. (2020, May 28). Executive order on preventing online censorship. https://www.federalregister.gov/documents/2020/06/02/2020-12030/preventing-online-censorship

Fábrega, J., & Vega, G. (2013). The impact of TV rating on Twitter's activity: Evidence for Chile based on the Telethon 2012. *Cuadernos Info, 33*, 43–52.

Fallis, D. (2015). What is disinformation? *Library Trends, 63*(3), 401–26.

Ferrara, E., Varol, O., Davis, C., Menczer, F., & Flammini, A. (2016). The rise of social bots. *Communications of the ACM, 59*(7), 96–104.

Gasparino, C. (2019, September 11). Chinese official to Fox Business: China won't lose face by compromising on trade. *Fox Business News*. https://www.foxbusiness.com/economy/chinese-official-to-fox-business-china-wont-lose-face-by-compromising

Guo, L., Vargo, C. J., Pan, Z., Ding, W., & Ishwar, P. (2016). Big social data analytics in journalism and mass communication: Comparing dictionary-based text analysis and unsupervised topic modeling. *Journalism and Mass Communication Quarterly, 93*(2), 332–59.

Ha, L., Andreu-Perez, L., & Ray, R. (2019). Mapping recent development in scholarship on fake news and misinformation, 2008 to 2017: Disciplinary contribution, topics, and impact.

American Behavioral Scientist. 1–28. https://doi.org/10.1177/0002764219869402

Hardy, B. W., & Scheufele, D. A. (2005). Examining differential gains from internet use: Comparing the moderating role of talk and online interactions. *Journal of Communication, 55*(1), 71–84.

HarperCollins (n.d.). Fake news. In *Collins Online Dictionary.* https://www.collinsdictionary. com/us/dictionary/english/fake-news

Horgan, J. (2008). From profiles to pathways and roots to routes: Perspectives from psychology on radicalization into terrorism. *ANNALS of the American Academy of Political and Social Science, 618*(1), 80–94.

Hyun, Y., & Kim, N. (2016). Detecting blog spam hashtags using topic modeling. Proceedings of the 18th Annual International Conference on Electronic Commerce E-Commerce in Smart Connected World: ICEC '16, 1–6.

Keith, T. (2016, November 18). Commander-in-tweet: Trump's social media use and presidential media avoidance. *National Public Radio.* https://www.npr. org/2016/11/18/502306687/commander-in-tweet-trumps-social-media-use-and-presidential-media-avoidance

Kick Factory. (2016, June 23). The average Twitter user now has 707 followers. *Kick Factory Blog.* https://kickfactory.com/blog/average-twitter-followers-updated- 2016/

Konkes, C., & Lester, L. (2017). Incomplete knowledge, rumor and truth seeking: When conspiracy theories become news. *Journalism Studies, 18*(7), 826–44.

Kushin, M. J., & Yamamoto, M. (2010). Did social media really matter? College students' use of online media and political decision making in the 2008 election. *Mass Communication and Society, 13*, 608–30.

Kwak, H., Lee, C., Park, H., & Moon, S. (2010, April). What is Twitter, a social network or a news media? In Michael Rappa (Ed.), *Proceedings of the 19th international conference on World Wide Web* (pp. 591–600). Association for Computing Machinery.

Loper, E., & Bird, S. (2002). *NLTK: The natural language toolkit.* Cornell University. http://arxiv. org/abs/cs/0205028

Lu, Y., Ray, R., Ha, L., & Chen, P. (2020). Social media news consumption and opinion polarization on China's trade practices: Evidence from a US national survey. *International Journal of Communication, 14*, 3478–95.

Markoff, J. (2016, November 18). Automated pro-Trump bots overwhelmed pro-Clinton messages, researchers say. *New York Times.*

Marwick, A., & Boyd, D. (2011). I tweet honestly, I tweet passionately: Twitter users, context collapse, and the imagined audience. *New Media & Society, 13*, 96–113.

McCombs, M. E. (2005). A look at agenda-setting: Past, present and future. *Journalism Studies, 6*, 543–57.

Morrison, K. (2015, June 11). Report: Journalists make up a quarter of all verified Twitter accounts. http://www.adweek.com/digital/report-journalists-make-up-a-quarter-of-all-verified-twitter-accounts/

O'Sullivan, D. (2019, May 22). Twitter co-founder calls Trump 'master of the platform.' *CNN Business.* https://www.cnn.com/2019/05/22/tech/president-trump-twitter-ev-williams/index.html

Porat, T., Garaizar, P., Ferrero, M., Jones, H., Ashworth, M., & Vadillo, M. A. (2019). Content and source analysis of popular tweets following a recent case of diphtheria in Spain. *European Journal of Public Health, 29*(1), 117–22.

Radzikowski, J., Stefanidis, A., Jacobsen, K. H., Croitoru, A., Crooks, A., & Delamater, P. L. (2016). The measles vaccination narrative in Twitter: A quantitative analysis. *JMIR Public Health and Surveillance, 2*(1), e1. https://publichealth.jmir.org/2016/1/e1

Ratkiewicz, J., Conover, M., Meiss, M., Gonçalves, B., Flammini, A., and Menczer, F. (2011). Detecting and tracking political abuse in social media. In N. Nicolov & J. G. Shanahan (Eds.), *Proceedings of the Fifth International AAAI Conference on Weblogs and Social Media* (pp. 297–304). AAAI Press. https://www.aaai.org/ocs/index.php/ICWSM/ICWSM11/paper/view/2850/3274

Rehurek, R., & Sojka, P. (2010). Software framework for topic modelling with large corpora. *In Proceedings of the LREC 2010 Workshop on New Challenges for NLP Frameworks*, 45–50.

Roberts, A., Choer Moraes, H., & Ferguson, V. (2019, May 21). The U.S.–China trade war is a competition for technological leadership. *Lawfare.* https://www.lawfareblog.com/us-china-trade-war-competition-technological-leadership

Sayre, B., Bode, L., Shah, D., Wilcox, D., & Shah, C. (2010). Agenda setting in a digital age: Tracking attention to California Proposition 8 in social media, online news and conventional news. *Policy & Internet, 2*(2), 7–32.

Seib, P. M. (2012). *Real-time diplomacy: Politics and power in the social media era.* Palgrave Macmillan.

Seward, Z. (2014, August 11). Twitter admits that as many as 23 million of its active users are automated. *Quartz.* https://qz.com/248063/twitter-admits-that-as-many-as-23-million-of-its-active-users-are-actually-bots/

Shearer, E., & Matsa, K. (2018). News use across social media platforms 2018. *Pew Research Center.* https://www.journalism.org/2018/09/10/news-use-across-social-media-platforms-2018/

Šimunjak, M., & Caliandro, A. (2019). Twiplomacy in the age of Donald Trump: Is the diplomatic code changing? *The Information Society, 35*(1), 13–25.

Smith, K. (2020, January 2). 60 incredible and interesting Twitter stats and statistics. Brandwatch. https://www.brandwatch.com/blog/twitter-stats-and-statistics/

Swaine, J. (2018, January 19). Twitter admits far more Russian bots posted on election than it had disclosed. *Guardian*.

Sundar, S. S. (2008). The MAIN model: A heuristic approach to understanding technology effects on credibility. In M. J. Metzger & A. J. Flanagin (Eds.), *Digital media, youth, and credibility* (pp. 73–100). MIT Press.

Sunstein, C. R., & Vermeule, A. (2009). Conspiracy theories: Causes and cures. *Journal of Political Philosophy, 17*(2), 202–27.

Takahashi, B., Tandoc Jr., E. C., & Carmichael, C. (2015). Communicating on Twitter during a disaster: An analysis of tweets during Typhoon Haiyan in the Philippines. *Computers in Human Behavior, 50*, 392–98.

Twitter. (2021, April). Number of monetizable daily active Twitter users (mDAU) worldwide from 1st quarter 2017 to 1st quarter 2021 (in millions) [Graph]. In *Statista*. https://www.statista.com/statistics/970920/monetizable-daily-active-twitter-users-worldwide/

Twitter. (2021, January 8). Permanent suspension of @realDonaldTrum. https://blog.twitter.com/en_us/topics/company/2020/suspension

Valenzuela, S., Puente, S., & Flores, P. M. (2017). Comparing disaster news on Twitter and television: An intermedia agenda setting perspective. *Journal of Broadcasting & Electronic Media, 61*(4), 615–37.

Varol, O., Ferrara, E., Menczer, F., & Flammini, A. (2017). Early detection of promoted campaigns on social media. *EPJ Data Science, 6*(1), 1–19.

Wojcik, S., Messing, S., Smith, A., Rainie, L., & Hitlin, P. (2018, April 9). Bots in the Twittersphere. *Pew Research Center*. https://www.pewresearch.org/internet/2018/04/09/bots-in-the-twittersphere/

Zeitzoff, T. (2017). How social media is changing conflict. *Journal of Conflict Resolution, 61*(9), 1970–91.

Zhao, W. X., Jiang, J., Weng, J., He, J., Lim, E. P., Yan, H., & Li, X. (2011). Comparing Twitter and traditional media using topic models. In P. Clough, C. Foley, C. Gurrin, G. Jones, W. Kraaij, H. Lee, & V. Murdock (Eds.), *Advances in Information Retrieval* (pp. 338–49). Springer.

PART 3

Media Coverage of the Trade War in China

How the Chinese News Media Present the U.S.–China Trade War

Peiqin Chen and Ke Guo

Since the collapse of the Soviet Union in 1991, the world's attention has gradually shifted to the Middle East, where major world powers support various nations in the war on terrorism. However, in the twenty-first century, China has been anointed as the new U.S. rival owing to its growing power and rapid development (Stone & Xiao, 2007). In his lecture at the Woodrow Wilson Center on October 24, 2019, U.S. Vice President Mike Pence regarded the United States' relationship with China as "a subject on which much of the destiny of the 21st Century hinges" and stated that "the United States now recognizes China as a strategic and economic rival." He also said Trump "does not seek a confrontation with China" (Pence, 2019, para 8). Within hours, Chinese foreign spokeswoman, Hua Chunying, responded to Pence's remarks by noting that "China expresses strong indignation and firm opposition" (Hua, 2019). The state-run *Global Times* cited Hua's responses, dismissing Pence's talk as a typical Trumpian blast of "lies with arrogance" (Bai, 2019). This tit-for-tat rhetoric became routine after the U.S.–China trade war escalated in early 2018 and subsequently affected the relationship between the two

The data collection and coding were funded by the National Social Science Fund of China (NSSFC), Project #14ZDB162.

nations significantly. A report released by the Pew Research Center in 2018 showed that 58 percent of Americans consider China as a significant economic threat to the United States (Wike & Devlin, 2019). A few observers even believed that the trade war indicated the start of a new "cold war" between the United States and China (Rudd et al., 2019).

This chapter relies on framing theory to explore how the Chinese mainstream media covered the U.S.–China trade war. Entman (1993) defined framing as the process of cherry-picking and highlighting a few aspects of the perceived reality. The selected elements then become more noticeable and meaningful to audiences, affecting their understanding, evaluation, and action toward a problem. There are four aspects that a news story can be framed: problem definition, identification of forces that cause the problem, evaluation of the causal agents, and effects and treatment recommendations.

Media frames play a crucial role in influencing public opinion, especially in international news, because few people have direct experiences of foreign countries. While addressing international news, Semetko and Valkenburg (2000) found five common media frames, namely, human interest (provides a human example or "human face" to the issue or emphasizes how individuals and groups are affected by the issue), conflict (reflects disagreement between parties, individuals, groups, or countries; one party, individual, group, or country explicitly blames the other), morality (places the issue in the context of moral basis), economic consequences, and attribution of responsibility. Because the present chapter focuses on international news, we follow Semetko and Valkenburg's five frames to evaluate the frames used by Chinese media outlets in their coverage of the U.S.–China trade war.

We performed a content analysis of the U.S.–China trade war stories published by four major Chinese media outlets and sought to identify the frames used in these stories. Three of these platforms were party media outlets: CCTV, the largest official TV platform in China; the WeChat accounts of *People's Daily*, the mouthpiece of the Communist party; and its subsidiary, the *Global Times*, an influential tabloid on global news coverage. In addition, *The Paper*, a more market-driven mobile news app, was selected so that we could compare whether its content differed from that of the party media outlets. Our findings indicate, in contrast to the assumption that China's media ecosystem is monolithic and authoritarian, that Chinese media are undergoing a rapid transformation fueled by social media and market-driven news apps, which are creating a diverse media landscape marked by a diversity of opinions and perspectives, including those about the U.S.–China trade war.

Social Media in China's Media Landscape

China's news media is undergoing the same digitalization processes as the news media elsewhere in the world. According to the 2020 Report of the China Internet Network Information Center (CNNIC, 2020), China had 904 million internet users in 2020, amounting to about 64.5 percent of its total population. Among them, 80.9 percent receive news through the internet, of whom 81 percent receive news through their mobile phones. In 2017, mobile phones (51 percent) and the internet (15 percent) accounted for most of the revenue in the Chinese media market (compared to 6 percent for print media and 13 percent for broadcast media), indicating that the majority of the media market has moved online, especially to mobile applications (Cui, 2018). Meanwhile, the mobile internet is turning out to be the most profitable medium. In 2018, the revenue generated by mobile internet platforms reached RMB 667.46 billion, approximately nineteen times higher than that of newspapers (Cui, 2019).

Meanwhile, China's newspaper revenues have dropped dramatically since 2013. Advertising revenues of newspapers in 2018 were approximately 15.7 percent of the revenues in 2011 (Cui, 2019). In 2014, media convergence was established as a national strategy, and most mainstream news media outlets in China have developed an active online presence across multiple platforms, including online news sites, mobile news apps, Weibo, and WeChat (Lu, 2017).

Social media are also affecting China's media landscape by providing platforms for both individuals and media organizations to release information. Compared with emerging commercial media producers, traditional mainstream media have unique advantages because they have inherited professional teams for news production and government licenses to cover major political news and international affairs. As a result, China's news media landscape is characterized by the convergence of new and traditional media platforms and an oligopoly comprising a few national and official social media outlets. During the past decade, China's mainstream media have become more commercialized and digitalized and are increasingly delivered on multiple platforms. In 2019, most media outlets posted news stories to their news apps (Cui, 2019). Party media, such as the *Xinhua News Agency*, *People's Daily*, and *Global Times*, now use mobile phones as their primary channel for distributing news, appealing to technology-savvy and entertainment-driven audiences (Xin, 2018). While these new social media platforms have enabled the party to share its message more widely, they have also enabled critics to offer counter-narratives and alternative frames of interpretation, hence adding new layers of complexity to China's media ecosystem.

Within this diversifying system, WeChat is the largest social media platform in China, and it is used by more than one billion monthly users (Gray, 2018). The WeChat accounts of *People's Daily*, Xinhua News Agency, CCTV, *People's Daily Online*, and *Global Times* were named the top five WeChat accounts in 2018 by two leading new media ranking companies, NewRank and TalkingData. Because of their multiplatform news delivery strategies, digital news brands such as *The Paper* from Shanghai, *Today's Headlines* from Beijing, and Tencent News Apps from Shenzhen, are also prospering in the new media environment in China. These news apps function like search engines, and artificial intelligence is used to automatically select and push news stories or information to individual users. These commercialized, native digital news outlets provide more diversified and alternative information to ordinary Chinese users than the party media because they are market-driven and cater more to the digital media environment. Indeed, studies have found that the commercialization and rapid modernization of the Chinese media have dramatically increased the size and diversity of news coverage since the 1990s (Tang & Iyengar, 2011; Zeng & Sparks, 2020). Contrary to some American stereotypes, then, the media ecosystem in China is evolving in exciting new ways that enable Chinese users to access a wide variety of opinions and perspectives—including those on the U.S.–China trade war.

China's View of the U.S.–China Trade War

While a vital role of the Chinese media is helping the Chinese government set the public agenda for political discourse, scholars have found that Chinese media outlets are relatively diversified due to media commercialization and new technologies (Tang & Iyengar, 2011). All media organizations in China, including party media, such as *People's Daily* and *Global Times*, are required to generate profits from the market. New communication technologies, such as the internet, mobile phones, and satellites, have reshaped the Chinese media, bringing about a revolution in information channels. In a very competitive market and with most Chinese people accessing news through these new media, all media outlets need to find their niches to cater to their audiences' diverse needs. Based on a content analysis of national news from five Chinese newspapers—*People's Daily, China Youth Daily, Chengdu Economic Daily, Xinmin*

Evening, and *Southern Metropolis Daily*—Wang et al. (2017) confirmed that mainland Chinese press organizations are significantly different from each other in presenting their news stories, and they follow rather different models of journalism practice.

A prevalent view is that the Chinese government often deliberately promotes nationalism in the media to mobilize public support for foreign policy (Stockmann, 2011). One reason for the frequent use of nationalism in the Chinese media is the still vivid memory of Japan's invasion of China (Wang, 2012). Scholars have found that over the past forty years, when American or Japanese foreign policy targeted China, outbursts of anti-American or nationalistic movements erupted in China (Johnston, 2003; 2006; Shirk, 2011). Clearly, at times, the demands of nationalism pressure the Chinese government to take stricter stands on international affairs. Meanwhile, the commercialization of Chinese media may have pushed news producers to turn to nationalism and force the Chinese government to act more aggressively when managing conflicts with foreign countries (Shirk, 2011). Based on a textual analysis of two major Chinese newspapers from 1999 to 2003, Stockmann (2011) noted that while the Chinese Foreign Ministry portrayed the United States more positively, China's news media covered the United States more negatively. Also, commercial apps of Chinese media outlets tend to offer more balanced reporting (combining positive and negative spins) over issues of conflict with the United States to attract greater numbers of Chinese users.

In some cases, the official party newspaper covered the United States with a more positive tone. In contrast, the more market-driven newspapers were more inclined to report negatively about the United States. Similarly, a recent study involving *Global Times* concluded that nationalism could be a central factor in the tabloid's coverage of the U.S.–China trade war because *Global Times* is considered to employ a nationalistic frame in its international coverage. In the studied sample, the tone of the coverage was very negative toward the United States (Zeng & Sparks, 2020). Thus, whereas previous chapters have noted the ways American nationalism, fueled by President Trump, drove U.S. responses to the trade war, we ask here about the ways Chinese media may color the Chinese response to the trade war.

Hypotheses and Research Questions

We selected CCTV, *People's Daily*, *Global Times*, and *The Paper* to represent the Chinese mainstream news media's coverage of the U.S.–China trade war. For television news, we selected CCTV because CCTV News has always been the leading TV news platform in China. The entire nation watches it, and its audience continues to grow with the increasing penetration of television in rural areas. In 2017, the ratings of CCTV News rose to 44.5 percent from 40.7 percent in 2016, indicating its domination of the TV news market in China (Cui, 2018). *Evening Newsline* (*Xinwen Lianbo*), a news program on CCTV 1, is the top news program echoing Chinese government policies. *People's Daily* has the same role as CCTV 1 in representing government voices. However, as a traditional official party newspaper, it has more in-depth reporting, and its editorials serve as a banner for government policies. *Global Times*, by contrast, is more like a tabloid. Even though it closely follows the Chinese government in its overall news policy, it mainly focuses on international news and often turns to sensationalism to attract larger audiences. This tabloid is considered one of China's top media outlets focused on international news and global issues. The news app, *The Paper*, which is under the umbrella of Shanghai United Media Group, was selected in this chapter to represent nonofficial popular news outlets. Founded on July 22, 2014, as an experimental new media organization, *The Paper* has focused on news analysis and in-depth reporting. It is a local digital news brand from Shanghai with no print or TV affiliations. *The Paper* is considered a popular and rising new media outlet in China, and it has attracted considerable attention both from media practitioners and researchers (Bao, 2018). According to TalkingData (2018), between January 1 and December 31, 2018, *The Paper* ranked twenty-fourth on average among all news apps in China (most of which are news aggregators), but it was one of the top apps with original news gathering and reporting. Its primary users are men (62.7 percent of users) and young people of ages twenty-six to thirty-five years (47.8 percent of the users) (Bao, 2018).

Because an important function of Chinese media is to convey government information to Chinese audiences, we hypothesized that CCTV, *People's Daily Online*, *Global Times*, and *The Paper* would support China's official policies and blame the trade conflict on the United States. We also hypothesized that the Chinese news media would blame the trade conflict on the United States and would support China's official trade policies. Meanwhile, we hypothesized that with China's evolving media environment, driven in large part by the commercialization of media and massive migrations of users to social media, the four media outlets would use different strategies to cater to their respective audiences' needs. Thus, we hypothesized that there would be significant differences in their news coverage of the U.S.–China trade conflict.

Our hypotheses were informed by the 2018 White Paper released by China's Information Office of the State Council, which indicated that the Chinese government places considerable emphasis on "win-win" cooperation in the U.S.–China trade relationship (ISOC, 2018). Assuming this White Paper speaks for the government, we predicted CCTV, the official television station with the largest audience in the country, would be more cautious in its reporting and would focus more on mutual interests and pursuing the win-win orientation. On the other hand, we assumed that *People's Daily*, the most traditional, elite party newspaper with a long publishing heritage as the mouthpiece of the Communist Party of China, would be more partisan than CCTV.

Global Times was founded as a branch of *People's Daily* to cater to popular audiences and generate more profits from the market. We hypothesized that *Global Times* would therefore be more nationalistic, as its coverage is catering to a market-driven audience. Indeed, *Global Times* tends to use a more sensational reporting style and has been called "China's hawkish, belligerent state tabloid" (Huang, 2016).

Finally, as a commercially oriented and internationally aware outlet, we assumed that the Shanghai-based news app, *The Paper*, would likely present the U.S.–China trade war with different frames than the other outlets and would adopt a more neutral tone, based, in part, on its drawing upon diversified, non-elite sources. We began our analysis by exploring how these Chinese news media framed the trade war and then asked whether their frames were significantly different in the news coverage.

Method

For this study, we selected CCTV, the social media (WeChat) accounts of two major party newspapers (*People's Daily* and *Global Times*), and a market-oriented news app, *The Paper*, to represent the Chinese news coverage of the U.S.–China trade conflict. For CCTV newscasts, three keywords ("美国," the United States; "贸易," trade; and "关税," tariffs) were used to retrieve news items by searching the archive of news videos on the CCTV website. Because the website only includes videos broadcast in the past year, our search was limited to 2018. We retrieved a total of 253 newscasts related to the U.S.–China trade conflict. A random sample of one hundred videos was selected as the final sample for coding. The coders transcribed the newscasts related to the trade conflict and, subsequently, coded the newscasts' transcripts.

WeChat is the most popular mobile social media platform in China, similar to Facebook in the United States, and it allows users to read news for free and share it with other users. The annual report of Tencent company showed that as of September 2019, WeChat had a total of 1.15 billion users (Qqtech, 2020). Among them, 660 million people used mobile phones to access news (CNNIC, 2019). The news items featured in the WeChat accounts of the media outlets are more likely to be read and shared by people than newspaper items because they are freely available on mobile phones. Hence, we used WeChat accounts in studying newspapers. The *People's Daily* and *Global Times* were among the top five WeChat news accounts in 2018, and *People's Daily* was the top WeChat account in 2018. Though ranked fifth, the *Global Times* focused on international news and China's foreign policy (NewRank, 2018). The other three most popular WeChat news accounts not included in this study are CCTV (which would duplicate CCTV newscasts), *Xinhua News* (China's official news agency), and *People's Daily Online* (which would duplicate *People's Daily*).

Wisers, a leading Chinese media database, was employed to retrieve samples of the two WeChat accounts (*People's Daily* and *Global Times*) and the news app (*The Paper*) between January 1, 2018, and December 31, 2018. While we initially used the same keywords as the ones used for our CCTV searches ("the United States" and "trade" or "tariffs"), we found that many articles would be omitted unless we included the term "trade war" in our searches. Therefore, we added this term to the three original keywords to retrieve the relevant articles. One hundred news stories were selected randomly from the search results of each news media outlet for coding. Only news reports were included in the sample. Editorials and commentaries were excluded.

Measures

Frame. To identify the news frames used by the various media outlets included in this study, we coded the stories in five categories: human interest, conflict, morality, economic consequences, and attribution of responsibility, following Semetko and Valkenburg's (2000) five frames of international news.

Attribution of Responsibility. To understand how the Chinese media outlets assigned responsibility for the trade conflict, we further coded the following four categories: (1) The United States is responsible for the trade deficit, (2) China is responsible for the trade deficit, (3) both the United States and China are responsible for the trade deficit, and (4) not applicable/no responsibility reference.

Elite and Non-elite Sources. Elite sources include government officials and agencies, think tanks, and academics. Non-elite sources include industry representatives, ordinary people, or people employed in sectors affected by the trade war.

Tone. To examine a news story's tone of coverage in general, we coded four categories: (1) supportive or mostly supportive of the policy (tariff sanction against China), (2) opposing the policy, (3) neutral, and (4) partly supportive and partly opposing the policy.

Conflict-Focus (mutual interest and partisanship). To examine the conflict-focus in the news besides the five frames, we coded specific mentions of mutual interest and partisanship (favoring the ruling party) in the news stories as four separate items: (1) discussion of similarities/mutual interests between the countries involved, (2) win-win orientation, (3) presentation of diversity (giving voice to many parties in the conflict), and (4) nonpartisan coverage.

Coding

A total of 400 non-duplicated news stories, with one hundred news stories from each outlet, were randomly chosen between January 1, 2018, and December 31, 2018. Five graduate students from Shanghai International Studies University were hired as coders for this study. An additional graduate student was employed to double-code 10 percent of a randomly chosen news media sample to compute the inter-coder reliability. Several training sessions were conducted to ensure that the coders understood the coding scheme and employed the necessary coding process. Moreover, the coders were responsible for checking for duplicate samples and excluding them from the final analysis. The presence of frames and the use of non-elite sources both achieved 95 percent agreement. The coder agreement in terms of the tone of the coverage was 80 percent.

Findings

We found that the news coverage of *Global Times* (68 percent) and *People's Daily* (81 percent) mostly attributed the responsibility for the trade conflict to the United States.

However, the news coverage of CCTV (90 percent) and *The Paper* (95 percent) mostly did not attribute the responsibility for the U.S.–China trade conflict to any party. The difference among the news outlets was statistically significant (χ^2 = 216, df = 6, p < .001).

As for the tone of coverage, an overwhelming majority of the news stories published by CCTV, *People's Daily*, and *Global Times* opposed the U.S. policy of imposing tariffs on China (CCTV 82 percent, *People's Daily* 93 percent, and *Global Times* 71 percent). Only 34 percent of the news stories published by *The Paper* opposed the U.S. tariffs, with 66 percent adopting a neutral viewpoint regarding the tariffs (χ^2 = 93.81, *df* = 3, p < .001). Therefore, our hypothesis that all mainstream Chinese news outlets would blame the trade war on the United States was not supported.

Regarding whether the media coverage focused on similarities and mutual interests between the two countries, the results showed that the media outlets did not predominantly concentrate on mutual interests. As summarized in table 1, 43 percent of the stories published by *People's Daily* focused on mutual interests, the highest among all the media outlets studied here, followed by *The Paper* with 36 percent, and *Global Times* with 21 percent. Only 8 percent of the stories published by CCTV focused on mutual interests, the lowest among the media outlets considered in this study.

Fewer stories across all the four media outlets mentioned the win-win orientation (CCTV 14 percent, *People's Daily* 32 percent, *Global Times* 16 percent, *The Paper* 9 percent), although the differences among the four papers were significant (p < .01). Therefore, the "win-win orientation" expectation was not supported. CCTV did not focus more on mutual interests between the two countries or the "win-win orientation."

Additionally, we measured the relationship between party affiliation, commercialization, and coverage of the trade war across the four media outlets by analyzing whether the commercial outlets were neutral and balanced without taking sides. A comparison of the four media outlets' partisanship showed that *The Paper*, a commercial news outlet, was the most nonpartisan media outlet among the four, with 98 percent of its stories being nonpartisan. *People's Daily* and *Global Times* were equally partisan, with 59 percent of the stories from both outlets being partisan. CCTV tended to be more neutral, with 57 percent nonpartisan stories. As expected, *People's Daily* and *Global Times* were more partisan and nationalistic than *The Paper* in reporting on the trade war.

Although *People's Daily* was as partisan as *Global Times*, of all the four media outlets, *Global Times* was the only media outlet that played up the zero-sum game

TABLE 1. Mutual Interests and Nonpartisanship (in percentages)

	CCTV	PEOPLE'S DAILY	GLOBAL TIMES	THE PAPER	**TOTAL**
	$N = 100$	$N = 100$	$N = 100$	$N = 100$	$N = 400$
Discussing mutual interests between countries involved**	8	43	21	36	108
Win-win orientation**	14	32	16	9	71
Presenting diversity**	12	38	30	7	87
Nonpartisan focus**	57	41	41	98	237

Note: **$p < .01$

frame, that is, an international focus where one nation can win a conflict, such as a trade war, only if another loses it. Our data pertaining to the presentation of a zero-sum game frame indicated that CCTV and *The Paper* did not present this frame in their stories. By contrast, 72 percent and 11 percent of the stories published by *Global Times* and *People's Daily* used the zero-sum game frame, respectively. Therefore, our expectation that *Global Times* was the most partisan and nationalistic media outlet among those analyzed in this study was supported.

The varying degrees of partisanship and nationalism among the Chinese media outlets indicate that they were not uniform in their coverage of the U.S.–China trade war. Instead, they demonstrated a fairly diversified coverage, similar to what other studies of Chinese foreign affairs coverage found (Jaros & Pan, 2018). While these findings indicate more openness and fluidity in Chinese foreign affairs news, China's media are still dominated by the government's perspective (Ma & Lu, 2020). While our data do not point to any firm conclusions in this regard, we nonetheless want to highlight this key finding: that counter to the prevalent U.S. narrative of China's media ecosystem as homogeneous and authoritarian, we found a wide diversity of frames, opinions, and arguments, indicating a robust media sphere.

Media Frames of Mainstream Media

By coding the presence of four main frames, namely human interest, conflict, morality, and economic consequences, we found that the Chinese media outlets presented the U.S.–China trade war mostly by using the frames of conflict and

TABLE 2. Frames of Four Chinese Media Outlets (in percentages)

	CCTV	PEOPLE'S DAILY	GLOBAL TIMES	THE PAPER
	$N = 100$	$N = 100$	$N = 100$	$N = 100$
Human interest**	19	66	4	31
Conflict**	63	97	75	10
Morality**	—	81	1	—
Economic consequence**	59	78	55	78

Note: **$p < .01$

economic consequences (see table 2). Of all the stories we examined, 61.3 percent used conflict frames, while 67.5 percent used the frame of economic consequences. Only 30 percent and 20.5 percent of the stories used the frames of human interest and morality, respectively. The proportion of the stories using competing news frames was very low, meaning the majority of the news stories used only one frame or no frame at all. Only one story on CCTV contained competing frames. *The Paper*, too, had very few stories with competing frames (8 percent). The outlets with the highest proportion of stories with competing frames were *Global Times* (26 percent) and *People's Daily* (24 percent). The difference across the news outlets in this regard was significant ($\chi^2 = 34.9$, $df = 3$, $p < .001$). This might indicate that the Chinese media preferred—at least during the period under study—to present the U.S.–China trade war without much interpretation, but in line with the Chinese government's views regarding the trade conflict.

There were significant differences ($p < .01$) across the media outlets using specific news frames. A total of 97 percent of the stories from *People's Daily* used the conflict frame, while only 10 percent of the news stories from *The Paper* used the conflict frame. In 78 percent of the stories by *People's Daily* and *The Paper*, frames of economic consequences were used. Meanwhile, 59 percent of the stories by CCTV and 55 percent of the stories by *Global Times* used the frame of economic consequences. Hence, the commercial news app, *The Paper*, focused more on economic consequences, while the three party-media outlets focused more on conflict. Overall, 97 percent, 75 percent, 63 percent, and 10 percent of the stories published by *People's Daily*, *Global Times*, CCTV, and *The Paper* used the conflict frame, respectively. Of all the four media outlets, only *People's Daily* (81 percent) used the morality frame. All the media outlets used the frame of human interest the least. More than half of news stories published by *People's Daily* (66 percent) used the frame of human interest. Other media outlets used this frame only occasionally (CCTV 19 percent, *Global Times* 4 percent, and *The Paper* 31 percent).

Conclusions

This chapter showed that the Chinese news media are not homogeneous, consistent with previous studies (Tang & Iyengar, 2011; Wang et al., 2017). As expected, party media outlets were more supportive of the government and were less likely to offer competing frames. Moreover, party-media outlets such as *Global Times* and *People's Daily* were more likely to use conflict frames than market-oriented media outlets such as *The Paper*. As the news media outlet with the largest audience, CCTV was more neutral than the *Global Times* and *People's Daily*. This trend might indicate that the Chinese government was cautious about presenting an overly politicized image of the U.S.–China trade war to its sizeable domestic TV audience.

Our content analysis showed that while the different Chinese media outlets had much in common, such as their focus on economic consequences and heavy reliance on elite sources, significant differences existed across the four media outlets. The two official newspapers, *People's Daily* and *Global Times*, attributed responsibility for the trade war to the United States and focused extensively on the conflict between the two countries. By contrast, the state-run CCTV and the more commercially oriented *The Paper* did not attribute responsibility to the United States. Among the four outlets, *The Paper* used the conflict frame the least (10 percent of the time), offered the most nonpartisan news stories (96 percent nonpartisan), and deployed objective and moderate wording.

Our results show that the four media outlets present the U.S.–China trade war with a greater emphasis on the frames of economic consequences and conflict. Although the Chinese government condemned the U.S. administration for protectionism, bullying, and improper practices (ISCO, 2019), most Chinese media outlets presented the U.S.–China trade conflict in 2018 using economic rather than political frames. The market-oriented news app *The Paper* presented the U.S.–China trade conflict in the most neutral and nonpartisan manner, while *People's Daily* and *Global Times* were more partisan and more nationalistic. In conclusion, the Chinese media helped promote the government's agenda in the public discourse of the trade war while offering a range of perspectives.

Although China's media landscape has dramatically changed, mirroring the past forty years of social development in the country, many Western discussions on China's media system and media operations still occur under the monolithic framework of ideological Communism. As Hartnett et al. (2017) pointed out, ignoring Chinese society's complexity would be a mistake, similar to treating the United States as a homogeneous democracy. A review of the decision made in the fourth session of the Nineteenth Central Committee of the Communist Party of China, on October 31, 2019, shows that China insists that the media should be under the Chinese Communist Party's leadership. However, this decision also emphasizes the diversity of media content, new technology development, and the media's role as a watchdog (Xinhua News Agency, 2019). Many studies of the Chinese media treat the leadership of the CCP as propagandistic (Hong 2013; Tang & Iyengar, 2011; Wang et al., 2017) while ignoring its role of providing information and checking corruption. This might make it difficult for academics from outside China to truly understand China's changing media development patterns, especially when Chinese media outlets cover a major international event, such as the U.S.–China trade war. Our results present a considerably more diverse and complex picture of how different Chinese news media outlets framed the U.S.–China trade war, depicting a media ecosystem that is evolving rapidly, with social media platforms and mobile news apps driving a wide range of opinions and perspectives.

Overall, this chapter provided a new way to examine the Chinese media, which have often been analyzed from a Western perspective only (Ooi & D'Arcangelis, 2017; Yang, 2019). Now that China has become the second-largest economy globally, there is a growing tendency in China to maintain its distinct cultural identity (often termed "Chinese characteristics") while trying to establish a cultural and political identity that is different from the West. A careful study of Chinese journalism ideology in line with the Communist party's internal operations may provide an alternative understanding of a complex Chinese media system and media practices from a Chinese perspective.

REFERENCES

Bai, Y. (2019, October 25). Hua Chunying's responses towards Pence's speech about China: China expresses strong indignation and firm opposition [in Chinese]. *Global Times.* http://hqtime.huanqiu.com/share/article/9CaKrnKnqFp

Bao, D. H. (2018). The Paper: A showcase of how traditional media are shifting their battle to social media [in Chinese]. *Media, 4,* 40–43.

Bao, Y. L. (2016). Gender analysis of contemporary college students' attention to international current affairs [in Chinese]. *Business, 28,* 77.

Beattie, P., & Milojevich, J. (2017). A test of the "news diversity" standard: Single frames, multiple frames, and values regarding the Ukraine conflict. *International Journal of Press/Politics, 22*(1): 3–22.

CNNIC (2020, September). Statistical report on internet development in China. http://www.cnnic.com.cn/IDR/ReportDownloads/202012/P020201201530023411644.pdf

Cui, B. G. (2019). Development report on China's media industry, 2018–2019 [in Chinese]. In Baoguo Cui, Xu Lijun Xu, & Mai Ding (Eds.), *Report on the development of China's media industry* (2019 ed.). Social Science Academic Press.

Cui, B. G. (2018). Development report on China's media industry, 2017–2018 [in Chinese]. In B. Cui (Ed.), *Report on the development of China's media industry.* Social Science Academic Press.

Entman, R. M. (1993) Framing: Toward clarification of a fractured paradigm. *Journal of Communication, 43*(4), 51–58.

Gray, A. (2018, March 21). Here's the secret to how WeChat attracts 1 billion monthly users. https://www.weforum.org/agenda/2018/03/wechat-now-has-over-1-billion-monthly-users/

Guo, K. (2020). China's international news coverage and world images [in Chinese]. *China Media Report, 19*(3), 37–41.

Hartnett, S. J., Keränen, L. B., Conley, D. (Eds.). (2017). *Imagining China: Rhetorics of nationalism in an age of globalization.* Michigan State University Press.

Hong, S. C. (2013). Scare sells? A framing analysis of news coverage of recalled Chinese Products. *Asian Journal of Communication, 23*(1), 86–106.

Huang, Z. (2016, August 9). Inside the *Global Times,* China's hawkish, belligerent state tabloid. *Quartz.* https://qz.com/745577/inside-the-global-times-chinas-hawkish-belligerent-state-tabloid/

Hua, C. (October 25, 2019) Foreign Ministry Spokesperson Hua Chunying's Regular Press Conference. https://www.fmprc.gov.cn/mfa_eng/xwfw_665399/s2510_665401/2511_665403/t1710842.shtml

ISOC (Information Office of the State Council of the PRC). (2018, September 25). *The facts and China's position on China-US trade friction* [White Paper]. http://english.scio.gov.cn/whitepapers/2018-09/25/content_63998615.htm

ISOC (Information Office of the State Council of the PRC) (2019, June 2). *China's position on the China-US economic and trade consultations.* http://www.scio.gov.cn/zfbps/32832/

Document/1655934/1655934.htm

Jaros, K., & Pan, J. (2018). China's newsmakers: Official media coverage and political shifts in Xi Jinping era. *China Quarterly, 233,* 111–36.

Johnston, A. I. (2003). *The correlates of nationalism in Beijing public opinion* [Working paper]. Institute of Defense and Strategic Studies.

Johnston, A. I. (2006). The correlates of nationalism in Beijing public opinion toward the United States, 1998–2004. In A. I. Johnston & R. S. Ross (Eds.), *New directions in the study of Chinese foreign policy.* Stanford University Press.

Lu, N. (2017). The exploration of media organization under convergence [in Chinese]. *Shanghai Journalism Review, 5,* 54–60.

Ma, D. Y., & Lu, Y. Z., (2020). Media framing effects in foreign policy issues: An experimental study on China-US trade war [in Chinese]. *Chinese Journal of Journalism and Communication, 42*(5), 99–120.

NewRank (2018). *Annual report of 500 popular WeChat accounts.* https://mp.weixin.qq.com/s/PQDOBVTwVo7ZPlG8-GKA7Q

Ooi, S. M., & D'Arcangelis, G. (2017). Framing China: Discourses of othering in US news and political rhetoric. *Global Media and China, 2*(3–4), 269–83.

Qqtech (January 9, 2020). *WeChat Annual Report of 2019.* https://mp.weixin.qq.com/

Pence, M. (2019, October 24). *Remarks by Vice President Pence at the Frederic V. Malek Memorial Lecture.* U.S. Embassy and Consulate in Vietnam. https://vn.usembassy.gov/remarks-by-vice-president-pence-at-the-frederic-v-malek-memorial-lecture/

Rudd, K., & Clark, H., & Bildt, C. (2019, October 12). Why we worry about the trade war. *New York Times.*

Semetko, H. A., & Valkenburg, P. M. (2000). Framing European politics: A content analysis of press and television news. *Journal of Communication, 50*(2), 93–109.

Shirk, S. L. (2011). Changing media, changing foreign policy. In S. L. Shirk (Ed.), *Changing media, changing China.* Oxford University Press.

Stockmann, D. (2011). Race to the bottom: Media marketization and increasing negativity toward the United States in China. *Political Communication, 28*(3), 268–90.

Stone, G. C., & Xiao, Z. W. (2007). Anointing a new enemy: The rise of anti-China coverage after the USSR's demise. *International Communication Gazette, 69*(1), 91–108.

TalkingData (2018). *The Paper* [in Chinese]. http://mi.talkingdata.com/search.html?keyword=%E6%BE%8E%E6%B9%83

Tang, W., & Iyengar, S. (2011). The emerging media system in China: Implications for regime change. *Political Communication, 28,* 263–67.

Wang, H., Sparks, C., Lu, N., & Huang, Y (2017). Differences within the mainland Chinese press: A quantitative analysis. *Asian Journal of Communication, 27*(2), 154–71.

Wang, Z. (2014). *Never forget national humiliation: Historical memory in Chinese politics and foreign relations.* Columbia University Press.

Wang, Z. (2015). The issues and strategies in Chinese media reporting international events [in Chinese]. https://xueshu.baidu.com/usercenter/paper/show?paperid=e61183ab7b9b15d1d3abc4bfe360de80&site=xueshu_se

Wike, R., & Devlin, K. (2019, October 11). As trade tension rise, fewer Americans see China favorably. *New York Times.*

Xin, X. (2018). Popularizing party journalism in China in the age of social media. *Global Media and China, 3*(1), 3–17.

Xinhua News Agency. (2019). The decision of the CPC Central Committee on major issues concerning upholding and improving the system of socialism with Chinese characteristics and advancing the modernization of china's system and capacity for governance. http://www.xinhuanet.com/politics/2019–11/05/c_1125195786.htm

Yang, L. R. (2019). On the construction method of media images of the other [in Chinese]. *Anyang Normal Institute Journal, 6*, 151–54.

Zeng, W., & Sparks, C. (2020). Popular nationalism: *Global Times* and the US–China trade war. *International Communication Gazette, 82*(1), 26–41.

Comparing U.S. and Chinese Media Coverage of the U.S.–China Trade War

War and Peace Journalism Practice and the Foreign Policy Information Market Equilibrium Hypothesis

Louisa Ha, Yang Yang, Rik Ray, Frankline Matanji, Peiqin Chen, Ke Guo, and Nan Lyu

P roposed by peace studies scholar Johan Galtung to highlight journalists' roles in promoting world peace (Lee & Maslog, 2005), peace journalism emphasizes balanced and nonpartisan news coverage focusing on the common people and the promotion of peace initiatives. Under this ideal, reporters are expected to show empathy for the parties in conflict. By contrast, war journalism escalates a conflict by focusing on violence, siding with elites, and serving as a government propaganda tool to achieve "victory" for the home country (Galtung, 2003). Peace journalism studies have traditionally focused on military conflicts or violent protests. However, trade wars can have destructive consequences as well. Using tariffs and economic sanctions as national security and protectionist measures, trade wars can cause serious harm by raising the cost of products, discouraging and prohibiting foreign investments in specific industries, and damaging

An earlier version of the chapter appeared as Ha, L., Yang, Y., Ray, R., Matanji, F., Chen, P., Guo, K., & Lyu, N. (2020). How US and Chinese media cover the US–China trade conflict: A case study of war and peace journalism practice and the foreign policy equilibrium hypothesis. *Negotiation and Conflict Management Research.* https://doi.org/10.1111/ncmr.12186. This revised version appears here with permission of *Negotiation and Conflict Management Research.* The data collection and coding in China were funded by the National Social Science Fund of China (NSSFC), Project #14ZDB162.

economic development. Such economic conflict can then escalate into political and military confrontations (Hoekman, 2020; Rapoza, 2019). Media representations of the U.S.–China trade war can therefore offer a unique opportunity for studying the adoption of war and peace journalism in a nonmilitary power conflict.

Ray and Lu ("U.S. Television News Coverage of the Trade War" in this volume) and Chen and Guo ("How the Chinese News Media Present the U.S.–China Trade War" in this volume) have shown how U.S. and Chinese news media outlets presented the U.S.–China trade war. This chapter compares how news media outlets in China and the United States practiced war and peace journalism during the trade war. We study how the roles of the United States as the initiator of the trade war and China as the responder in the trade war influenced the use of war and peace journalism frames in news coverage. We also investigate whether media formats (television vs. newspapers) and media partisanship affected the coverage of government policies related to the trade war. Consequently, this study contributes to the literature on peace journalism by testing the applicability of peace journalism in different press systems for nonmilitary conflicts and by analyzing how different media formats and partisanship influence the practice of war and peace journalism.

While war and peace journalism is useful for showing how the news media cover international conflicts, it overlooks the different stages of a conflict and how competing frames might relate to foreign policymaking. The *foreign policy information market equilibrium* hypothesis explains how the information gap between the government and the public can be reduced—and it illustrates the changing relationship between the news media and the government over time. By tracking and comparing the use of news sources in U.S. and Chinese media across time, and by analyzing the dynamics of media coverage in support of and/or opposition to the U.S. trade war, this chapter presents the first empirical test of the foreign policy information market equilibrium hypothesis in a cross-national context. Understanding how news media frame foreign policy news and how such frames change over time can demonstrate how the news media interpret foreign policy, inform the public, and support or challenge their governments in conflicts with other nations.

War and Peace Journalism

Conflict is a major theme in international news (Galtung & Ruge, 1965). Peace journalism advocates a more proactive role for the news media to quell rather than escalate conflict (Colbert, 2009). A review of forty-one studies from the literature on peace journalism (Gouse et al., 2018) demonstrated its evolution from quantitative analyses of news articles to qualitative and quantitative studies that analyze journalists' attitudes toward war and peace journalism (e.g., Neuman & Fahmy, 2016). These studies illustrate the variations in journalistic norms and values across countries and the different ways war and peace journalism have been conceptualized.

In reporting violent conflicts, peace journalism practices can set international norms and improve professional ethical standards (Nohrstedt & Ottosen, 2015). Howard (2009) advocated conflict-sensitive reporting by training journalists to contribute to dialogue among the belligerent parties' communities. Such reporting avoids stereotypes and maintains professionalism with accuracy, fairness, balance, and responsible conduct. Although the peace journalism ideal has received support from some journalism scholars (e.g., Demarest & Langer, 2018; Keeble et al., 2010; Lynch & McGoldrick, 2013; Youngblood, 2017), others have criticized the underlying assumptions of peace journalism. Hanitzsch (2004), for example, argued that journalists are not as powerful as the advocates of peace journalism assume. He noted that peace journalism shifts the responsibility for peace from governments and the military to journalists. In a subsequent study, Tenenboim-Weinblatt et al. (2016) proposed an alternative conflict narrative framework to replace peace journalism, which grouped the narrative into four clusters: political-diplomatic, interactional narrative; political-diplomatic, outward-looking narrative; violence-centered, inward-looking narrative; and violence-centered, outward-looking narrative. The four-cluster framework was applied to Israeli news media outlets' coverage of the Israel–Palestine conflict and violent struggles in Syria and Iran. However, as the authors admitted, the coding was highly complex and difficult to replicate. Moreover, the new framework remained focused on violence (war) versus nonviolence/diplomacy (peace), which is the basic premise of the peace and war journalism dichotomy.

Herein, we propose that peace journalism can promote critical thinking and transparency by prompting journalists to acknowledge the limitations of elite sources and, thus, attempt to diversify their sources. Additionally, war and peace journalism's dual nature implies that news stories may contain both war and peace attributes. For example, a story can primarily use elite sources represented by the government (war journalism) with a "win-win orientation" (peace journalism) (Galtung, 2003, p.187). A greater emphasis on "peace" than "war" items in a news report can encourage people to seek a more peaceful resolution to a conflict.

The recent trade conflict between the United States and China provides opportunities for both war and peace journalism framing by journalists. In order to punish China for engaging in unfair trade practices (such as intellectual property theft, currency manipulation, or government subsidies), the U.S. government announced tariffs on Chinese imports and pressured China to concede to its demands (Executive Office of the United States President, 2018). China saw this as an attempt by the United States to impede its economic growth and stall its technological advancement (Liu & Woo, 2018). In response to the U.S. trade tariffs imposed on China, both U.S. and Chinese journalists aroused nationalist sentiments by megaphoning the government's stance to generate favorable public opinion for their government's decisions, hence practicing war journalism. At the same time, our data show that some journalists also provided critical perspectives on U.S.–China relations by utilizing alternative sources of information and reflecting on their own country's economic and technological development, hence practicing peace journalism. We would like to emphasize the following key finding: our data shows that U.S. and Chinese news media deployed war and peace journalism in roughly equivalent levels, which lead to news coverage of the trade war in both nations that was ambivalent, mixed, and often times counter to their respective government's narratives.

The Foreign Policy Information Market Equilibrium Hypothesis

Studies of the effects of media coverage on foreign policy decision-making have been mainly conducted in Western democracies (Baum & Potter, 2008). The news media play an important role in enhancing the public's understanding of foreign policy issues and can help policymakers become more receptive to public opinion. Soroka (2003) demonstrated this process by conducting longitudinal studies in the United Kingdom and the United States, comparing the public's grasp of foreign policy in both countries. His analysis indicated a positive correlation between increased public understandings of policy changes, which, in turn, influenced how policymakers responded to public opinion. To theorize this process, Baum and Potter (2008) proposed the concept of *foreign policy information market equilibrium*. The concept explains the media's role through different stages of a conflict by tracking the changing information gap between foreign policymakers and the public. In the initial stage, the media will follow the government's narrative and rally around the flag, as political leaders are the main source of information on foreign policy. An equilibrium stage is reached when policymakers do not have much information advantage over the public on a specific foreign policy issue, and the public has sufficient knowledge of the policy. At this stage, policymakers are bound to respond to public needs; thus, both the media and the public influence foreign policy.

The equilibrium hypothesis can be studied by analyzing the changes in the media's role in supplying information to the public. In the beginning, most people do not have sufficient information about a foreign policy matter or are simply disinterested, while the policymakers and elites have an information advantage. The theory assumes that the media play the role of a conveyor belt, helping the government legitimize their actions at this stage by reporting the government's viewpoints without reporting contesting voices. However, as the issue develops, the media are more likely to incorporate alternative news sources, hence providing competing frames that enrich the public's understanding of foreign policy. After exposure to different media frames, the public may question the policy and demand changes from the policymakers. At this stage of equilibrium in the foreign policy information market, policymakers no longer hold a large information advantage over the public.

However, the foreign policy information market equilibrium hypothesis does not consider the specifics of news framing practices used by journalists, such as language usage and explanation of the conflict's consequences. By examining both the war and peace journalism frames of the U.S. and Chinese news media and the changes in sources and frames throughout the conflict, this study contributes to a more comprehensive understanding of how news coverage can reduce or increase the information gap between the government and the public over time. Moreover, examining the news source and frame diversity from both peace journalism and foreign policy information market equilibrium make them useful complementary perspectives for explaining the U.S.–China trade war and other conflicts.

Chinese and U.S. Journalistic Traditions and Press Systems

To compare journalistic practices between China and the United States, we first need to understand the journalistic traditions within their respective media systems. While the U.S. media operate independently from the government and are driven in large part by commercial interests (Akhavan-Majid & Wolf, 1991; Hallin & Mancini, 2004; Pickard, 2015), the Chinese media have been traditionally understood as a close approximation of the Soviet-Communist media under party control (Josephi, 2005). However, media outlets in contemporary China have changed. The authoritarian state leadership of the media is more prominent than party leadership in contemporary China (Zhao, 2012). Moreover, Chinese journalists have been exposed to Western journalism practices, and many of them have been trained at Western universities, resulting in the emergence of new forms of professionalism among journalists in China (Simons et al., 2017). Although the Chinese media still play a primary role in promoting the government's views, it is impossible to ignore the increasing commercialization of news media. Over the past forty years of economic development, Chinese news media outlets have transitioned from being dependent on government subsidies to greater dependency on advertising revenues; therefore, they have to appeal to their audiences' interests. Cao (2007) classified China's news media into two types: the party press and the market-oriented press. The two types differ substantially in terms of their coverage of foreign affairs. The party press outlets focus on the leaders and the government, indoctrinating the public with the party's policies. In contrast, the market-oriented news press outlets provide more contextual information and use nongovernmental sources, including an ever-burgeoning range of social media.

Although the roots of American journalism can be traced to the eighteenth century, the modern ideals of nonpartisan and objective journalism developed only in the twentieth century (McChesney, 2003). Kaplan (2003) noted that the two World Wars provided the foundation for most American journalistic practices by reinforcing national identity. Moreover, he argued that even in the context of war journalism, objectivity never entirely replaced partisanship as a journalistic value; only the locus shifted from conflicts within the nation to "the actions of the president in confrontation with our national enemies" (p. 215). The journalistic objectivity ideal was catalyzed by the structure of media ownership in the United States, which was mostly profit-driven and heavy on sensationalism (McChesney, 2003).

As media technologies develop rapidly, scholars have examined media convergence as a process involving shifts in power, industries, markets, production genres, and the blurring relationship between users and producers (Jenkins, 2004, Jensen, 2010). While scholars hoped media convergence would foster dialogues and audience participation, Hartnett et al. (2020) noted that digital platforms have become the incubator of misinformation and a forum for manipulation. In the United States, news media convergence is the fusion of user-generated content and professional content in news delivery. In China, media convergence means using different platforms to deliver content from the same media institution to serve different audiences. Dodge (2020) describes the communication convergence in China as the fusion of government, party, and state media characterized by unquestionable party domination, with President Xi as the paramount "core."

In 2014, media convergence became a national strategy in China requiring mainstream news media outlets to develop an active online presence on multiple platforms, including online news sites, mobile news apps, the microblogging platform Weibo, and the messaging app WeChat (Lu, 2017). By 2017, online (15 percent) and mobile news consumption (51 percent) surpassed news consumption through traditional print (6 percent) and broadcast (13 percent) sources, demonstrating vividly that the Chinese media market had moved online (Cui, 2018). Although the speed with which breaking news can be published online makes it impossible to censor all items before they appear online, in China, political control is achieved through journalists' use of government sources and a delay in publishing sensitive and investigative topics in print. However, journalists are still the gatekeepers of published news despite the presence of user-generated leads from social media (Li, 2018). Compared to emerging commercial news media, traditional media outlets have unique advantages because they have inherited professional teams for news production, and, most importantly, government licenses to cover major political news and international affairs. Thus, when examining foreign policy-related matters, such as the U.S.–China trade conflict, it is important to consider the role of the Chinese mainstream media because of their greater access to government sources and information.

Media Coverage of China and the United States

How the U.S. and Chinese media cover each other's nation is greatly influenced by their political relations. X. Lu's (2011) rhetorical analysis of U.S. coverage of China from the 1940s to the 1990s, for example, reflected the change in U.S.–China relations from "military allies" to "ideological enemies" and from "moral adversaries" to "strategic partners." Similarly, a comparative study of ABC news broadcasts in the United States and CCTV news broadcasts in China indicated that social and cultural norms dictate the framing of news content about domestic and international affairs

(Chang et al., 1998). Indeed, news framing and reporting in a given society usually follow dominant opinions, ideas, and political powers (Krumbein, 2015). Therefore, it is reasonable to assume that the different ideologies and interests of the United States and China influence how the media in each country cover international news. For example, in a study comparing how U.S. and Chinese newspapers covered the 1999 NATO airstrikes in Yugoslavia, Yang (2003) found that newspapers in each country used different frames to describe the NATO intervention. *China Daily* and *People's Daily Online* framed the NATO military action as an intervention in the former Yugoslavia's territory and a violation of its sovereignty. In contrast, the *Washington Post* and the *New York Times* covered the airstrikes as humanistic assistance to curtail the Serbians from massacring the Albanians (Yang, 2003). Likewise, the issue of human rights has been repeatedly utilized by the U.S. media and policymakers to criticize China. Yin (2007) described the U.S. and Chinese media discourses surrounding human rights as a struggle for "authority to define this issue" (p.89). As these examples demonstrate, most scholars agree that the news media usually frames foreign policy issues via narratives that reflect a national bias.

Since the fall of the Soviet Union, China's portrayal in the United States has increasingly become negative (Peng, 2004; Shambaugh, 2003; Xu, 2018). Peng (2004) asserted that the U.S. media's coverage of China mostly consists of three different news frames—ideological, political, and economic. While the use of ideological and political frames by the U.S. media has been fairly consistent, China's growing economic prominence should increase the use of economic frames by the U.S. media. Yang and Liu (2012) drew upon the "China threat" narrative to add another dimension to these three frames: the military or strategic frame. Therefore, the question is how did the media frame the U.S.–China trade war in each nation, and how were their framing strategies inflected by distinctly national perspectives?

Influences on News Coverage of the U.S.–China Trade War

Based on the above discussion, we argue that the news coverage of the U.S.–China trade war depended on the role each country played in the conflict as an initiator or defender, the type of media reporting on the trade war, the relationship between a media outlet and the government, and media partisanship. In this particular case, the United States can be considered the "initiator" of the trade war because it first imposed the trade tariffs. On June 15, 2018, President Trump declared that the

United States would impose a 25 percent tariff on $50 billion of Chinese exports. We assumed the U.S. media would be more likely to play up this conflict and, thus, more likely to employ war journalism frames. In contrast, China played the role of the "defender" by retaliating with its own tariffs on U.S. products. Because China strongly desired a quick resolution of this trade dispute to avoid an economic downturn, we expected the state-controlled media in China would be more likely to employ peace journalism frames. In short, we expected that the U.S. news media would be more likely to use war journalism to report the U.S.–China trade war, whereas the Chinese news media would be more likely to use peace journalism to report this conflict.

Moreover, we expected different media outlets would engage in different peace and war journalism practices. Because CCTV is China's official party broadcaster, we expected it to be cautious in its reporting and less likely to emphasize the differences and confrontations with the United States. In contrast, we assumed that the broadcast TV networks in the United States, for instance, ABC (commercial TV network) and PBS (public broadcast TV network), reflecting the general American public's concern for the large trade deficit and job losses from manufacturing relocations to China, would be more likely adopt an aggressive position that framed China as an economic rival. Consequently, we hypothesized that U.S. television broadcasters (PBS and ABC) would be more likely to use war journalism in their coverage of the U.S.–China trade war than their Chinese television counterparts.

Elite newspapers might play different roles in covering the U.S.–China trade war than television because they can contain more information. Moreover, elite-newspaper readers tend to be better educated and informed than those who rely primarily on television for their news (Grabe et al., 2009). We therefore speculated that elite U.S. newspapers, such as the *New York Times*, would be more likely to use war journalism frames than their Chinese counterparts because of the anti-Communist ideology in their coverage of China in the past (Peng, 2004; Lueck et al., 2014). In contrast, official Chinese newspapers, such as *People's Daily*, serve as the party organ and mostly target party followers. The party wanted to negotiate the elimination of the trade tariffs with the United States and to avoid direct confrontation. Therefore, we expected that the *New York Times* would be more likely than *People's Daily* to use war journalism to cover the U.S.–China trade war.

In addition to comparing elite U.S. and Chinese newspaper and television coverage, we examined whether the type of media influences the use of war and peace journalism frames. Because newspapers have headlines and more space to frame the news, while television news scripts are much shorter and do not include a headline, the presence of war and peace journalism indicators should be stronger in newspapers than in television news, regardless of country. Thus, we expected newspapers to have higher war journalism and peace journalism scores than television news in the coverage of the U.S.–China trade war.

While the Chinese news media are not allowed to challenge or oppose the national government, U.S. news media are more likely to have a diverse role because they are expected to serve a watchdog role and because of the political pluralism of news media ownership. Due to the high animosity between the Trump administration and large sections of the U.S. news media, we hypothesized that the U.S. news media would be more likely to challenge or oppose the tariffs rather than support them. In contrast, we assumed the Chinese news media would only oppose the U.S. tariffs, following the Chinese government's policy.

In the United States, the liberal news media frequently criticize the Trump administration. Therefore, we expected liberal news media organizations would be more likely to oppose government policies regarding the trade war, perhaps even more than the Chinese party press. Therefore, we hypothesized that the liberal U.S. news media (MSNBC, PBS, CNN) would be more likely to challenge or oppose the U.S. official government policies related to the U.S.–China trade war than the Chinese party press (*Global Times, People's Daily*). Here again, our hypothesis reflected our sense that the U.S. media enable a much wider range of perspectives than do the Chinese media, with U.S. outlets varying from strong support for Trump's tariffs to equally strong opposition against them.

Moreover, this study combined the concept of war and peace journalism with the foreign policy information market equilibrium hypothesis to examine how the U.S. and Chinese news media reported the trade conflict. According to Baum and Potter's (2008) foreign policy market equilibrium hypothesis, the longer a conflict lasts, the more competing frames and non-elite news sources would be used by the news media to report the conflict. Because no previous studies have tested the foreign policy information market equilibrium hypothesis in a Communist media system, we asked the following research question: can the foreign policy market information equilibrium hypothesis be applied in both China and the United States within the context of the U.S.–China trade war?

Method

We performed a content analysis of U.S. and Chinese media outlets to examine the U.S.–China trade war coverage. In selecting the media outlets in these two countries, we considered the number of online followers, audience ratings, and the outlets' reputation as elite news media. Given the high prevalence of social media use as news sources in China (CNNIC, 2018) and the United States (Shearer, 2018), and considering the ease of sharing news articles with others on social media, we selected online articles from newspapers featured on their official newspaper social media pages to represent newspaper media coverage. We used "China" and "trade" or "tariffs" as the keywords for all the sampled U.S. media outlets and "United States" and "trade" or "tariffs" to retrieve Chinese news media items, except those from newspapers and mobile news apps because we found that many such articles would be omitted unless we included the term "trade war" in our searches. Consequently, we added this term to the three original keywords to retrieve the relevant articles.

For the Chinese media, we chose one TV channel, online news articles posted through the social media (WeChat) accounts of two official party newspapers, and news articles from one market-oriented news app with original news reports. For the TV channel, we chose CCTV News, the leading news program in China, which reaches almost the entire nation. In 2017, the rating of CCTV News rose to 44.5 percent from 40.7 percent in 2016, indicating its domination of the Chinese TV news market (Cui, 2018). To select news stories from the CCTV video archive, we used the keywords "the United States" and "trade" or "tariffs." Because the website provided videos for the past year only, we searched the archive from January 1, 2018, to December 31, 2018, for relevant news stories. Overall, we found a total of 253 video newscasts related to the U.S.–China trade war for the year 2018. A random sample of one hundred videos was selected as the final sample for coding. The coders transcribed the newscasts related to the trade conflict and then coded the transcripts.

WeChat is the largest social media platform in China, with more than one billion daily active users (Lee, 2019). We selected the WeChat accounts of *People's Daily* and *Global Times* because they were among the top five WeChat news accounts in 2018. *People's Daily* was the top WeChat news account in 2018. *Global Times*, ranked fifth, focuses on international news and China's foreign policy, and it was therefore deemed the most relevant to our study (NewRank, 2018). For mobile news apps, we chose *The Paper*, the top market-oriented news app with original news gathering and reporting. Its primary users are men (62.7 percent) and young people aged twenty-six to thirty-five (47.8 percent). *Wisers*, a leading Chinese media database, was employed to retrieve samples of the two WeChat accounts (*People's Daily* and *Global Times*) and *The Paper* from the period January 1, 2018, to December 31, 2018. We randomly selected one hundred news stories from each news outlet for coding.

In the United States, we selected two elite newspapers, the *New York Times* (on Facebook) and the *Wall Street Journal* (on Twitter). These newspapers have the largest number of followers on Facebook and Twitter, respectively. CNN's social media page is one of the most visited news media pages with an online audience larger than its TV audience (Boland, 2018; CNN Business, 2017). Therefore, we decided to examine its online version featured on Facebook rather than its TV broadcasts. For television, we selected several TV news outlets to include the entirety of the political spectrum. We selected the conservative Fox News; ABC, the commercial broadcast news channel with the highest ratings (Battaglio, 2018); public broadcast TV news (PBS); and the more liberal MSNBC (Engel, 2014).

As a result of this strategy, we used seven news outlets to represent the U.S. news coverage of the trade war (ABC, PBS, Fox News, CNN, MSNBC, the *New York Times*, and the *Wall Street Journal*). For TV news (except CNN for reasons explained above), we downloaded transcripts of newscasts from January 1 to December 31, 2018, from Nexis Uni. Because many shows on Fox News and MSNBC are not newscasts but talk shows, we limited the coding to *The Beat with Ari Melber* (MSNBC) and the *Special Report with Bret Baier* (Fox News) for the sake of comparison with other news broadcasts. All TV newscasts we analyzed aired at 6:00 p.m. or 6:30 p.m. as the main evening newscast.

We located the news stories posted by the *New York Times*, the *Wall Street Journal*, and CNN on social media by using a search algorithm on Facebook and Twitter with the same keywords, "China" and "trade." We restricted the period from January 1, 2018, to December 31, 2018. All databases and algorithms ranked the articles by relevance. Thus, to build a list of the population of articles posted during the period, the coders checked the most relevant articles in the order listed by Facebook and Twitter until they found the articles to be not relevant. With this comprehensive approach, we still found a small number of U.S. news items covering the trade war. Therefore, instead of sampling, we used all the news items identified as relevant to the topic from each selected outlet (PBS, $N = 42$; CNN, $N = 48$; ABC, $N = 38$; Fox, $N = 75$; MSNBC, $N = 18$; *New York Times*, $N = 71$, *Wall Street Journal*, $N = 47$), resulting in a total of 339 U.S. news articles about the U.S.–China trade war. This number of sampled U.S. news articles was slightly lower than the total number of sampled Chinese news articles (N = 400). The unequal sample sizes indicate the different emphasis placed on the trade war by each nation's media.

Coding

Five graduate students at Shanghai International Studies University in China and four graduate students and two faculty members at Bowling Green State University in the United States served as coders. The first author and a Chinese graduate student double-coded 10 percent of the U.S. and Chinese samples respectively to compute intercoder reliability. Several training sessions were conducted to make sure the coders understood the coding scheme and employed the coding process correctly. The coding of competing frames and the use of non-elite sources both achieved 95 percent agreement. The coding agreement of the tone of the coverage was 80 percent. The coding agreement of war journalism practices reached 82.5 percent (from 70 percent to 95 percent for individual indicators) and 84.4 percent for peace journalism practices (from 75 percent to 100 percent for individual indicators).

Measures

War and Peace Journalism Practice. We employed the coding scheme of war and peace journalism practices used by Lee and Maslog (2005), with thirteen items each for war and peace journalism (see tables 1 and 2). In addition to listing the frequency of war and peace journalism practices, we computed a peace journalism score and a war journalism score by summing up the presence of war and peace journalism indicators (1–13). Moreover, we calculated a "war-peace journalism differential" by subtracting the war journalism score from the peace journalism score, similar to the method used by Lynch (2014). A negative differential indicates that the article is more oriented toward peace journalism practices.

   Use of the Term "Trade War" in the News. To corroborate the war and peace journalism item analysis, we counted whether the term "trade war" was used in each news story from the reporter or the interviewees, not whether the term "trade war" was used by Trump. While this term provided an additional indicator of the war journalism frame used in each news story, it was not used in the computation of war journalism score.

Types of Sources. Another indicator of war and peace journalism practice is the type of news sources used—elite sources in war journalism and non-elite sources in peace journalism. Elite sources included political leaders, government officials, academics, and think-tank experts. Non-elite sources included nongovernment organizations, industry representatives, and common people.

Number of Sources. This measure represents the count of the number of sources included in a news story. To provide evidence for the diversification of sources, we compared the numbers and types of sources used by each news media outlet in each conflict stage.

Presence of Competing Frames. An objective and fair report should contain competing frames that are equally persuasive (Beattie & Milojevich, 2017). In an ongoing conflict, a greater number of competing frames should be included in news stories over time. Therefore, each story was coded for the presence of more than one frame and for whether the frames were competing.

Position of the News Story. We examined the position of each news story in general based on four categories: (1) supportive or mostly supportive of the policy (tariff sanctions against China), (2) opposing the policy, (3) neutral, and (4) partly supportive or partly opposing the policy.

Trade Conflict Stages. We divided the trade conflict into three stages to test the foreign policy information market equilibrium hypothesis. The "beginning stage" (stage 1) started January 22, 2018, when U.S. President Donald Trump imposed tariffs on solar panels and washing machines imported from China (which represent two of China's largest exports to the United States). This stage ended in April 2018, when China responded by imposing tariffs on 128 products imported from the United States. The "combative stage" (stage 2) started in May 2018 when China's vice premier visited the United States for trade talks, and it ended in July 2018 when U.S. tariffs on $34 billion of Chinese goods came into effect, and China imposed retaliatory tariffs on U.S. goods of similar value. The "truce stage" (stage 3) started on August 8, 2018, when the Office of the U.S. Trade Representative published a list of 279 Chinese goods worth $16 billion to be subjected to a 25 percent tariff starting August 23, 2018, and China responded with its own tariffs of equal value. This stage ended on December 1, 2018, when Chinese President Xi and U.S. President Trump announced a temporary truce in tariffs at the G-20 Summit in Argentina.

Findings

We analyzed a total of 739 articles, including 400 Chinese and 339 U.S. articles. The scores for each peace and war journalism practice indicator in the U.S. and Chinese news media are shown in tables 1 and 2, respectively. For peace journalism practices, Chinese news media were significantly more likely to use neutral language. They reported the damages, causes, and consequences of the conflict and discussed the areas of agreement that might resolve the conflict.

To test the hypothesis that the war journalism scores of the U.S. news media would be higher than those of Chinese news media, we performed an independent sample t-test. The hypothesis was supported for both war journalism and peace journalism scores. The mean war journalism scores for the Chinese and the U.S. data were 3.38 and 4.07, respectively, $t(737) = -4.22, p < .001$. In contrast, the mean values of the peace journalism scores for the Chinese and the U.S. data were 4.8 and 4.44, respectively, $t(737) = 2.21, p = .03$. The mean differential between war and peace journalism within each Chinese news story was -1.08. The mean differential between war and peace journalism within each U.S. news story was $-.74$. Because higher values indicate more dominant war journalism, the U.S. news media included more elements of war journalism than the Chinese news media. In addition, the U.S. media outlets were significantly more likely to use the term "trade war" ($M = .72$) in their stories compared to the Chinese media ($M = .61$), $t(729) = -3.08, p = .02$. Overall, the findings indicate that the U.S. news media were more likely to use war journalism in their stories about the U.S.–China trade war than the Chinese news media.

Next, we compared the type of media in which the stories about the U.S.–China trade war appeared. To test the hypothesis that U.S. broadcast TV news media would be more likely to employ war journalism than CCTV, we conducted an independent sample t-test comparison. The mean score of war journalism for PBS and ABC was 3.88, which was significantly higher than that of CCTV, which was only 2.75, $t(178) = 4.58, p < .001$. This implies that U.S. TV news outlets were more likely to use war journalism than CCTV, supporting the hypothesis.

We also found that elite newspapers in the United States were more likely to use war journalism than their Chinese counterparts, as hypothesized. The mean war journalism score of the *New York Times* was 5.66, which was significantly higher than the mean score of 4.91 for *People's Daily*, $t(169) = 2.62, p = .01$.

To examine whether news articles published in newspapers were more likely to have higher war journalism scores than television newscasts, we compared

TABLE 1. Peace Journalism Comparison between Chinese and U.S. News Media

PEACE JOURNALISM INDICATORS	CHINA		U.S.		TOTAL	
	N	%	*N*	%	*N*	%
Reporting on damage to society and culture**	35	8.8%	56	16.5%	91	12.3%
Reporting on psychological damages	4	1.0%	14	4.1%	18	2.4%
Focusing on non-elite sources	32	8.0%	42	12.4%	74	10.0%
Discussing similarities/mutual interests between the countries involved**	107	26.8%	79	23.3%	186	25.2%
Reporting causes and consequences of the conflict**	153	38.3%	178	52.5%	33	44.8%
Win-win orientation**	71	17.8%	76	22.4%	14	19.9%
Presenting diversity (giving voice to many parties in the conflict)**	87	21.8%	108	31.9%	195	26.4%
Proactive reporting**	10	2.5%	93	27.4%	10	13.9%
Nonpartisan	237	59.3%	199	58.7%	43	59.0%
Reporting the areas of agreement that might lead to a solution to the conflicts**	38	9.5%	73	21.5%	111	15.0%
Avoiding victimizing language**	326	81.5%	241	71.1%	567	76.7%
Avoiding demonizing language**	376	94.0%	264	77.9%	640	86.6%
Objective and moderate wording**	305	76.3%	207	61.1%	512	69.3%

Note: **p < 0.01

the average war journalism scores of newspaper articles and television newscast samples in both countries. Indeed, there was a significant difference depending on the medium. The war journalism score of newspapers (M = 3.70, SD = 2.30) was significantly higher than that of television (M = 3.20, SD = 1.7) $t(662)$ = 2.98, p = .003. For peace journalism, the opposite was true. Television newscasts had a higher peace journalism score (M = 4.82, SD = 2.24) than newspapers (M = 4.36, SD = 2.01) $t(662)$ = 2.77, p = .006.

Contrary to our expectation that the U.S. news media are more likely to oppose the U.S. tariffs imposed on China, while all Chinese news media outlets would oppose the U.S. tariffs, we found that the tariffs received almost equal support and opposition from the U.S. media. Overall, 70 percent (280 articles) of the Chinese media outlets opposed the U.S. tariff policy, 30 percent (120 articles) were neutral,

TABLE 2. War Journalism Comparison between Chinese and U.S. News Media

WAR JOURNALISM INDICATORS	CHINA		U.S.		TOTAL	
	N	%	N	%	N	%
Reporting economic damages (visible effects)**	140	35.0%	252	74.3%	392	53.0%
Reporting material damages**	44	11.0%	76	22.4%	120	16.2%
Focusing on elite sources (leaders and intellectuals)**	271	67.8%	229	67.6%	500	67.7%
Focusing on differences that lead to the conflict**	66	16.5%	144	42.5%	210	28.4%
Focusing mainly on the here and now (present happenings)**	253	63.2%	106	31.3%	359	48.6%
Dichotomies between "good" and "bad guys"**	61	15.3%	36	10.6%	97	13.1%
Presenting a zero-sum game**	83	20.8%	61	18.0%	144	19.5%
Reactive reporting**	77	19.3%	102	30.1%	179	24.2%
Stopping reports after conflict**	125	31.3%	90	26.5%	215	29.1%
Loss of voter/public support**	36	9.0%	34	10.0%	70	9.5%
Using victimizing language**	73	18.3%	57	16.8%	130	17.6%
Using demonizing language on sources	18	4.5%	28	8.3%	46	6.2%
Using emotive words**	104	26.0%	163	48.1%	267	36.1%

Note: **$p < .01$

and none of the articles supported the U.S. tariffs. In contrast, 17.8 percent (60 articles) of the U.S. media opposed the tariff policy, 18 percent (61 articles) supported the policy, and the majority (64 percent) were neutral. These findings indicate that while the Chinese media strongly opposed Trump's tariffs, the U.S. news media was split between a majority of outlets taking no position and equal subsets both supporting and opposing the tariffs.

Another unexpected result was the fact that even the liberal U.S. news media, which was critical of the Trump administration on most domestic and international issues, did not oppose the trade tariffs. We found 21 percent of the news stories from the U.S. liberal news media explicitly opposed the Trump's trade tariffs, while another 64 percent remained neutral. In contrast, 82 percent of Chinese party news media opposed the U.S. trade tariff policy. Here again, our findings confirm that

TABLE 3. Comparison of Types of Sources in Stories about U.S.–China Trade War

	U.S. *N* = 339	CHINA *N* = 400
Government sources	78.7%	74.3%
Think tank/consultant**	39.0%	28.3%
Academic/university*	11.9%	18.5%
Agriculture sector**	7.3%	13.5%
Retail/trade sector**	23.7%	40.6%
Manufacturing sector*	11.9%	17.5%
General public	8.3%	7.8%
Other sources	11.1%	14.4%

Note: *$p < .05$, **$p < .01$

the Chinese news media spoke in a more unilateral manner, with 82 percent of the stories taking an anti-tariff position, while the U.S. media, like the nation itself, was split along competing responses and frames.

Because news sources are an important indicator both for peace journalism and the foreign policy information market equilibrium hypothesis, we explored which sources were used by the U.S. and Chinese news media. As shown in table 3, except for the dominance of government sources in both countries, the U.S. and Chinese news media differed significantly in their use of non-elite sources. The Chinese media were more likely than their U.S. counterparts to use sources from sectors affected by the trade war, such as retail and trade (40.6 percent), manufacturing (17.5 percent), and agriculture (13.5 percent). In terms of elite sources, the Chinese media were more likely to use academics (18.5 percent), while the U.S. media were more likely to use think tanks and consultants (39 percent). We should note that the revolving door between academia, think tanks, government offices, and the media—a phenomenon as prevalent in China as it is in America—rendered these "elite" sources difficult to differentiate at times.

To answer the research question related to the foreign policy information market equilibrium hypothesis, we compared the changes in the number of sources, the use of non-elite sources, and the presence of competing frames during the three stages of the U.S.–China trade war by performing one-way analysis of variance. In addition, we compared the scores of war and peace journalism in each stage of the conflict. Overall, the findings indicated a significant difference between the U.S.

and Chinese news media in terms of changes in their news source diversity and the presence of competing frames across stages.

For the U.S. news media, the highest numbers of sources were used in the first and third stages, with a dip in the middle (table 4). Thus, the result did not support the hypothesis that the number and types of news sources increase and diversify over time. Moreover, the number of sources was not related to the use of non-elite sources ($r = .01$, $p = .66$).

Next, we looked specifically at non-elite sources. There was no significant difference in the use of non-elite sources across different stages. In terms of competing frames, we found some differences across the stages, and these differences approached statistical significance. Yet, the stage with the greatest number of competing frames was the second rather than the last stage. Thus, the findings did not show a diversification of sources over time as hypothesized, but rather fluctuated by event and stage. Nonetheless, when we examined China and the United States separately, the use of non-elite sources and competing frames by China's news media outlets increased over time, which provides some support for the foreign policy information market equilibrium hypothesis. However, U.S. news media outlets did not follow the foreign policy information market equilibrium hypothesis.

Finally, we compared the war and peace journalism scores of the U.S. and the Chinese news media across the three stages. Overall, the U.S. news media had a higher war journalism score than China throughout the three stages. In the initial stage, the U.S. new media's war journalism score was the highest, highlighting a more combative framing of its news reports than its Chinese counterparts. At the same time, the U.S. news media's peace journalism score was higher than its Chinese counterparts in the first two stages. Here again, our data confirm that the range of perspectives in U.S. media outlets was wider than in Chinese media outlets, as the U.S. media scored higher in both war and peace journalism. In fact, our findings indicate that in many U.S. stories war and peace frames were present at the same time, leaving readers with clashing views of the U.S.–China trade war.

For example, a *New York Times* news story that discussed how the trade war hurt Michigan's automobile industry illustrates how war and peace journalism frames can coexist in foreign affairs news reporting. The story begins by expressing a desire for peace between the United States and China, with the headline "Trump's Trade War with China Pierces the Heart of Michigan." It continues by noting that President Trump's attempts to punish China with trade tariffs has led to Michigan

TABLE 4. Diversity of Sources, Competing Frames, War and Peace Journalism Scores by Stages of Conflict

	U.S.			CHINA		
	NUMBER OF SOURCES PER NEWS STORY					
	M	SD	N	M	SD	N
Stage 1	4.16	2.24	92	4.79	2.31	200
Stage 2	3.79	2.08	104	4.20	2.22	100
Stage 3	4.32	2.15	143	4.53	2.03	100
Total	4.11	2.16	339	4.58	2.29	400
	$F = 1.79, p = 0.17$			$F = 2.25, p = 0.11$		
	USE OF NON-ELITE SOURCES					
	M	SD	N	M	SD	N
Stage 1	0.16	0.37	92	0.06	0.24	200
Stage 2	0.15	0.36	104	0.04	0.27	100
Stage 3	0.08	0.27	143	0.16	0.35	100
Total	0.12	0.33	339	0.08	0.27	400
	$F = 2.55, p = 0.08$			$F = 6.12, p = 0.02$		
	PRESENCE OF COMPETING FRAMES					
	M	SD	N	M	SD	N
Stage 1	0.57	0.50	92	0.13	0.23	200
Stage 2	0.58	0.50	104	0.13	0.34	100
Stage 3	0.35	0.48	143	0.21	0.40	100
Total	0.48	0.50	339	0.15	0.36	400
	$F = 9.12, p < 0.001$			$F = 5.04, p = 0.007$		
	WAR JOURNALISM PRACTICE					
	M	SD	N	M	SD	N
Stage 1	4.42	2.15	92	3.27	2.02	200
Stage 2	4.16	2.63	104	3.55	2.06	100
Stage 3	3.76	2.25	143	3.42	2.19	100
Total	4.06	2.35	339	3.38	2.07	400
	$F = 4.61, p = 0.01$			$F = 0.64, p = 0.53$		

	U.S.			CHINA		
	PEACE JOURNALISM PRACTICE					
	M	SD	N	M	SD	N
Stage 1	5.50	2.53	92	4.55	1.43	200
Stage 2	4.66	2.66	104	4.01	1.73	100
Stage 3	4.47	2.62	143	4.70	2.00	100
Total	4.81	2.63	339	4.45	1.68	400
	$F = 2.36, p = 0.10$			$F = 5.00, p = 0.007$		

being "caught in the cross hairs, with its ability to remain competitive and develop emerging technologies like autonomous vehicles, robotics and artificial intelligence highly dependent on ties to international markets, including China." However, the story also includes more aggressive references by pointing out that even though Michigan might see China as an economic partner, "President Trump sees an 'economic enemy'—one intent on overtaking America's competitive edge by stealing technology, trade secrets and jobs from domestic companies" (Swanson, 2018). The article thus deploys both peace and war journalism, offering readers a mixed perspective for making sense of the trade war.

Overall, these types of competing frames were quite common in many of the nonpartisan news media reports we analyzed. Interestingly, the "phase one" trade agreement signed by the United States and China on January 15, 2020, was hailed as a win-win agreement by both governments. However, it was criticized by the U.S. and Chinese media as conceding too much to the other nation. The U.S. news website Vox, for example, noted that "President Donald Trump is selling this deal as an enormous win, but the administration did not get the structural changes to China's economy that it wanted, including tackling things like Beijing's huge subsidies to Chinese companies" (Kirby, 2020, para. 9). Similarly, the *Global Times* wrote that "on each side are people that argue their country made too many concessions or did not gain enough from the deal" (Wang, 2020, para. 19). "At a time of celebration and historic importance, there have been some domestic concerns, alleging that the trade deal is largely made out of China's concessions to America" (Gong, 2020, para. 2). As these examples illustrate, war and peace journalism was deployed in both U.S. and Chinese media outlets, indicating a sense of ambivalence and even confusion about the trade war.

Conclusions

This comparative analysis of the U.S.–China trade war coverage in China and the United States shows that more news stories about this conflict used peace journalism frames rather than war journalism frames. Similar to the findings by Lee and Maslog (2005), a here-and-now focus and an elite orientation dominated the war journalism practices in both countries. However, the proportion of war journalism indicators in the U.S.–China trade conflict was higher than those in the Asian military conflict articles analyzed by Lee and Maslog (2005). Contrary to their findings, we also found more frequent usage of peace journalism language in the U.S. and Chinese news media. As expected, the U.S. news media were more eager to present the United States as the eventual victor of the trade war by making accusations against China and therefore were more likely to use war journalism in their news stories than their Chinese counterparts. However, we also found the U.S. news media deployed peace journalism frames roughly equally with war journalism frames, which ensured that neither perspective dominated the news coverage of the U.S.–China trade war.

Overall, this study confirmed that the use of peace and war journalism practices is affected by the country's roles in the conflict. We found that the U.S. media were more likely to use combative rhetoric during the trade conflict and more often referred to the conflict as a trade "war" than their Chinese counterparts. The U.S. media's more frequent use of emotive words and demonizing language toward China that led to higher war journalism scores. We should be cautious about this conclusion, however. For example, while Trump's aggressive statements toward China were reported by U.S. journalists, such quotes do not necessarily indicate an endorsement of his positions. However, it also should be noted that while some journalists disputed Trump's claims regarding the possible effects of trade tariffs, other journalists—especially those working for Fox News—clearly supported his political views.

As the responding party in this conflict, the Chinese news media were more likely to discuss mutual interests between the two nations and cover economic sectors most affected by the tariffs, such as manufacturing, retailing, and agriculture. Moreover, as state-controlled press outlets, they followed the government's cautious approach to trade negotiations and employed the style of peace journalism frequently. This finding has important implications for the research on peace journalism and international conflicts because it highlights the roles of the conflict initiator and the responder as factors that should be considered in explaining news coverage in addition to culture, journalistic, and institutional constraints. Thus, in order to facilitate conflict resolution, journalists in the country initiating a conflict should minimize their use of war journalism framing and instead increase their peace journalism framing.

The most surprising finding was that the foreign policy information market equilibrium hypothesis, which was originally proposed within the context of Western democracies, was supported by the Chinese rather than the U.S. data. We initially suspected that the unequal proportions of news in each stage between China and the United States might be responsible for the difference in the results. However, after we randomly sampled the same number of stories from each country in each stage, the result remained the same. Upon further examination, the U.S. news media's overall emphasis was limited mostly to elite sources—especially the Trump administration—across all stages of the trade war. These media outlets invested more effort and used diverse sources (especially during the first and the second stages) only after the U.S. and Chinese governments made big moves on the tariffs. Despite the use of a greater number of competing frames across all the conflict stages by the U.S. news media, the trend diminished instead of strengthened over time. Instead of presenting more varying perspectives, the U.S. news media outlets increasingly focused on one particular frame: China's unfair trade practices.

When we further analyzed the amount of news coverage at different stages, the U.S. media initially provided limited coverage of the trade war, which gradually increased over time. This might indicate that the U.S. news media initially considered the trade war as a topic of low interest to the U.S. public. The increase in the U.S. news coverage during the third stage likely was linked to the 2018 national midterm election.

In contrast, the Chinese news media paid immediate attention to the trade war. The Chinese media also diversified their sources and provided other frames of reference for their audiences, which included reflections on China's international position and technological developments. Thus, while China moved toward a foreign policy information market equilibrium during the U.S.–China trade war, the United States did not.

This study also shows that peace journalism can be practiced in Western democratic and Chinese Communist media during a conflict. Governments might promote peace journalism when they are interested in resolving conflicts through negotiation rather than direct confrontation. In the case of the U.S.–China trade conflict, peace journalism frames were more prevalent than war journalism frames based on the news items' scores in both the United States and China. But relatively speaking, the U.S. media had higher war journalism scores than the Chinese media. Whether the truce between the United States and China in December 2018 had anything to do with the peace journalism practices of Chinese and U.S. news media cannot be determined because many other factors could have contributed to the truce.

The foreign policy information market equilibrium hypothesis proposed by Baum and Potter (2008) received some preliminary empirical support in China but not in the United States. Even though the U.S. news media initially used more non-elite sources and competing frames than the Chinese news media, its diversity decreased over time. In contrast, the Chinese news media increased their use of non-elite sources and competing frames as the trade war developed. Although the Chinese government is not elected by the people, it needs to monitor public opinion and manage people's support of government policies. The more frequent use of peace journalism in the Chinese news media is consistent with the Chinese government's tactic of negotiating a better deal for China during the trade war by creating a vision for common grounds and emphasizing the benefits of free trade. The Chinese government framed its retaliation against the tariffs as a defense against attacks by the United States, which, as the party claimed, wanted to contain China's economic growth and technological advancement. The heavy media coverage of the trade war in the Chinese media helped create salience toward the Chinese government's position, shape the public's understanding of the conflict, and facilitate reflection on China's economic and technological development by providing competing frames on the topic as the conflict progressed.

REFERENCES

Akhavan-Majid, R., & Wolf, G. (1991). American mass media and the myth of libertarianism: Toward an "elite power group" theory. *Critical Studies in Media Communication, 8*(2), 139–51.

Battaglio, S. (2018, September 25). ABC wins the morning and evening ratings races, but network news is still losing viewers overall. *Los Angeles Times*.

Baum, M. A., & Potter, P. B. (2008). The relationships between mass media, public opinion, and foreign policy: Toward a theoretical synthesis. *Annual Review of Political Science, 11*(1), 39–65.

Beattie, P., & Milojevich, J. (2017). A test of the "news diversity" standard: Single frames, multiple frames, and values regarding the Ukraine conflict. *International Journal of Press/Politics, 22*(1), 3–22.

Boland, G. (2018, October 11). The top Facebook publishers in September 2018. *Newswhip.* https://www.newswhip.com/2018/10/the-top-facebook-publishers-september/

Bradsher, K., & Myers, S. L. (2018, August 14). Trump's trade war is rattling China's leaders. *New York Times.*

Cao, Q. (2007). Confucian vision of a new world order? Culturalist discourse, foreign policy and the press in contemporary China. *International Communication Gazette, 69*(5), 431–50.

Chang, T.K., Wang, J., & Chen, C. (1998). The social construction of international imagery in the post-Cold War era: A comparative analysis of US and Chinese national TV news. *Journal of Broadcasting & Electronic Media, 42*(3), 277–96.

CNN Business. (2017, September 28). CNN Digital #1 in audience, video, mobile, social and millennial reach [Press release]. http://cnnpressroom.blogs.cnn.com/2017/09/28/cnn-digital-biggest-audience-video-mobile-social-millennial/

CNNIC (China Internet Network Information Center) (2018). *The 42nd China Internet development statistical report* [in Chinese]. http://www.cnnic.net.cn/hlwfzyj/hlwxzbg/hlwtjbg/201808/t20180820_70488.htm

Colbert, A. M. (2009). Peace journalism. In C. H. Sterling (Ed.), *Encyclopedia on Journalism* (pp. 1047–1048). SAGE.

Cui, B. (2018). Development report on China's media industry, 2017–2018 [in Chinese]. In B. Cui (Ed.), *Report on the development of China's media industry.* Social Science Academic Press.

Demarest, L., & Langer, A. (2018). Peace journalism on a shoestring? Conflict reporting in Nigeria's national news media. *Journalism, 22*(3), 671–88. https://doi.org/10.1177/1464884918797611

Dodge, P. S.-W. (2020). Communication convergence and "the core" for a new era. In P. S.-W. Dodge (Ed.), *Communication convergence in contemporary China: International Perspectives on Politics, Platforms, and Participation* (pp. ix—xxxii). Michigan State University Press.

Engel, P. (2014, October 21). Here's how liberal or conservative major news sources really are. *Business Insider.* https://www.businessinsider.com/what-your-preferred-news-outlet-says-about-your-political-ideology-2014–10

Executive Office of the United States President. (2018). Findings of the investigation into China's acts, policies, and practices related to technology transfer, intellectual property and innovation under section 301 of the Trade Act of 1974. Office of the United States Trade Representative. https://ustr.gov/sites/default/files/enforcement/301Investigations/301%20 Draft%20Exec%20Summary%203.22.ustrfinal.pdf

Galtung, J. (2003). Peace journalism. *Media Asia, 30*(3), 177–80.

Galtung, J., & Ruge, M. H. (1965). The structure of foreign news: The presentation of the Congo, Cuba and Cyprus crises in four Norwegian newspapers. *Journal of Peace Research, 2*(1), 64–90.

Gong, J. (2020, January 18). China's phase one trade deal with US is a landmark agreement. *CGTN.* https://global.chinadaily.com.cn/a/202001/18/WS5e22bd74a310128217271e00.html

Gouse, V., Valentin-Llopis, M., Perry, S., & Nyamwange, B. (2018). An investigation of the conceptualization of peace and war in peace journalism studies of media coverage of national and international conflicts. *Media, War & Conflict, 12*(4), 435–49.

Grabe, M. E., Kamhawi, R., & Yegiyan, N. (2009). Informing citizens: How people with different levels of education process television, newspaper, and web news. *Journal of Broadcasting & Electronic Media, 53*(1), 90–111.

Hallin, D. C., & Mancini, P. (2004). *Comparing media systems: Three models of media and politics.* Cambridge University Press.

Hanitzsch, T. (2004). Journalists as peacekeeping force? Peace journalism and mass communication theory. *Journalism Studies, 5*(4), 483–95.

Hartnett, S. J., Hu, Z., Dong, Q., Li, S., & Dodge, P. S.-W. (2020). On the paradox of convergence and fragmentation in the age of globalization. In P. S.-W. Dodge (Ed.), *Communication convergence in contemporary China: International Perspectives on Politics, Platforms, and Participation* (pp. 3—17). Michigan State University Press.

Hoekman, B. (2020). Trade wars and the World Trade Organization: Causes, consequences, and change. *Asian Economic Policy Review, 15*(1), 98–114.

Howard, R. (2009). Conflict-sensitive reporting: State of the art. *Communication and Information.* UNESCO http://www.unesco.org/new/en/communication-and-information/resources/publications-and-communication-materials/publications/full-list/conflict-sensitive-reporting-state-of-the-art-a-course-for-journalists-and-journalism-educators/

Jenkins, H. (2004). The cultural logic of media convergence. *International Journal of Cultural Studies, 7*(1), 33–43.

Jensen, K. B. (2010). *Media convergence: The three degrees of network, mass and interpersonal communication.* Routledge.

Josephi, B. (2005). Journalism in the global age: Between normative and empirical. *Gazette, 67*(6), 575–90.

Kaplan, R. L. (2003). American journalism goes to war, 1898–2001: A manifesto on media and empire. *Media History, 9*(3), 209–19.

Keeble, R., Tulloch, J., & Zollman, F. (Eds.). (2010). *Peace journalism, war and conflict resolution.* Peter Lang.

Kirby, J. (2020, January 15). Trump signed a "phase one" trade deal with China: Here's what's in it—and what's not. *Vox.* https://www.vox.com/world/2020/1/15/21064070/trump-china-phase-one-trade-deal-signing

Krumbein, F. (2015). Media coverage of human rights in China. *International Communication Gazette, 77*(2), 151–70.

Lee, C. (2019 January 9). Daily active users of WeChat exceed 1 billion. *ZDNet.* https://www.zdnet.com/article/daily-active-user-of-messaging-app-wechat-exceeds-1-billion/

Lee, S. T., & Maslog, C. C. (2005). War or peace journalism? Asian newspaper coverage of conflicts. *Journal of Communication, 55*(2), 311–29.

Li, K. (2018). Convergence and de-convergence of Chinese journalistic practice in the digital age. *Journalism, 19*(9–10), 1380–96.

Liu, T., & Woo, W. T. (2018). Understanding the U.S.-China trade war. *China Economic Journal, 11*(3), 319–40.

Lu, N. (2017). The exploration of media organization under convergence [in Chinese]. *Shanghai Journalism Review, 5,* 54–60.

Lu, X. (2011). From "ideological enemies" to "strategic partners": A rhetorical analysis of U.S.-China relations in intercultural contexts. *Howard Journal of Communications, 22*(4), 336–57.

Lueck, T. L., Pipps, V. S., & Lin, Y. (2014). China's soft power: A *New York Times* introduction of the Confucius Institute. *Howard Journal of Communications, 25*(3), 324–49.

Lynch, J., & McGoldrick, A. (2013). Responses to peace journalism. *Journalism, 14*(8), 1041–58.

Lynch, J. (2014). *Peace journalism.* Hawthorn Press.

McChesney, R. W. (2003). The problem of journalism: A political economic contribution to an explanation of the crisis in contemporary US journalism. *Journalism Studies, 4*(3), 299–329.

Neuman, R., & Fahmy, S. (2016). Measuring journalistic peace/war performance: An exploratory study of crisis reporters' attitudes and perceptions. *International Communication Gazette, 78*(3), 223–46.

NewRank (2018) *Annual report of 500 popular WeChat accounts.* https://mp.weixin.qq.com/s/PQDOBVTwVo7ZPlG8-GKA7Q

New York Times (2018, July 6). How the 'biggest trade war in economic history' is playing out.

Nohrstedt, S, A., & Ottosen, R. (2015). Peace journalism: A proposition for conceptual and methodological improvements. *Global Media and Communication, 11*(3), 219–35.

Peng, Z. (2004). Representation of China: An across time analysis of coverage in the *New York Times* and *Los Angeles Times*. *Asian Journal of Communication, 14*(1), 53–67.

Pickard, V. (2015). *America's battle for media democracy: The triumph of corporate libertarianism and the future of media reform*. Cambridge University Press.

Rapoza, K. (2019, June 26). The unintended consequences of the China trade war. *Forbes*. https://www.forbes.com/sites/kenrapoza/2019/06/26/the-unintended-consequences-of-the-china-trade-war/#2fcaa7be6ba0

Seib, G. (2018, November 28). A history of discord fuels today's U.S.-China trade relations. *Wall Street Journal*.

Shambaugh, D. (2003). Introduction: Imagining demons; The rise of negative imagery in U.S.-China relations. *Journal of Contemporary China, 12*(35), 235–37.

Shearer, E. (2018, December 10). Social media outpaces print newspapers in the U.S. as a news source. *Pew Research Center*. http://www.pewresearch.org/fact-tank/2018/12/10/social-media-outpaces-print-newspapers-in-the-u-s-as-a-news-source/

Simons, M., Nolan, D., & Wright, S. (2017). 'We are not North Korea': Propaganda and professionalism in the People's Republic of China. *Media, Culture & Society, 39*(2), 219–37.

Soroka, S. N. (2003). Media, public opinion, and foreign policy. *Harvard International Journal of Press/Politics, 8*(1), 27–48.

Swanson, A. (2018, July 12). Trump's trade war with China pierces the heart of Michigan. *New York Times*.

Swanson, A., & Rappeport, A. (2020, January 15). Trump signs China trade deal, putting economic conflict on pause. *New York Times*.

Tenenboim-Weinblatt, K., Hanitzsch, T., & Nagar, R. (2016). Beyond peace journalism: Reclassifying conflict narratives in the Israeli news media. *Journal of Peace Research, 53*(2): 151–65.

Xu, K. (2018). Painting Chinese mythology: Varying touches on the magazine covers of *Time, The Economist, Der Spiegel*, and *China Today*. *International Communication Gazette, 80*(2), 135–57.

Wang, C. (2020, January 15). China, US to sign phase one trade deal. *Global Times*. https://www.globaltimes.cn/content/1176933.shtml

Yang, J. (2003). Framing the NATO air strikes on Kosovo across countries: Comparison of Chinese and US newspaper coverage. *Gazette, 65*(3), 231–49.

Yang, Y. E., & Liu, X. (2012). The 'China Threat' through the lens of US print media: 1992–2006. *Journal of Contemporary China, 21*(76), 695–711.

Yin, J. (2007). The clash of rights: A critical analysis of news discourse on human rights in the United States and China. *Critical Discourse Studies, 4*(1), 75–94.

Youngblood, S. (2017). *Peace journalism principles and practices: Responsibly reporting conflicts, reconciliation, and solutions.* Routledge.

Zhao, Y. (2012). Understanding China's media system in a world historical context. In D. Hallin & P. Mancini (Eds.), *Comparing media systems beyond the Western world* (pp. 143–176). Cambridge University Press.

How Weibo Influencers and Ordinary Posters Responded to the U.S.–China Trade War

Louisa Ha, Peiqin Chen, Ke Guo, and Nan Lyu

I n this chapter, our goal is to understand Chinese public opinion leaders' views on the U.S.–China trade war and to ask whether their views align with those of the party's news media. We examined Weibo posts to study what the Chinese people and public opinion leaders thought of the U.S.–China trade war, hoping to ascertain whether key influencers and ordinary users differed in their views from news media and how news media content was used in Weibo posts.

Weibo was launched in August 2009 as the Chinese equivalent to Twitter. Ordinary people can set up a Weibo account to read what others think about public issues, disseminate information, and post their opinions on those issues. Weibo has thus become a significant source for keeping track of Chinese public opinion (Ha, 2010). By 2019, Weibo represented the largest microblogging social media platform in China, with 469 million monthly active users (CIW Team, 2019; Wan, 2019). While Weibo offers English-language versions, most users (73 percent) are from mainland China (Thomala, 2019). The majority (57 percent) of users are male, and 40 percent are twenty-three to thirty years old (Hutchinson, 2019). As a social media platform

The data collection and coding were funded by the National Social Science Fund of China (NSSFC), Project #14ZDB162.

under Chinese government control, Weibo is subject to post-publishing censorship. Accounts can be deleted and access to specific posts can be blocked (Yang, 2012). As we note below, as much as 15 percent of the trade war commentary on Weibo has been deleted—still, we argue that studying Weibo posts offers unique opportunities for gauging Chinese public opinion.

Unlike the bots (or automated accounts) found on Twitter, Weibo bots are usually fake follower accounts that boost the number of followers for influencers who seek financial gain (Y. Zhang & Lu, 2016). There are also Weibo "bots" who are real people pretending to be bots (Bai, 2018). As a result, these Weibo bots usually do not disseminate thousands of messages to amplify original posts, as is done by the Twitter bots discussed in Ha, Ray, Matanji, and Yang, "How News Media Content and Fake News about the Trade War Are Shared on Twitter," in this volume. In addition, the total number of Weibo bots is much smaller than the number of automated bots found on Twitter (Bolsover & Howard, 2019). We do not believe Weibo bots have polluted our analysis.

Moreover, it is important to note that Weibo has become a symbolic political arena in China, and to some degree, a key public arena for spotlighting official corruption. Those who expose government corruption on Weibo have been viewed as whistleblowers who provide disciplinary bodies with tips about government officials' corrupt and unprofessional activities (Xinhua News Agency, 2015). In fact, Qin et al. (2017) found more than five million corruption-related Weibo posts between 2009 and 2013. Although most corruption cases posted on Weibo take place at local levels, they serve as powerful tools to investigate and publicize corruption in China.

Anti-corruption, nicknamed "beating the tiger," has been a theme in Chinese President Xi Jinping's administration, which means that Weibo posts can criticize specific party members for corrupt acts. Even China's central leaders acknowledge the use of Weibo to expose corruption in local governments as a form of constructive criticism for local governments (Gan, 2016). Such posts are called cyber-vigilantism and have had considerable political and social effects on Chinese society (e.g., Cheong & Gong, 2010). Chinese scholars have documented how Weibo users reported corrupt officials and collaborated with other users to find and publicize corruption cases. For example, the journalist Ji Xuguang brought down former Chongqing party chief Lei Zhengfu by exposing his sex tape with an eighteen-year-old woman on Weibo (CNTV, 2013). As Sullivan (2014) noted, the Chinese government also has used Weibo to maintain control by enhancing the government's legitimacy through solving individual corruption cases, circumscribing dissent by crushing political mobilization efforts, monitoring online public opinion to formulate policy adaptations, and developing propaganda efforts by engaging paid commentators (King et al., 2017).

Weibo therefore serves as both a public opinion outlet and an instrument of party control. At the same time, Weibo has become an alternative news source for many Chinese people. A Weibo usage study reported that getting news is the most important reason for Chinese citizens to use Weibo (CIW, 2016), especially because social media provides outlets for topics not widely covered by the mainstream media (Rogstad, 2016). Weibo also serves as a community business marketing platform for users to sell their services or products through their accounts. Users can set up accounts to promote their businesses and share information with their followers. In 2019, there were over 1.5 million business accounts on Weibo (Wan, 2019). Some of these accounts serve as storefronts, while many others are merely marketing sites for major Chinese companies. Yang (2021) characterized this mix of political, commercial, and technological logics of social media in China as "state-sponsored platformization," which resulted in "depoliticization of Chinese online discourse." (p.13). While Weibo includes individual and business accounts, we focused on individual accounts to analyze public perceptions of the U.S.–China trade war. As our data show, the public deliberation on Weibo about the trade war reveals how Chinese opinion, contrary to stereotypical assumptions, is multilayered, both supporting and opposing the government's policies.

Weibo as Limited Public Deliberation

Posting on Weibo allows Chinese users to express their views publicly on a wide variety of topics. Moreover, the ability to comment on Weibo posts and share them increases user engagement (Z. Zhang & Negro, 2013). However, most people do not create original posts on social media because it takes more effort than simply reading posts. Hence, we expected more shared posts from Weibo users than original content; our data confirms the hunch that most Weibo posts related to the U.S.–China trade war were shared posts rather than original posts. The past literature on active social media posters explains that their motivations to post are for self-expression, reinforcement, elaboration of information, self-affirmation, or influencing others (Cho et al., 2018; Yoo et al., 2017). Social media posting is both a process of reinforcing one's own beliefs and attempting to influence others.

Therefore, the posts that Weibo users share or repost from media accounts mostly support their views instead of opposing them. Based on this literature, we expected that Weibo posters would be more likely to share posts with opinions that they support rather than views they oppose. Much like what happens on Facebook and Twitter, then, we found that public deliberation on Weibo tended to serve a conveyor belt, reproducing dominant ideals without challenging assumptions, offering fresh perspectives, or risking alternative interpretations of the news.

Intermedia Agenda-Setting and Framing

The relationship between social media and the news media has been examined through the intermedia agenda-setting theory, which proposes that the mainstream news media influence the salience of topics on social media. A study conducted by the University of Oxford showed that the mainstream media are the lifeblood of conversations on social media because almost three-quarters of Twitter links originate from mainstream media (Newman, 2011). Neuman et al. (2014) compared twenty-nine different political issues in the United States by using time-series data and found that social media and traditional media employ similar frames. For a few issues, such as abortion and immigration, the frames used by social media and mainstream media were more alike than those used for other issues. This similarity was attributed to the public nature of microblogs and the generally scant use of frames.

In China, the mainstream media have official reporting licenses and therefore special access to information—which gives them an advantage over social media. Consequently, they are more likely to set the agenda for Weibo posters. As the primary sources of information, news media outlets set the public agenda (McCombs & Shaw, 1972). The creation of issue salience is the first level of agenda-setting. At the second level of agenda-setting, news stories' affective attributes or frames are transferred from the media to individuals (McCombs et al., 1997). Framing research shows that the news media frame the public understanding of foreign policy (Entman, 2004). Thus, based on the intermedia agenda-setting theory, we hypothesized that the trade war frames employed by Weibo posters will be similar to the frames presented by the Chinese mainstream media, hence reiterating our sense that Weibo functions largely as a conveyor belt for foreign policies (Baum & Potter, 2008).

The Different Types of Individual Weibo Posters

There are two types of individual Weibo posters. The first type includes Weibo influencers who have large numbers of followers (fans), while the other type consists of ordinary users who post on Weibo and read posts but do not have many followers. By Chinese standards, users with 100,000 followers or more are considered "key online influencers" (KOL) (Tan, 2019). These influencers have verified accounts with an orange "V" badge (for verified) to ensure authenticity and avoid other people using their account names. Many of these influencers (or "Big Vs") are movie and TV stars, famous journalists, or book authors (Boster et al., 2011). As influencers, they can disproportionately affect the spread of information and related behaviors. In China, influencers have played an important role in controversial social and political issues (Bi et al., 2015). For studying how these influencers might have shaped public opinion about the U.S.–China trade war, it is crucial to investigate how they discussed the trade war on Weibo. However, it is reasonable to assume that these influencers affect "ordinary" posters, who do not have large numbers of followers, as well as "quiet" users, who do not post anything but merely read the influencers' posts.

Journalists and commentators are influencers with often large numbers of followers on Weibo. However, their Weibo posts do not necessarily reflect their news organizations' viewpoints, and some prominent investigative journalists even campaign for societal causes on Weibo (Bei, 2013). Moreover, Weibo influencers often are the initiators, agenda-setters, and disseminators of news and information (Nip & Fu, 2016). However, Tong and Zhou (2014) found that both "elite" (influencers and journalists) and ordinary posters can initiate social protest discussions on Weibo. According to the authors, local social protest discussions on Weibo often are dominated by ordinary people, while elites tend to dominate national social protest discussions on this platform. Thus, it is likely that influencers and journalists are more influential and active than ordinary users in leading discussions about international issues.

While influencers play a dominant role on Weibo, many other users have fewer followers but post regularly on Weibo. It would therefore be a mistake to underestimate their potential influence on their followers. L. Zhang et al. (2015) noted that more attention should be paid to the role of ordinary users because their early participation in a topic can lead to extensive propagation of the topic compared to the early participation of key influencers. The spread of a so-called "lingo" (popular terms used on the internet), for example, can start small but then become popular quickly once the lingo becomes viral and is shared with others.

Past research on online activism has shown that most Weibo activists are male (Nip & Fu, 2016). In recent years, though, an outspoken group of nationalistic Weibo users has emerged that is defending China against any foreign criticism with patriotic posts. This group, known as the "Little Pink" in China, consists mostly of young women whose online behavior has been publicly applauded by state authorities (Jiang, 2019). Therefore, our first research question examines who the Weibo posters are in terms of gender and the proportion of key influencers and ordinary posters in posts related to the trade war.

Past research on influencers' roles in crises, such as the fake vaccine scandals in China (Bi et al., 2018), shows that influencers can be critical of the government's handling of domestic crises. However, in the context of international conflicts, it is unknown whether Chinese influencers hold more independent views or act as government supporters. Consequently, we investigate whether ordinary posters and influencers in China are more or less supportive of the Chinese government's position regarding the U.S.–China trade war.

Influence of Media Sources on Online Posters

Prior research on social media posts has found that people often use media sources in their posts (Nip & Fu, 2016). Many intermedia agenda-setting studies have shown that the mainstream news media can influence the issue agenda of social media posts (e.g., Harder et al., 2017; Neuman et al., 2014). Moreover, research has shown that public opinion leaders are heavy news media users—and consequently are often influenced by the news media (Bobkowski, 2015). In China, however, the mainstream news media represent the government's viewpoints. For most people, Weibo serves as an alternative news source and a forum for opinion expression. Thus, to gain attention and support from their followers, Weibo posters may not be inclined to use mainstream media as their sources because those who follow them probably would not be interested in seeing the same content. Instead, Weibo users are likely to look for new perspectives on the same topic. In such circumstances, it would be interesting to determine whether influencers and ordinary posters would be inclined to create original posts to show that they are different and not under the government's influence as a way to demonstrate their creativity and independence.

However, ordinary posters may not worry about their posts' consequences because they have a limited number of followers. Therefore, they may be inclined to be more independent of the mainstream media than the influencers—who are often scrutinized by the government because of their large numbers of followers. Because of such scrutiny and pressure on influencers, we examine whether influencers are more or less likely to use media sources than ordinary Weibo posters.

People influence each other in several different ways on social media. One way is to post views as original posts (as agenda-setters do) by initiating and discussing a topic without external sources as support. Another way is to share posts with or without personal comments (as disseminators do) by spreading other people's comments and information and using them as evidence or support to the poster's arguments (Nip & Fu, 2016). Thus, our last research question focuses on the differences between the posting strategies of influencers and regular posters by asking which group is more likely to share (disseminators) or write posts (agenda-setters) related to the U.S.–China trade war.

Method

We employed a quantitative content analysis to study the Weibo posts of influencers and ordinary posters and compared them with the party media's coverage of the trade war. Because of the large number of posts on Weibo, we focused on fifteen major events related to the U.S.–China trade war, which occurred between January 1, 2018, and December 31, 2018 (see the trade war timeline in the introduction of this volume). We randomly selected forty posts for each event (twenty posts from the day of the event and twenty posts from the following day) to capture the immediate public response to each of the fifteen events. We downloaded all Weibo posts created during these selected dates by using the keywords "the United States" and "trade" or "trade war" (including deleted Weibo posts) in Chinese from Wiser, the largest news database company in China. Five Chinese graduate students from Shanghai International Studies University coded the posts. Of the 600 Weibo posts we collected initially, ninety-one Weibo posts (15 percent) were deleted and replaced with other randomly selected posts from the same day.

To ensure that all analyzed Weibo posts were created by human accounts, the coders identified and recorded the posters' profiles. Several training sessions were

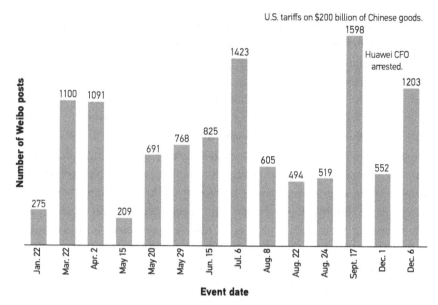

FIGURE 1. Number of Weibo Posts on Major Events during the U.S.–China Trade War in 2018

conducted to ensure that all the coders understood and agreed upon the coding scheme. Another trained coder double-coded 10 percent of the sample to compute the intercoder reliability for this analysis.

Only posts from individual accounts containing information about the number of followers were used to compare influencers with ordinary posters. All media organization accounts were excluded from the study. Figure 1 lists the event dates and the number of Weibo posts for each period. The event that generated the most Weibo posts (N = 1,598) was the U.S. government's announcement on September 18, 2018, to impose a 10 percent tariff on $200 billion worth of Chinese goods. China promptly retaliated on the same day by announcing a 10 percent tariff on $60 billion worth of U.S. goods.

Three party media outlets were selected to represent the news media/government frames for comparison with the Weibo posts, namely, CCTV, the central broadcast TV station, and two party newspapers, *People's Daily* and *Global Times*. Because of the multiplatform delivery of party newspapers and the importance of WeChat for accessing and sharing news in China, we decided to use the WeChat online accounts of the two newspapers instead of the print versions. One hundred articles published between January 1, 2018, and December 31, 2018, were randomly selected from the WeChat accounts of each of the two newspapers. For CCTV, 100 news video clips were randomly selected from the CCTV's online video archive during the same period that was used for the newspaper sample. The keywords "United States" and "trade" were used to retrieve the news articles and newscasts (see Ha, Yang, Ray, Matanji, Chen, Guo & Lyu, "Comparing U.S. and Chinese Media Coverage of the U.S.–China Trade War," in this volume, for more details of sampling procedures and choice of party media).

Measures

Identity of Weibo Posters. Five identities of Weibo posters were coded: non-media related verified accounts, ordinary people, commentators or journalists, academics, and government officials. The average coder agreement was 82.5 percent.

Source Use and Originality of Posts. Posts were coded as either original posts (without reposts or linking to any source), partly original posts (original post + repost of news media post, original post + repost of non-news media post, original post + repost of news media posts + non-news media post, original post + comment + repost of others' posts), or non-original posts (reposts of others' posts without comments). The average coder agreement was 77.5 percent.

Support of Government Policy. Both the Weibo posts and the party media's news stories were coded to reflect their stance toward the Chinese government's policies regarding the U.S.–China trade war: 1) supporting China's policy of not conceding to the United States' demands with retaliatory tariffs, 2) opposing China's policy of not conceding to the United States' demands with retaliatory tariffs, 3) expressing no opinion, and 4) partly supporting and partly opposing China's policy. The average coder agreement was 80 percent.

Frames Employed to Describe the U.S.–China Trade War. Seven frames were used to analyze the party media's news stories and the Weibo posts. These frames were identified based on a review of the Chinese news coverage and Weibo posts related to the issue before coding: 1) China is the envy of the United States, 2) the trade war is unfair to China, 3) U.S. protectionism is justified, 4) free trade is good for China, 5) the trade war is just a means to curtail China, 6) President Xi is heading in the right direction by not yielding to U.S. demands, and 7) the trade war is hurting the United States. The average coder agreement was 85.3 percent.

Views on the U.S.–China Trade War. Seven items were used to measure the presence of views and opinions regarding the trade war: 1) China is the victim in this trade war, 2) China needs to defend itself against U.S. pressures, 3) China is more successful than the United States, 4) China is a threat to U.S. power in the world, 5) China supports free trade and globalization, 6) the United States benefits from Chinese exports, and 7) the United States wants to suppress China's growth. The average coder agreement was 75 percent.

Results

Among the 600 Weibo posts we sampled, 43 percent were posted by general influencers, 12.3 percent by journalists or commentators, and 39.8 percent by ordinary posters. Thus, influencers, including journalists as well as general influencers, accounted for the largest subset of posts related to the U.S.–China trade war. The majority of these posters were men (68.7 percent), while 6.5 percent were women (for 24.8 percent of the posts, the poster's gender could not be determined because the posts were by non-media organizations, not individuals).

Source Use and Originality of Posts

The majority of Weibo posts about the trade war were shared posts of other users (54.5 percent), while 45.5 percent were original posts. Consequently, our first hypothesis that most Weibo posts on the trade war were shared posts was supported. Next, we examined the individuals who shared posts by others to check whether they supported or opposed the views of the people whose posts they reposted. A majority of the reposts (64.4 percent) did not include any original comment by the reposters. Those who commented on the reposts mostly did so to support their own views (58 percent) rather than opposing or criticizing the views of others. Only 6 percent opposed or criticized the views of the posts they reposted. Thirty-six percent of the reposters did not express any opinions in their reposts. Consequently, sharing content on Weibo can be viewed mostly as an act of affirmation rather than as an act for stimulating critical thinking. Thus, our second hypothesis, that posters would be more likely to share media posts that they support, was confirmed by the findings. Moreover, the fact that a majority of users did not create new content, and merely

TABLE 1. Post Originality Comparison between Ordinary Posters and Influencer Posters (in percentages)

	ORDINARY POSTERS (N = 213)	INFLUENCERS (N = 313)
Original posts	51.4	40.8
Partly original posts		
Original post + reposting news media post	28.5	24.6
Original post + reposting non–news media post	10.7	18.6
Original post + reposting news/non–news media posts	2.3	4.8
Original post + comments and reposting others' posts	1.4	3.3
Nonoriginal post (reposting others' posts only)	5.6	7.8

Note: x^2 = 15.91, d.f. = 6, p < .05

reposted materials they agree with, seems to confirm the hunch that Weibo works mostly as an echo chamber and not as a tool for enriching our civic discourse.

As shown in table 1, ordinary posters (51.4 percent) were more likely to create original posts than influencers (40.8 percent). News media posts were common sources for influencers and ordinary posters. In contrast, influencers were more likely to repost non–news media posts (18.6 percent) than ordinary posters (10.7 percent). Overall, influencers were more likely to use a variety of sources, including news media, non–news media sources, adding their comments, or simply reposting other people's posts and showing additional third-party support for their own posts. They were skillful users of other people's content, maintaining their high visibility by highlighting major news events.

Chinese Media, Influencers, and Ordinary Posters' Frames of the Trade War

When we analyzed the specific frames employed by the party news media outlets, ordinary posters, and influencers, we found that they were similar, except in two aspects: the party media outlets more frequently framed the trade war as hurting the United States (46.7 percent) and free trade as being good for China (25.3 percent). In contrast, both ordinary posters (8 percent) and influencers (4 percent) rarely

TABLE 2. Comparison of Trade War Frames between Party Media and Weibo Posters (in percentages)

	PARTY MEDIA (N = 300)	ORDINARY POSTERS (N = 214)	INFLUENCERS (N = 332)
China is the envy of the United States.	10.3	12.0	8.0
Tariffs are unfair to China.	9.3	11.0	14.0
U.S. protectionism is justified.	3.0	1.0	3.0
Free trade is good for China.*	25.3	8.0	4.0
Trade war is just a means to curtail China.	8.0	11.0	8.0
Xi is right not to yield to U.S. demands.	6.0	4.0	4.0
Trade war is hurting the United States.*	46.7	22.0	9.0

Note: *$p < .01$

expressed that free trade is good for China, and fewer ordinary posters (22 percent) and influencers (9 percent) thought the trade war was hurting the United States (see table 2). Overall, our third hypothesis, which stated that the frames used by Weibo posters to discuss the U.S.–China trade war would correspond to the frames used by the Chinese mainstream media, was partly supported.

Comparison of Party Media and Weibo Posters' Support for the Trade War

Despite similar frames used by the party media and the Weibo posters, a comparison of ordinary posters' and influencers' stances on the trade war with those of the party news media outlets in China (CCTV, *Global Times*, and *People's Daily*) revealed a significant difference in views between online opinion leaders and government officials. As shown in table 3, while the party media outlets overwhelmingly supported the government's policy in their news coverage (82.3 percent), only 16 percent of ordinary posters and 10.5 percent of the influencers exhibited explicit support for the government's policy in their posts. Most influencers (83.8 percent) adopted a neutral stance on the issue or used their posts to talk about something else, such as the stock market or U.S.–China relations. Only a few influencers (2.1 percent) opposed the government's policy in their Weibo posts. Thus, our data clearly indicate that the vast majority of Weibo posts we analyzed, even when ostensibly addressing the U.S.–China trade war, did not explicitly support the

TABLE 3. Support of Government Policy by Party Media and Weibo Posters (in percentages)

	PARTY MEDIA (N = 300)	ORDINARY POSTERS (N = 213)	INFLUENCERS (N = 313)
Support government policy*	82.3	16.0	10.5
Oppose government policy	—	—	2.1
Neutral/no opinion*	17.7	82.2	83.8
Partly support/oppose government policy	—	1.9	3.6

Note: *$p < .01$

TABLE 4. Comparison of Views between Ordinary Posters and Influencers (in percentages)

	ORDINARY POSTERS (N = 214)	INFLUENCERS (N = 332)
China is the victim in the trade dispute.*	10.0	17.0
China needs to defend itself against U.S. pressure.	15.0	18.0
China is more successful than the United States.	3.0	1.0
China is the threat to U.S. power in the world.	1.0	2.0
China supports free trade & globalization.	5.0	2.0
The United States benefits from Chinese exports.	4.0	3.0
The United States wants to suppress China's growth.	12.0	16.0

Note: *$p < .01$

Chinese government. The chasm between the party-run outlets' support for the government's trade policies (82.3 percent) and Weibo users' support for these policies (26.5 percent, counting both ordinary posters and influencers) illustrates that Weibo does offer a more grassroots, open, and genuine forum for the discussion of foreign policy such as the trade war.

We also compared the views of influencers and ordinary posters regarding the trade war (see table 4). Among the seven items we compared, only one item yielded a significant difference: influencers (17 percent) were more likely than ordinary posters (10 percent) to believe that China was the victim in the U.S.–China trade war. These results reaffirm a high consensus between the views of influencers and ordinary posters regarding the negative effects of the trade war.

We need to be clear that our analysis, and the data it is based upon, depends in part on the fact that even within the tightly controlled media spaces of China, many posts critical of the trade war were *not* deleted from Weibo. The following post, for example, notes that "Under the manipulation of the Soviet Union, China has been under the leftist ideological control of Mao. Gaining billions of trade surplus from the U.S., China still tried to launch a global anti-U.S. campaign and directly confront the U.S. military, do you think the U.S. is an idiot?" (June 16, 2018, male influencer with 145,378 followers). While such posts were uncommon, they indicate that some criticism of China's trade war policy was permissible on Weibo. Our research was not initiated with the intention of commenting on the overall status of the media ecosystem in China, but this finding points to an emerging culture of free discussion, wherein criticism of the government's policies is possible.

Conclusions

This study of Weibo posters found that the frames used by influencers and ordinary posters were mostly similar to those used by the party news media when the trade tariffs were framed as a threat from the Western world. Yet, the posters sampled in this analysis did not follow the party media's frame about "free trade is good for China" and "the trade war is hurting the United States." They also did not express strong support for the Chinese government's trade policy. The large number of neutral posts (over 80 percent) that did not show any support or opposition to the government's trade policy indicates that many posters only disseminated information to their followers rather than trying to influence public opinion regarding the trade war. Another interpretation of the low number of opinionated posts could be that it was too early for the posters to take a stance on this issue. Thus, instead of being an active supporter or critic of the trade war, they might have preferred to play the roles of disseminators and agenda-setters by posting information about this economic dispute.

Weibo posts provide a somewhat different perspective of the U.S.–China trade war compared to the party media, which clearly support the government's policies. Based on the large number of nonopinionated posts found in this study, Weibo provided an alternative news source for Chinese audiences interested in events related to the trade war. However, alternative news does not mean that the views of the posters were substantially different from those of the news media outlets—mostly because both used similar frames to describe the trade war. Thus, the intermedia agenda-setting hypothesis, which predicted a high similarity between the trade war frames used by the news media and on social media in China, was mostly confirmed by the data gathered in this study.

However, we did find a few different posting patterns between the influencers and the ordinary posters. The influencers posted more often than the ordinary posters about the U.S.–China trade war, which might indicate that the trade war was more of an elite topic. However, the influencers mostly reposted the posts of others instead of writing original posts. These tactics allow the influencers to maintain their visibility through regular postings and their involvement in major issues, while minimizing their effort for creating original content. Our findings matched those of Nip and Fu (2016), who found that in social crises, Weibo influencers are disseminators rather than agenda-setters, while ordinary posters function more as trendsetters by breaking news stories through original posts. Ordinary posters usually do not need to worry about their reputation as much as influencers do. Therefore, they might be more likely to post their thoughts without support from other sources.

Given that more than half of the posts shared by the influencers were reposts of mainstream media content rather than other individuals' posts, the importance of the mainstream media as a source for Weibo influencers cannot be understated. By sharing mainstream news media content and showing their support for the content, Weibo influencers indicated that their agendas were either influenced by or aligned with those of the mainstream media.

The gender distribution found in this study reinforced the fact that posts on Weibo are dominated by men (Nip & Fu, 2016) and therefore likely reflected a more male perspective of the trade war. Moreover, there was no evidence for the Little Pink nationalist activism mentioned earlier. As Fang and Repnikova (2018) noted, the Little Pink label is just "a convenient shield for liberal intellectuals to take a political stance against radical nationalism, as well as to channel more subtle criticisms of the party-state" (p. 2174). Thus, male Weibo users are still more likely to share their opinions on current affairs than female Weibo users.

Notably, 15 percent of the posts related to the U.S.–China trade war were deleted during the process of retrieving them from the Wiser database. Assuming that most of these posts opposed the government's stance on the trade war, this systematic erasure of critical perspectives indicates the party's discomfort with political dissent. The fact that we mostly saw consensus regarding the U.S.–China trade war on Weibo indicates a strong alignment of views among the news media outlets, influencers, and ordinary posters, yet this conclusion may be tempered by the censoring of many posts that we assume were critical of the party.

Finally, we also need to acknowledge that there are individuals who are paid by the Chinese government to post supportive propaganda on Chinese social media sites. These online commentators are known as the "50 Cent Army" because they are reportedly paid fifty cents per post. However, as King et al.'s (2017) noted, the Chinese government does allow a certain number of critical Weibo posts as long as they do not mobilize collective action. Of course, we do not know if our Weibo sample contained posts by commentators who belonged to this 50 Cent Army. However, the lack of Weibo posts strongly supportive of the government or extreme nationalism in our analysis might indicate that cyber-nationalism (Jiang, 2012; Yang, 2019) does not have to dominate all foreign affairs issues.

While we found some posts that expressed strong opinions, they represented only a small fraction of the trade war posts. Instead, what we found was a large number of fairly rational posts, which likely represent Weibo users who are genuinely supportive of the Chinese government and occasionally use sarcasm against foreign opponents. For example, one post noted that "we need to thank the U.S./Trump for the trade war to stop the (Chinese) import of U.S. waste, putting the U.S. in crisis." Another post stated, "if Americans had a lot of cards, they would have already used them, instead of such trials one at a time." Thus, Weibo might be more of an "acceptable public opinion" platform for those who address issues of interest and offer constructive criticism, albeit without challenging the party or the central government.

It is important to point out that the rise of WeChat as both a point-to-point messaging system and a mass-posting platform is threatening Weibo's dominance as a public opinion platform. This change can mostly be ascribed to the fact that people can form private discussion groups on WeChat rather than posting their opinions publicly, as they are required to do on Weibo. Future studies on opinion sharing must consider WeChat as an important social media platform that can influence and shape public opinion on foreign and domestic issues. However, because WeChat functions as a closed social network, public affairs discussions on this platform are difficult to study without violating individuals' privacy.

In addition, the posting of misinformation, rumors, and unauthorized news can mislead users on Weibo. Social media users do not need to conform to professional journalistic ethics and might not consider their posts as journalism products. Although there were some journalists in our influencer sample, their views did not necessarily represent those of their news organizations. Moreover, most journalists use their Weibo accounts to promote their online news articles rather than expressing their opinions.

The high similarity between the frames used by the party media outlets and the Weibo posters and the apparent alignment of views on the U.S.–China trade war between the influencers and the ordinary posters indicate a high degree of public consensus regarding this conflict. Undoubtedly, the U.S. trade tariffs imposed on China aroused nationalistic sentiment and pride in China's economic achievements among many Chinese citizens. In addition, the Chinese people were rallied by the government to stand firm against the U.S. tariffs and strive for further strengthening their country. A few observers (e.g., Li, 2018) even suggested that discussions of the U.S.–China trade war have helped the Chinese public and the government to reflect on the problems that have accumulated over the past forty years of social development, such as economic inequality between the urban and rural areas of China. Thus, despite Weibo's limitations as a public opinion forum, it can facilitate information exchange as an alternative news source to party media and public discussions on important social and international topics.

REFERENCES

Baum, M. A., & Potter, P. B. (2008). The relationships between mass media, public opinion, and foreign policy: Toward a theoretical synthesis. *Annual Review of Political Science, 11,* 39–65.

Bai, M. (2019, February 22). The "bots" of Weibo. *China Channel.* https://chinachannel. org/2019/02/22/bots-weibo/

Bei, J. (2013). How Chinese journalists use Weibo microblogging for investigative reporting [Reuters Institute Fellowship paper]. Reuters Institute for the Study of Journalism. The University of Oxford. https://reutersinstitute.politics.ox.ac.uk/sites/default/files/ research/files/How_Chinese_journalists_use_Weibo_microblogging_for_investigative_ reporting%25281%2529.pdf

Bi, N. C., Zhang, F. R., & Ha, L. (2018). The government's public health crisis response strategies and online opinion leaders in China: A case study of the 2016 illegal expired vaccine scandal. *China Media Research, 14*(2), 16–28.

Bobkowski, P. S. (2015). Sharing the news: Effects of informational utility and opinion leadership on online news sharing. *Journalism and Mass Communication Quarterly, 92*(2), 320–45.

Bolsover, G., & Howard, P. (2019). Chinese computational propaganda: Automation, algorithms and the manipulation of information about Chinese politics on Twitter and Weibo. *Information, Communication & Society, 22*(14), 2063–80.

Boster, F. J., Kotowski, M. R., Andrews, K. R., & Serota, K. (2011). Identifying influence: Development and validation of the connectivity, persuasiveness, and maven scales. *Journal of Communication, 61*, 178–96.

Cheong, P. H., & Gong, J. (2010). Cyber vigilantism, transmedia collective intelligence, and civic participation. *Chinese Journal of Communication, 3*(4), 471–87.

CIW (China Internet Watch). (2016, June 28). *Weibo usage study 2016*. https://www.chinainternetwatch.com/18051/weibo-usage-study-2016/

CIW Team (2019, March 6). *Weibo monthly active users grew to 462 million in Dec 2018: 93% on mobile*. https://www.chinainternetwatch.com/tag/weibo/

Cho, J., Ahmed, S., Keum, H., Choi, Y. J., & Lee, J. H. (2018). Influencing myself: Self-reinforcement through online political expression. *Communication Research, 45*(1), 83–111.

CNTV (2013, March 11). *Weibo: An eye on corruption*. http://www.china.org.cn/china/NPC_CPPCC_2013/2013-03/11/content_28201650.htm

Entman, R. M. (2004). *Projections of power: Framing news, public opinion, and US foreign policy.* University of Chicago Press.

Fang, K., & Repnikova, M. (2018). Demystifying "Little Pink": The creation and evolution of a gendered label for nationalistic activists in China. *New Media & Society, 20*(6), 2162–85.

Gan, N. (2016 April 21). Xi Jinping calls for greater tolerance of criticism online about China's government . . . and comments about his remarks are barred or censored. *South China Morning Post*. https://www.scmp.com/news/china/policies-politics/article/1937518/xi-jinping-calls-greater-tolerance-criticism-online

Ha, L. (2010). Emerging media and challenges in Chinese communities. *Chinese Journal of Communication, 3*(4), 377–83.

Han, R. (2015). Defending the authoritarian regime online: China's voluntary fifty-cent army. *China Quarterly, 224*, 1006–25.

Harder, R. A., Sevenans, J., & Van Aelst, P. (2017). Intermedia agenda setting in the social media age: How traditional players dominate the news agenda in election times. *International Journal of Press/Politics, 22*(3), 275–93.

Hatton, C. (2015). Is Weibo on the way out? *China Blog*, BBC News. https://www.bbc.com/news/blogs-china-blog-31598865

Hutchinson, A. (2019, April 23). *10 statistics you need to know about Weibo for influencer marketing*. https://www.dragonsocial.net/blog/chinese-social-media-weibo-and-twitter-comparison/

Jiang, X. (May 7, 2019). Online nationalism in China and the "Little Pink" generation. *The SAIS Observer*. https://saisobserver.org/2019/05/07/

online-nationalism-in-china-and-the-little-pink-generation/

Jiang, Y. (2012). *Cyber-nationalism in China.* University of Adelaide Press.

King, G., Pan, J., & Roberts, M. E. (2017). How the Chinese government fabricates social media posts for strategic distraction, not engaged argument. *American Political Science Review, 111*(3), 484–501.

Lu, J., & Qiu, Y. (2013). Microblogging and social change in China. *Asian Perspective, 37*(3), 305–31.

Li, Y. (March 24, 2018). *The US-China trade war has a large positive impact on China in the long run.* http://www.nifd.cn/MediaCoverage/Details/161

McCombs, M. E., & Shaw, D. L. (1972). The agenda-setting function of mass media. *Public Opinion Quarterly, 36*(2), 176–87.

McCombs, M., Llamas, J. P., Lopez-Escobar, E., & Rey, F. (1997). Candidate images in Spanish elections: Second-level agenda-setting effects. *Journalism and Mass Communication Quarterly, 74*(4), 703–17.

Neuman, R. W., Guggenheim, L., Mo Jang, S., & Bae, S. Y. (2014). The dynamics of public attention: Agenda-setting theory meets big data. *Journal of Communication, 64*(2), 193–214.

Newman, N. (2011). Mainstream media and the distribution of news in the age of social media. Reuters Institute for the Study of Journalism. Oxford University Research Archive. https://ora.ox.ac.uk/objects/uuid:94164da6-9150-4938-8996-badfdef6b507

Nip, J. Y., & Fu, K. W. (2016). Challenging official propaganda? Public opinion leaders on Sina Weibo. *China Quarterly, 225*, 122–44.

Qin, B., Strömberg, D., & Wu, Y. (2017). Why does China allow freer social media? Protests versus surveillance and propaganda. *Journal of Economic Perspectives, 31*(1), 117–40.

Rogstad, I. (2016). Is Twitter just rehashing? Intermedia agenda setting between Twitter and mainstream media. *Journal of Information Technology & Politics, 13*(2), 142–58.

Smith, C. (2019, September 6). *70 amazing Weibo statistics and facts by the numbers.* https://expandedramblings.com/index.php/weibo-user-statistics/

Sullivan, J. (2014). China's Weibo: Is faster different? *New Media & Society, 16*(1), 24–37.

Tan, J. (2019, June 5). Nearly 80% of the influencers in Asia are micro influencers. *Marketing Interactive.* https://www.marketing-interactive.com/nearly-80-of-the-influencers-in-asia-are-micro-influencers/

Thomala, L. L. (2019, Nov 8). Number of Weibo users in China, 2017–21. *Statista.* https://www.statista.com/statistics/941456/china-number-of-sina-weibo-users

Tong, J., & Zuo, L. (2014). Weibo communication and government legitimacy in China: A computer-assisted analysis of Weibo messages on two 'mass incidents.' *Information,*

Communication & Society, 17(1), 66–85.

Wan, V. (2019, April 9). The ultimate guide to Sina Weibo: The largest microblogging platform in China. *Dragon Social.* https://www.dragonsocial.net/blog/chinese-social-media-weibo-and-twitter-comparison/

Xinhua News Agency (2015, May 9). Social media encouraging corruption whistleblowing. *China Daily.* https://www.chinadaily.com.cn/china/2015-05/09/content_20665420.htm

Xu, W. W., Sang, Y., Blasiola, S., & Park, H. W. (2014). Predicting opinion leaders in Twitter activism networks: The case of the Wisconsin recall election. *American Behavioral Scientist, 58*(10), 1278–93.

Yang, G. (2012). A Chinese internet? History, practice, and globalization. *Chinese Journal of Communication, 5*(1), 49–54.

Yang, G. (2019). Performing cyber-nationalism in twenty-first-century China: The case of Diba Expedition. In Hailong Liu (Ed.), *From Cyber-Nationalism to Fandom Nationalism* (pp. 1–12). Routledge.

Yang, G. (2021). Introduction: Social media and state-sponsored platformization in China. In G. Yang, & W. Wang (Eds.), *Engaging social media in China: Platforms, publics and production* (pp. 6–22). Michigan State University Press.

Yoo, S. W., Kim, J. W., & Gil de Zúñiga, H. (2017). Cognitive benefits for senders: Antecedents and effects of political expression on social media. *Journalism and Mass Communication Quarterly, 94*(1), 17–37.

Zhang, L., Zhao, J., & Xu, K. (2015). Who creates trends in online social media: The crowd or opinion leaders? *Journal of Computer-Mediated Communication, 21*(1), 1–16.

Zhang, Y., & Lu, J. (2016). Discover millions of fake followers in Weibo. *Social Network Analysis and Mining, 6*, 16.

Zhang, Z., & Negro, G. (2013). Weibo in China: Understanding its development through communication analysis and cultural studies. *Communication, Politics & Culture, 46*(2), 199.

Conclusion

The Roles of Professional and User-Generated Media in Shaping U.S.–China Relations in the Digital Age

Louisa Ha and Lars Willnat

n this book, we have examined the roles of news framing and agenda-setting during the U.S.–China trade war through a collection of diverse empirical studies addressing how the U.S. and Chinese news media covered Chinese investment in the United States (see Bean), how the U.S. and Chinese media reported the trade war using peace and war journalism framing (see Ha, Yang, Ray, Matanji, Chen, Guo & Lyu, "Comparing U.S. and Chinese Media Coverage of the U.S.–China Trade War"), how the different domestic U.S. and Chinese media presented the trade war differently to their audiences (see Ray & Lu and Chen & Guo), how news about the trade war affected public opinion in China and the United States (see Willnat, Tang, Shi & Zhan and Zhang, Ha & Bi), and how U.S. and Chinese social media networks interacted with traditional media in the creation of news about the trade war (see Ha, Ray, Matanji & Yang, "How News Media Content and Fake News about the Trade War Are Shared on Twitter," and Ha, Chen, Guo & Lyu, "How Weibo Influencers and Ordinary Posters Responded to the U.S.–China Trade War").

We believe this multimethod approach provides deeper insights into the roles of the news media in foreign affairs than single-method studies, which are often too focused on one characteristic of international news and thus miss other important factors. Moreover, such a multimodal approach provides insights into the interactions of professional journalism with user-generated content, which can significantly affect the creation and impact of global news.

As Beckman and Hartnett's review of economic conflicts between China and the United States shows, the United States should untangle the *China knot* carefully while addressing the distress of those American workers who, suffering the unintended consequences of globalization, supported Trump and his "America first" policies. It is clear that the United States and China experienced significant economic losses during the trade war. In fact, the United Nations Conference on Trade and Development (UNCTAD, 2019) declared the trade war a "lose-lose" for both the United States and China. According to a 2019 Federal Reserve report, U.S. manufacturing industries, which the tariffs were supposed to protect, had to lay off workers and faced increased production costs due to higher tariffs on imports from China. In addition, China's retaliatory tariffs put U.S. firms at a disadvantage relative to their foreign competitors (Flaaen & Pierce, 2019).

The U.S. agriculture industry was hit particularly hard (Flaaen & Pierce, 2019). The Tax Foundation reported that $80 billion of Trump's trade tariffs had been passed on to Americans as an additional cost on consumer products imported from China. Overall, the tariffs reduced GDP in the United States by 0.23 percent and cost 180,000 full-time jobs (York, 2020). The Brookings Institution sharply criticized the economic cost of the trade war to the United States, flagging the large number of jobs lost, the stagnation of U.S. manufacturing, and the devastating effects of the tariffs on American farmers (Hass & Denmark, 2020). Several automobile manufacturers, such as Tesla, Volvo, Ford, and Mercedes-Benz, filed lawsuits against the U.S. government over additional tariffs on Chinese goods, demanding customs duties paid on imports to be returned with interest (Agence France-Presse, 2020). Thus, while the trade war served Trump's nationalist rhetoric, it made little economic sense.

While the trade war decreased the U.S. trade deficit with China to $352 billion in 2019, this reduction was not due to an increase in U.S. exports, but to a shift of U.S. imports from nations other than China (Hass & Denmark, 2020). Because of the trade war, China's exports to the United States fell by 12 percent in 2019, and its overall industrial output shrank to its lowest level in seventeen years (Myers et al., 2020). To compensate for these losses, Chinese firms started absorbing some of the U.S. tariffs by reducing the prices of their exports (UNCTAD, 2019) and by focusing more on building China's domestic markets. Any damage Trump's trade war inflicted on China was therefore ephemeral, while coming at great cost to

American workers and consumers. As we have shown herein, the most damaging consequences of the trade war were rhetorical. By escalating conflict between the United States and China, the trade war fueled longstanding threat narratives, thus making it even harder to imagine international peace and understanding.

How the News Media Framed the U.S.–China Trade War

To make sense of how the American and Chinese media presented this unfortunate episode in international relations, we focused on the news coverage of the U.S.–China trade war. As demonstrated in "Comparing U.S. and Chinese Media Coverage of the U.S.–China Trade War," the news media in both the United States and China relied mostly on government sources in their news stories about the trade war and framed the trade war typically from their governments' perspectives. While the Chinese media argued that the trade war was hurting the United States rather than China, the U.S. media were more likely to claim that the United States needed to protect itself from China's growing economic power. The U.S. media also focused more on economic competition and the idea that the United States has been a victim of China's unfair trade practices. As expected, critical views of the trade tariffs were found mostly in the more liberal U.S. news media. We should note again that our findings are based on limited data, as we surveyed only the leading mainstream news outlets in both nations. Especially in the American media ecosystem, this means we did not consider the wide range of sources on the fringes of mainstream news.

The U.S. government justified the additional trade tariffs on Chinese imports with the argument that China would eventually concede to U.S. demands by changing its trade practices, thus giving the United States an economic and political victory. It is therefore hardly surprising that both the U.S. government and the U.S. media framed the economic disagreements between the United States and China more in terms of a "war" rather than a simple economic dispute. Thus, as our authors argue in a number of chapters, the U.S.–China trade war represents more of a political power struggle between rival powers than a reasoned debate about international economics in the age of globalization.

For example, Bean highlighted how, even before the trade war began, U.S. newspapers often adopted a "China threat" narrative, while the state-run *China Daily* routinely defended the Chinese government's position—in both cases, nationalism and xenophobia colored pre–trade war reporting on the other nation.

Although some stories opposed the tariffs and questioned their effectiveness, negative portrayals of China dominated the U.S. coverage of the trade war, especially among conservative media such as Fox News (Ray & Lu) and in the reports produced by conservative think-tanks.

Other chapters showed how these negative depictions of China became part of four news frames used by U.S. journalists to report about the trade war: (1) competition from China, (2) unfairness to the United States, (3) need for protectionism, and (4) tariffs as the best way to reduce the trade deficit.

While a mutually acceptable trade agreement won't address the more fundamental political rivalry between the United States and China, our authors have argued that peace journalism could play a positive role in minimizing disputes between the two nations. Peace journalism's strength lies in its potential use as a global standard for framing news during international conflicts, thus transcending national boundaries and cultures (Lynch & McGoldrick, 2010) while looking for common ground. One obstacle to the successful use of peace journalism frames in reporting international conflicts is the need for journalists to decide whether it is more important to advance national interests or to promote peaceful solutions based on political compromises. The journalists' role as fair and objective global citizens is an essential component of peace journalism, but it remains unclear how many journalists have adopted such transcending "global" roles. For example, an international "win-win" agreement might still be considered a concession by more nationalistic journalists, who might prefer a win for their nation accompanied by losses in other nations. Thus, the question is how many journalists would be willing to advocate for compromises that might reduce conflict but might put their nation at an economic or political disadvantage.

We also argued that Baum and Potter's (2008) foreign policy information market equilibrium hypothesis allows for a better understanding of changes in media framing in the context of the U.S.–China trade war. According to Baum and Potter, as international disputes develop, the news media will shift from relying primarily on government sources to providing more diverse news sources in their news stories. This shift to more diverse news sources enables the public to become more knowledgeable about the conflict and thus reduces the knowledge gap between political leaders and the general public, achieving a so-called "information market equilibrium." However, as Ha and her colleagues show in "Comparing U.S. and Chinese Media Coverage of the U.S.–China Trade War," the U.S. media used more competing news frames and non-elite sources at the beginning of the trade conflict than they did in the later stages. This unexpected finding indicates a need to rethink the use of news frames and sources during international conflicts.

It is important to note that the likelihood of the use of war and peace journalism depends on the type of media. As "Comparing U.S. and Chinese Media Coverage of the U.S.–China Trade War" shows, online newspapers are more likely than television outlets to engage in war journalism because newspapers usually offer journalists more space to develop their arguments. Thus, future analyses should consider the characteristics of different news media that might influence the use of news frames. Moreover, previous studies on global news framing often did not account for the news media's political leaning within a country. Instead, most studies focused on the international news coverage of either the domestic elite press or national TV news networks that did not necessarily reflect the political diversity of each nation's media (e.g., Khasib & Ersoy, 2017; Lee, 2010; Lee & Maslog, 2005). This question of how different types of media in different nations impact the practice of peace journalism should be the focus of future research.

Media Formats and Framing of the U.S.–China Trade War

Today's news is mostly delivered on multiple digital media platforms that include websites, social media networks, and mobile news applications (apps). Although the news tends to be fairly similar across these platforms, each platform's characteristics (degree of professional vetting of news, level of audience interactivity, etc.) can significantly influence the audience's understanding and perception of news. Twitter users, for example, are more likely to discuss news by commenting on or retweeting news stories, while Google News audiences are more likely to passively consume the news. Our analysis shows that most social media users addressing the trade war tended to consume and/or repost stories rather than offering their own opinions or analyses.

The content analyses included in this book attempt to capture how the news media presented the U.S.–China trade war in the traditional news media (i.e., television) and on digital platforms (i.e., newspapers' websites, social media, and news apps). While traditional media present news to audiences in a mostly top-down mode, news on digital platforms is often shared among users in a more networked fashion. As a result, the process of digital news consumption has become more complicated because users now can discuss and share the news with others, which might either boost or suppress the effects of news on public opinion. These changes in news consumption also make it more difficult for governments and the news media to monopolize the flow and framing of information on important issues. Especially in the Chinese media ecosystem, our analysis shows an increasingly varied market for diverse ideas—even as party-run outlets attempt to use social media to spread their messages to more users.

Print and Online News: Discordant Effects of Headlines and News Content

Print and online news employ headlines to attract readers by highlighting a news story's main points. However, the headlines might not fully match the news stories' content, which is a common problem when editors—rather than reporters—write the headlines. For example, when the headline "Trump Hits China with Tariffs on $200 billion in Goods, Escalating Trade War" is followed by a lead paragraph noting that "President Trump, emboldened by America's economic strength and China's economic slowdown, escalated his trade war with Beijing on Monday" (Tankersley & Bradsher, 2018), readers who only read the first few paragraphs of this news story might get the impression that the U.S. economy is doing much better than China's economy. However, those who read the entire news story also learn that "retailers, manufacturers, and a wide swath of other American businesses have warned that the new tariffs could hurt their profits, hiring, and growth" (para. 8). Thus, only readers who read the entire story learn that the U.S. economy might be affected negatively by the trade tariffs in the long run.

Because readers often skim the news (Lin et al., 2004) or do not read past the first three paragraphs, discrepancies between confrontational headlines and the criticisms of the trade war contained in the news story might prevent readers from processing and comprehending media content (Andrew, 2007). Such discordant effects might have increased public support for Trump's trade policy, especially among readers who only skimmed the news. Thus, future analyses that focus on print or online news should consider the potential framing effects of headlines and the order in which content is placed in a news story.

TV and Video: Images and Personalities

Although TV news stories typically do not have headlines and are much shorter than newspaper stories, their framing power rests on the imagery and personalities featured in the videos. For example, interviews with ordinary people could be understood as a representation of public opinion (Beckers, 2019) and therefore might influence audience members with strong populist attitudes (Peter, 2019). On the other hand, if TV news focuses on political leaders, perceptions of these leaders might affect how audiences understand or process the news through a more political lens.

The U.S.–China trade war, of course, was more challenging to visualize than military conflicts or natural disasters, which often yield dramatic video footage. Thus, it is likely that for TV news about the trade war, the scripts were more important for shaping the understanding of the dispute than the actual video footage. However, newscasts that focused on how the tariffs affected people's daily lives in the United States or China might have enhanced people's understanding of the consequences of the tariffs by offering stories and relatable characters. Consequently, framing analyses of TV news should examine both the scripts and the audio-visual content featured in news stories. As seen herein, our analysis has been overwhelmingly textual, not visual. Future research therefore might want to address U.S. and Chinese media representations of international issues while focusing more on the visual aspects of news coverage.

Social Media: Liking, Sharing, and Commenting as Publicly Displayed Metrics

A growing number of people around the world use social media to access and consume news. A critical limitation of accessing news on social networking sites is that each platform has its own algorithm for providing news to its users. Facebook, for example, gives preference to friends' posts in its news feed. Consequently, the traditional news media have little control over what news is delivered to social media users. However, media outlets can track the number of views, likes, shares, and comments for each news item displayed on the users' social media news feeds. It is important to note that these publicly displayed user metrics can affect how audiences perceive these posts and whether they share them on social media. Specifically, news items that receive many likes or comments will be more likely to draw attention and be forwarded to others. As illustrated in Ha, Ray, Matanji, and Yang, "How News Media Content and Fake News about the Trade War Are Shared on Twitter," this "multiplier effect" of news sharing on social media is significant. In the context of the U.S.–China trade war, frequently shared posts often discussed conspiracy theories and originated from social media influencers with many followers. The widespread distribution of posts that contained rumors and conspiracy theories on social media might have increased their perceived credibility, making it more likely that people would share them. Moreover, the analysis indicated that automated bots were used to amplify certain news items through repeated posting and mass distribution. As this analysis makes clear, public discussions of the U.S.–China trade war were saturated with misinformation, further clouding the average news consumer's ability to make sense of U.S.–China relations in a reasoned, fact-based manner.

Mobile News Applications: Push and Alert Reminders

News applications (apps), such as Google News in the United States or Tencent News in China, provide users with a convenient way to consume news on their mobile devices. One key feature of mobile news apps is the pushing of news to users in so-called "news alerts." Users regularly receive news updates from their news apps, which usually contain a personalized summary of the day's most important news. These updates have become constant reminders for many users to keep up with breaking news around the clock. As a result, digital news consumption on mobile phones has increased dramatically in recent years (Kasinitz, 2015). For example, the Apple News app draws about 125 million monthly users in the United States (Matney, 2020). Given the large number of smartphone users in China and the United States, future studies on the effects of news consumption should consider the growing importance of mobile news apps in these two countries and users becoming passive recipients of news through news alerts.

Partisan Media Coverage of the U.S.–China Trade War

The effects of partisan media coverage on U.S. media audiences have been analyzed extensively for domestic issues such as race relations, police abuse of power, immigration, and gun control (Chon & Park, 2020; Gottfried & Grieco, 2019; Mitchell et al., 2014; Müller et al., 2017; Stamps & Mastro, 2020). The effects of partisan media coverage of foreign affairs, on the other hand, have been investigated less often (see Aday, 2014; Baum & Potter, 2019). Overall, our analyses indicate that U.S. media coverage of the trade war was politically more diverse than the Chinese media coverage. However, this diversity was driven mostly by partisan cable TV networks, such as Fox News and MSNBC. Ray and Lu show significant differences in how the U.S. broadcast and cable TV networks covered the trade war. The conservative Fox News supported Trump's tariff policy and adopted an aggressive narrative in their coverage, blaming China for the U.S. trade deficit and for ignoring established norms of international business. In contrast, the more neutral PBS and ABC News were more likely to use competing news frames and to attribute the responsibility for the U.S. trade deficit to both countries. Despite these differences, all TV news networks primarily relied on government officials and think tanks as sources in their coverage of the U.S.–China trade dispute.

In China, where media polarization is not an issue because of the government's control of the media, commercial news media such as *The Paper* can offer diverging views of foreign affairs (see Chen & Guo). Unlike official party media outlets (i.e., CCTV, *People's Daily*, and *Global Times*), which frequently focused on the economic and political conflict between China and the United States, *The Paper* rarely used conflict frames and focused instead on the economic consequences of the trade dispute. Thus, by choosing a more neutral political stance, *The Paper* offered Chinese audiences an alternative to the official media's nationalistic perspective regarding the trade war.

Toward the end of 2018, the midterm elections in the United States began to influence U.S. news coverage of the trade war by focusing public attention on how Trump's tariffs would affect American voters, especially Midwestern farmers. While the liberal media mostly attributed the harmful effects of the trade war to Trump's tariffs on Chinese products, the conservative media discussed how these tariffs could reduce the trade deficit, pressure China to remove state subsidies, and protect U.S. intellectual property rights through sanctions on U.S. technology exports. Indeed, it seems reasonable to argue that the trade war directly affected the 2018 midterm elections. Studies conducted by the National Bureau of Economic Research indicate that "Republican candidates lost support in the 2018 congressional election in counties more exposed to trade retaliation" and that these losses "were only partially mitigated by the US agricultural subsidies announced in summer 2018" (Blanchard et al., 2019, p. 1).

While the U.S. media focused more on the domestic consequences of the U.S.–China trade war throughout 2018, the Chinese media widened its perspective by slightly increasing the use of non-elite news sources and competing news frames in their trade war coverage in the latter part of 2018 (see "Comparing U.S. and Chinese Media Coverage of the U.S.–China Trade War"). Given the traditionally constrained coverage of international events by the Chinese news media, such an increase in diverse news sources and frames is intriguing. One possible explanation for this change could be that the U.S.–China trade war prompted the Chinese public to reflect on China's economic development and the reasons for the United States to increase economic pressure on China. Thus, by offering more diverse news sources, the Chinese government might have tried to build a more convincing case that justified the retaliatory trade tariffs. As noted in multiple chapters, China's social media also offered varied and sometimes critical perspectives, providing Chinese news consumers with a constrained yet expanding range of news options.

The Role of User-Generated Posts in the U.S.–China Trade War

We have argued that discussions of the news media's role in international conflicts need to consider the potential effects of user-generated content on news reporting and public opinion. While newspapers and television news networks still dominate the creation and framing of international news, posts by social media users can significantly influence how media outlets report foreign affairs.

The analysis of Weibo posts, presented in "How Weibo Influencers and Ordinary Posters Responded to the U.S.–China Trade War," indicates that Chinese social media users mostly mirrored the frames employed by the official news media in their posts about the trade war. Weibo users were somewhat less likely than professional news media outlets to stress the importance of free trade and the fact that the trade war was mostly hurting the United States. Weibo users also preferred using traditional news sources in their trade war posts rather than linking to alternative sources that might have provided different perspectives. As expected, most Weibo users adopted a neutral position toward the trade war or used their posts to discuss related issues, such as the stock market or international relations between the United States and

China. The findings also showed that Weibo influencers and ordinary users did not differ much in how they thought about the trade war, except that influencers were slightly more likely to see China as the victim of the trade war.

The analysis of Twitter posts about the trade war, presented in "How News Media Content and Fake News about the Trade War Are Shared on Twitter," yielded similar results. Twitter users in the United States relied heavily on the U.S. news media as sources in their trade war posts. Slightly more than half of the sources came from the news media, while government sources were found in only a small number of tweets about the trade war. This dominance of media sources indicates that American social media users—just as Chinese social media users—were strongly influenced by their domestic news media. Similar to what was found for the Weibo posts, most of the tweets were neutral in tone and did not explicitly support or oppose the trade war or the additional tariffs. However, tweets that included personal opinions were mostly opposed to Trump's trade policy.

Social Media Use and Perceptions of the U.S.–China Trade War

A significant part of this book focused on how traditional and social media might affect public opinion regarding the trade war in the United States and China. We have argued that public perceptions of the trade war were affected by traditional news coverage and related social media posts. Overall, it appears that social media users in both nations relied on the mainstream media as information sources for the trade war. Nonetheless, social media users exhibited more diverse views of the trade war than those presented by the news media in their respective nations. For example, Chinese Weibo users were much less nationalistic than the party media. In contrast, American Twitter users who expressed an opinion in their tweets generally held much more positive opinions of China than the U.S. news media.

Thus, although a majority of the social media posts did not contain strong opinions about the trade war, Weibo and Twitter might have intensified people's views of the trade war because they allowed users to publicly express their partisan opinions and find support for their positions among similar-minded users (Lu & Lee, 2019; Lu et al., 2020). Such a conclusion is supported by the findings presented in Willnat, Tang, Shi, and Zhan, which show that people's social media engagement correlated with stronger attitudes toward the trade war in the United States and China. Moreover, Americans who used social media more frequently exhibited greater concern about the trade war and stronger support for higher trade tariffs on Chinese products. Among Chinese, social media use also was associated with increased concern about the trade war—but was unrelated to their support of retaliatory trade tariffs on U.S. products.

Media and Public Opinion about the U.S.–China Trade War

As we have maintained in Willnat, Tang, Shi, and Zhan and Zhang, Ha, and Bi, stereotypical perceptions of other nations shaped by long-term exposure to foreign news can influence perceptions of foreign affairs. Grounded in international image theory (Herrmann & Fischerkeller, 1995), Willnat and his colleagues argue that individuals maintain general images (or schema) of foreign nations. In turn, these national images interact with traditional and social media news exposure to shape public perceptions of foreign policy issues. While their findings support the hypothesis that national images affect people's attitudes toward the U.S.–China trade war, perceptions among Americans were primarily driven by demographics and media exposure. Especially conservative men with higher incomes and more exposure to Trump-aligned Fox News were more supportive of tariffs on Chinese products. In China, by contrast, older respondents with higher levels of online news exposure were slightly more supportive of tariffs on U.S. products.

The stronger effects of media exposure on perceptions of the trade war observed among Americans might be due to the fact that the U.S. respondents generally knew much less about China than the Chinese respondents knew about the United States. For example, only 16 percent of the Americans knew that China's economy is smaller than the U.S. economy, while more than 63 percent of the Chinese respondents were aware of this fact. We also found that Chinese who knew more about the United States tended to be more concerned about the consequences of the trade war. In contrast, Americans with more knowledge about China did not exhibit greater concerns about the trade war.

Significant media effects on how Americans perceived the U.S.–China trade war were also found in the survey conducted by Zhang and her colleagues. Using schema (Castano et al., 2016) and attitude transfer theory (Glaser et al., 2015), the authors investigated the extent to which Americans' attitudes toward mainland Chinese and Chinese immigrants affected their views of the U.S.–China trade war. The findings indicate that more positive perceptions of Chinese immigrants and mainland Chinese people were associated with less favorable views of Trump's tariff policy. Moreover, only the perceptions related to economic competition of Chinese people (such as the belief that mainland Chinese people take jobs away from Americans or that Chinese immigrants exploit the U.S. social welfare system) were associated with increased support for trade tariffs on China. Thus, Americans who had more favorable perceptions of Chinese people were more likely to reject Trump's tariffs targeting Chinese imports.

The authors conclude that owing to the higher accessibility of attitudes toward Chinese immigrants, Americans' negative perceptions of Chinese immigrants were a stronger predictor of support for the tariffs than Americans' negative perceptions of the mainland Chinese people. The findings also indicate that exposure to more liberal news outlets (such as CNN or PBS) predicted more critical views of Trump's trade policies. In contrast, exposure to more conservative media outlets (such as Fox News) and business news channels (such as CNBC) predicted more positive views of Trump's trade policies.

Overall, our analyses of how the Chinese and U.S. news media covered the trade war and how this coverage affected public opinion of this issue show that professional and user-generated media are powerful forces in international affairs. This was especially true because both the Chinese and the U.S. news media generally adopted their respective government's framing of the trade war. Moreover, social media in both countries added what the professional news media did not provide: more diverse sources, grassroots perspectives, and plenty of rumors and conspiracies related to the trade war.

How the Media Can Help the United States and China Escape *Thucydides's Trap*

The rise of China as a challenger to America's global leadership perfectly exemplifies *Thucydides's Trap*. The term, coined by the American political scientist Graham Allison (2015, 2017) and named after the Athenian historian Thucydides (ca. 460–400 BC), describes the phenomenon that war will become inevitable when an established and dominant power fears being replaced by an emerging power. Trump's insistence on "blaming China first" underscores Allison's (2015) warning that China and the United States have been caught in this trap and are likely heading to war within the next decade. Similarly, former secretary of state Henry Kissinger recently warned that "America and China are now drifting increasingly toward confrontation, and they're conducting their diplomacy in a confrontational way. The danger is that some crisis will occur that will go beyond rhetoric into actual military conflict" (Martin, 2020). Our analysis of the narratives surrounding the trade war shows that threat and survival have become dominant political frames adopted by the U.S. and Chinese news media, hence fueling fears of *Thucydides's Trap*. We should note that this theory is a prime example of war journalism at work, as its very premise is that war is inevitable. However, it is also clear that the news media in both countries could reject these confrontational frames and instead stress the complex economic interdependences that characterize the relationship between China and the United States.

Our authors point to examples of alternative news frames in the coverage of U.S. farmers, who were deeply affected by China's retaliatory tariffs on agricultural products imported from the United States. These stories often described the plight of Midwestern farmers who have borne the brunt of Trump's trade war. Many of these farmers could not sell their agricultural products because of China's increase in tariffs on soybeans, feed grains, and pork imported from the United States. The result was a large number of farm bankruptcies and social and economic decline in small farming communities throughout the Midwest. As one cattle farmer from Towner, North Dakota, described it: "This lifestyle is harder for a young family to come and want to embrace. Your town shrinks in size. Your school shrinks in size and that makes it much harder for everyone who is left out on the land when your town is under that kind of stress" (Simpson, 2020).

We hope such stories about the human consequences of the trade war might help prevent the two countries from falling into *Thucydides's Trap* by cultivating mutual understanding and cooperation. Professional news media and user-generated content can support this process by providing audiences with more reflective accounts of how international conflicts affect the lives of regular people. The Oscar-winning Netflix documentary, *American Factory*, which describes the cultural adaptation of a Chinese glass company in the United States (Chianne, 2020), is a good example of how the media can provide audiences with a better understanding of the challenges that result from globalization and international trade.

We therefore argue that the U.S. and Chinese news media should avoid narratives of foreign threat and ethnocentrism in their international news reporting. Instead, the media should focus on stories that provide audiences with more diverse perspectives and a deeper understanding of how globalization affects people worldwide. We also hope that Chinese and American social media users will increasingly look beyond their national borders for alternative views on how important political and social issues—such as globalization, migration, or climate change—will affect their lives in the coming years.

National Security and U.S.–China Trade

In late 2020, the Trump administration increased economic pressures on China by linking the dispute over the U.S. trade deficit with concerns about U.S. technology exports and national security. In September 2020, the U.S. Commerce Department placed new restrictions on twenty-five Chinese state-owned companies, including Semiconductor Manufacturing International Corporation (SMIC), China's most advanced maker of computer chips and alleged supplier of the People's Liberation Army (Kelion, 2020). American companies trying to sell their technologies to these Chinese companies were now required to obtain an official export license, thus deepening technology-related conflicts between China and the United States.

President Trump also tried to ban the popular Chinese video-sharing app TikTok (or Douyin in China) and the social media app WeChat from operating in the United States (Swanson et al., 2020). The ban was intended to pressure TikTok's owner, ByteDance, to sell the app to an American company due to security concerns over the possible leaks of private and personally identifiable user data to the Chinese government. Consequently, ByteDance agreed to set up a new U.S.-based company in partnership with Walmart and Oracle, with a promise of 20,000 U.S. hires and user data stored in the United States. However, the deal was undermined by the U.S. government's demand for ByteDance to transfer control of the new company and TikTok's proprietary AI algorithm to the new majority U.S.-owned company. While the Committee on Foreign Investments in the United States (CFIUS) is still reviewing the deal at the time of writing this book (Qu et al., 2020), China updated its export restrictions by requiring TikTok to get official approval for its sale to a U.S. company (*China Daily*, 2020). Thus, the United States and China appear to be stuck in a tit-for-tat cycle of protectionism regarding intellectual property and media market access.

The U.S. government's national security concerns related to the global use of social media platforms mirror the concerns of U.S. companies, such as Google or Facebook, which refused to comply with Chinese censorship rules and provide information about dissidents on their platforms to Chinese authorities in 2009–2010 (Leskin, 2019). Google's accusation of a Chinese cyber-attack on its corporate infrastructure in China finally led to its decision to leave the Chinese market (Hartnett, 2011). While national security concerns are legitimate in the global trade of advanced technologies, standards for such trades should be negotiated through international organizations such as the United Nations' International Telecommunications Union rather than by unilaterally declaring national regulations that could undermine international trade and technological progress. While the trade war was largely about competing visions of manufacturing and market shares, these examples indicate how the future of U.S.–China trade relations will hinge on questions of technology, advanced research and development, and the accelerating "platformization" of communication (Yang & Wei, 2021).

COVID-19 and the U.S.–China Trade

As of November 2020, the trade war between China and the United States has not ended despite a "phase one" agreement signed on January 15, 2020. Because of the economic disruptions that followed the COVID-19 pandemic, China purchased only about a quarter of the U.S. products listed in the agreement, and both nations agreed to postpone the review of the agreement's implementation (Hass & Denmark, 2020; Ng & Wu, 2020). The pandemic also increased political tensions between the two countries, especially when President Trump accused China of downplaying the disease's severity in early 2020. In response, Chinese officials argued that the United States was slow in responding to the pandemic, despite China's early warning and extensive efforts to contain the virus (Fuchs, 2020).

 While the pandemic quickly became a global issue, news coverage of COVID-19 stoked the political rivalry between the United States and China. In the early stages of the pandemic, the U.S. media often criticized China for the severity of its lockdown in the pandemic's epicenter, Wuhan. By contrast, the Chinese media frequently blamed the United States for ignoring China's warnings and succumbing to xenophobia when President Trump suspended most flights from China to the United States in January 2020. Predictably, conspiracy theories about the source of the virus quickly emerged and thrived on social media. Some of these online rumors were later discussed in the U.S. and Chinese mainstream news media, lending them a flair of respectability and focusing public attention on the pandemic's origin (Brennan, 2020; DiResta, 2020;

Fisher, 2020; Leng & Wan, 2020). While our analysis did not focus on this question, future research might want to pursue the relationship between the trade war, rising threat narratives, and the ways the pandemic influenced such political rhetoric.

China-bashing has become a common tactic in U.S. politics and elections. During the 2020 presidential election campaign, a memo issued by the National Republican Senatorial Committee revealed that attacking China for its handling of the COVID-19 outbreak was adopted as an official strategy by the Republican party (Edmondson, 2020). President Trump quickly embraced the racist strategy by blaming China for the pandemic and referring to COVID-19 as the "China virus" in many of his incendiary public campaign rallies. The politicization of COVID-19 worried international health experts, who recognized that a successful fight against the pandemic would require cooperation rather than "political shadow boxing" (Chappell, 2020).

The World Health Organization also warned of an "infodemic" because of the rampant digital spread of false information and conspiracy theories related to the virus. Melissa Flemming, United Nations' under-secretary-general for Global Communications, noted in early 2020 that "our common enemy is a virus, but our enemy is also a growing surge of misinformation. So to overcome this virus, we need to urgently promote facts and science" (United Nations, 2020). As became apparent soon, lies and misinformation about COVID-19 quickly spread across the globe through social media, messaging apps, and websites dedicated to politically charged news and information.

It also became apparent in late 2020 that the pandemic disrupted the global economy to a much greater extent than the U.S.–China trade war. According to the World Trade Organization, global trade was forecasted to fall 9.2 percent in 2020, and global GDP to decline by 4.8 percent (WTO, 2020). More importantly, the World Health Organization reported almost 1.4 million deaths related to COVID-19 in late November 2020, a number projected to rise quickly in the following months (World Health Organization, 2020).

In light of the enormous loss of human lives and the profound disruption of the global economy that resulted from the pandemic, it seems obvious that the United States and China should have ended their political and economic rivalries to focus on the pandemic. As we have argued earlier, the news media in both countries should support bilateral cooperation by adopting more diverse and sophisticated news frames that stress both nations' interdependences rather than their political differences. Such a shift to peace journalism in international reporting likely would improve relations between the United States and China and help both governments to tackle the current and future crises that threaten the world.

President Biden and U.S.–China Relations

While the Biden victory in the November 2020 U.S. presidential election left some observers feeling hopeful about U.S.–China relations, the Biden White House inherited a strained U.S.–China relationship. For example, in July 2020, U.S. secretary of state Mike Pompeo denounced the past fifty years of engagement with China as a "failure" and declared that "securing our freedoms from the Chinese Communist Party is the mission of our time" (2020, para. 128). In response, Wang Wenbin, spokesperson of China's Foreign Ministry, denounced Pompeo's "Cold War mentality" and noted that "US politicians have deliberately stirred up ideological disputes, talked about changing China, denied China-US relations, and provoked China's relationships with other countries. Their purpose is to suppress China's development and divert the public's attention from their own country" (*Global Times*, 2020b). China also announced a "dual circulation" economic policy that would focus more on domestic market growth and less on exports to the United States and its allies. The dual circulation refers to integrating with the world's economy and self-reliance on domestic production and consumption of goods, especially in the technology area (McGregor, 2020).

While Biden's win ignited hopes for a more positive relationship between the United States and China, it was not clear how he would handle Trump's and Pompeo's foreign policy blunders. Most political observers expected Biden would replace Trump's inflammatory rhetoric with traditional diplomacy and dialogue, which would seek cooperation with Beijing on issues of mutual concern (Campbell, 2020). However, in early 2020, Biden wrote in *Foreign Affairs* that the United States has to be "prepared to lead again—not just with the example of our power but also with the power of our example." While he described the trade war as "ill-advised," Biden also noted that "China represents a special challenge" because "it is playing the long game by extending its global reach, promoting its own political model, and investing in the technologies of the future" (Biden, 2020, p. 70). Biden promised to confront "China's abusive behaviors" with a coalition of U.S. allies and partners who will represent strength and democracy: "When we join together with fellow democracies, our strength more than doubles. China can't afford to ignore more than half the global economy. That gives us substantial leverage to shape the rules of the road on everything from the environment to labor, trade, technology, and transparency, so they continue to reflect democratic interests and values" (p. 71).

Biden's essay likely caused anxiety in Beijing when it became clear that a Biden administration would not allow China's economic and political rise to continue unchallenged (Chaguan, 2020). China's initial hesitation in congratulating Biden after his win signaled that China was wary of a Biden presidency and did not want to anger President Trump before the lawsuits challenging the election outcome were resolved. However, China's state-controlled *Global Times* (2020a) later stated that China and the United States would collaborate on issues of mutual interest, such as the pandemic and climate change. However, it also expected the Biden administration to continue pressuring China on trade issues, which might eventually result in a gradual opening of the Chinese market to more U.S. industries.

The biggest challenge will be to reach an agreement between China and the United States in international organizations such as the World Trade Organization or the United Nations—rather than unilaterally deciding on what is best for each nation. Both Biden and Xi ostensibly are interested in ending the trade war and improving bilateral relations. The remaining question is how each nation will define its global leadership role in the coming years and how much power they are willing to relinquish to international organizations (Hurd, 2020).

Conclusions

Both professional and user-generated media shape the public's understanding of the United States and China, either through news, entertainment programs, or social media. Consequently, transcending national interests and promoting world peace should be a principal mission for professional journalists covering foreign news. In addition, journalists should highlight the importance of the news media to international relations, emphasize the respect of other cultures, and develop a deeper knowledge and understanding of other countries and international organizations.

Because the move toward greater globalization is unlikely to slow, it would be beneficial for the United States and China if products and services were allowed to compete freely in each other's market. International economic competition can be beneficial if both sides respect intellectual property rights and abide by international trade laws. If the news media were to report more frequently about the benefits of fair international competition and demonstrate more clearly how interconnected China and the United States are, both countries might avoid the *Thucydides's Trap*. In other words, rather than relying on a threat narrative that has dominated the U.S. and Chinese news media for decades, fostering mutual understanding and trust between China and the United States should be the ultimate goal.

Online news and social media will play a crucial role in the development of increased international cooperation. The internet allows national and international news organizations to reach people worldwide with news that is more accessible, timely, and diverse than ever before. News aggregators, such as Apple News or Google News, combine news from different media organizations and make them accessible through multiple platforms that include websites, social media, and news apps. At the same time, the global flow of news is increasingly facing internet censorship by governments that insist on defining how information is produced and consumed (Committee to Protect Journalists, 2019). Thus, while online news might affect people's understanding of the world, access to such news is becoming increasingly difficult in several nations, including China. Although tech-savvy Chinese citizens can circumvent online censorship by using virtual private networks (VPNs) to access Western news and entertainment media (Yang & Liu, 2014), most Chinese rely on Chinese websites and news apps for information.

However, our analyses have shown that even though social media offered users access to more diverse viewpoints and facts about the trade war, much of the information that was posted on social media came from each country's domestic news media. Moreover, a significant number of social media influencers spread misinformation and conspiracy theories about the trade war. Thus, as the COVID-19 "infodemic" vividly demonstrated, both the traditional news media and social media can foster xenophobia among audiences that are receptive to such messages.

Finally, it is important to note that the Chinese government's determination to dominate the global digital marketplace has led to the development of various key communication technologies that put China in direct competition with the United States. For example, China is racing to establish itself as the world leader in 5G, the fifth generation of cellular network technology. Dominating the global 5G market would allow China to increase its export of related technologies, products, and services to consumers and governments worldwide (Bartholomew, 2020).

It also seems clear that China's technological advancements cannot be contained by limiting trade with China. After Google shut down its Chinese search engine in 2010, for example, the Chinese-run Baidu quickly became China's most popular search engine. The popularity of social media apps such as WeChat and TikTok further underscores the competitiveness of large Chinese tech companies in today's global market. Because digital giants such as Google, Apple, Tencent, and ByteDance have become important news and entertainment sources, their use of algorithms and artificial intelligence will determine the future development of digital media for their home country and the world.

Considering China's rise as an economic superpower, the United States must learn to cooperate with China rather than contain it. Such cooperation must be based on the established norms of the international economic, financial, and technological system (Brown et al., 2020). Blocking China's access to technology would be counterproductive if the goal is to integrate China within global standards and jurisdiction. Moreover, isolating China might make it more difficult for the United States to track China's technological progress. The recent signing of the Regional Comprehensive Economic Partnership (RCEP), which includes fifteen Asian countries that generate one-third of the world's GDP, and the European Union–China Comprehensive Agreement on Investment announced on December 30, 2020, shows that a world order dependent on U.S. leadership may no longer be a realistic perspective (Emont & Gale, 2020; Fallon, 2021).

At the same time, though, we strongly believe that both the United States and China should use their political and economic clout to jointly face existential threats such as nuclear war, environmental destruction, and climate change. The global news media can play a significant role in this process by fostering mutual understanding and encouraging people in both nations to look at the world from different social, cultural, and political viewpoints. The United States and China need to learn to share their power in this world with many countries in different stages of economic development and political systems. While our chapters have addressed the U.S.–China trade war, their findings all point to one conclusion: it's time for both sides to offer an olive branch to the other.

REFERENCES

Aday, S. (2014). The US media, foreign policy, and public support for war. In K. Kenski &, K. Hall Jamieson (Eds.), *The Oxford Handbook of Political Communication* (Online ed.).

https://www.oxfordhandbooks.com/view/10.1093/oxfordhb/9780199793471.001.0001/
oxfordhb-9780199793471-e-025?print=pdf

Agence France-Presse. (2020, September 23). Automakers sue US government over tariffs
on Chinese imports. *Voice of America*. https://www.voanews.com/economy-business/
automakers-sue-us-government-over-tariffs-chinese-imports

Allison, G. (2015, 24 September). The Thucydides Trap: Are the U.S. and China headed for war?
Atlantic. https://www.theatlantic.com/international/archive/2015/09/united-states-
china-war-thucydides-trap/406756/

Allison, G. (2017). *Destined for war: Can America and China escape Thucydides's Trap?*
Houghton Mifflin Harcourt.

Andrew, B. C. (2007). Media-generated shortcuts: Do newspaper headlines present another
roadblock for low-information rationality? *Harvard International Journal of Press/Politics,
12*(2), 24–43.

Bartholomew, C. (2020). China and 5G. *Issues in Science and Technology, 36*(2). https://issues.
org/china-and-5g/

Baum, M. A., & Potter, P. B. (2008). The relationships between mass media, public opinion,
and foreign policy: Toward a theoretical synthesis. *Annual Review of Political Science,
11*(1), 39–65.

Baum, M. A., & Potter, P. B. (2019). Media, public opinion, and foreign policy in the age of
social media. *Journal of Politics, 81*(2), 747–56.

Beckers, K. (2019). What vox pops say and how that matters: Effects of vox pops in television
news on perceived public opinion and personal opinion. *Journalism and Mass
Communication Quarterly, 96*(4), 980–1003.

Biden, J. (2020). Why America must lead again: Rescuing foreign policy after Trump. *Foreign
Affairs, 99*(2), 64–76.

Blanchard, E. J., Bown, C. P., & Chor, D. (2019, November). Did Trump's trade war impact
the 2018 election? [Working paper, no. 26434]. *National Bureau of Economic Research.*
https://www.nber.org/papers/w26434

Brennan, M. (2020, April 17). U.S. explores theory virus spread started in Wuhan lab. *CBS News*.
https://www.cbsnews.com/video/us-explores-theory-virus-spread-started-in-chinese-lab

Brown, M., Chewning, E., & Singh, P. (April 2020). Global China: Assessing China's growing
role in the world. *Brookings Institution*. https://www.brookings.edu/research/preparing-
the-united-states-for-the-superpower-marathon-with-china/

Campbell, C. (September 29, 2020). Trump says China wants him to lose the U.S. presidential
election: The truth is more complex. *Time*. https://time.com/5894125/trump-biden-us-
election-china/

Castano, E., Bonacossa, A., & Gries, P. (2016). National images as integrated schemas: Subliminal primes of image attributes shape foreign policy preferences. *Political Psychology, 37*(3), 351–66.

Chaguan. (2020, November 7). No American election will change China's mind. *Economist.* https://www.economist.com/china/2020/11/07/no-american-election-will-change-chinas-mind

Chappell, B. (2020, April 8). 'Please don't politicize this virus,' WHO head says after Trump threatens funding. *National Public Radio.* https://www.npr.org/sections/coronavirus-live-updates/2020/04/08/829944795/please-don-t-politicize-this-virus-who-head-says-after-trump-threatens-funding

Chianne, B. (2020, February 10). *American Factory* is the 2020 Oscar winner for documentary. *ABC.* https://oscar.go.com/news/winners/american-factory-is-the-2020-oscar-winner-for-documentary-feature

China Daily. (September 23, 2020). No disguising proposed TikTok deal is a dirty and underhanded trick. https://global.chinadaily.com.cn/a/202009/23/WS5f6a2445a31024ad0ba7b1c9.html

Chon, M.-G., & Park, H. (2020). Social media activism in the digital age: Testing an integrative model of activism on contentious issues. *Journalism and Mass Communication Quarterly, 97*(1), 72–97.

Committee to Protect Journalists. (2019). *10 most censored countries.* https://cpj.org/reports/2019/09/10-most-censored-eritrea-north-korea-turkmenistan-journalist/

DiResta, R. (2020, April 11). For China, the 'USA Virus' is a geopolitical ploy. *Atlantic.* https://www.theatlantic.com/ideas/archive/2020/04/chinas-covid-19-conspiracy-theories/609772/

Edmondson, C. (2020, July 9). Faced with crisis and re-election, Senate Republicans blame China. *New York Times.*

Emont, J., & Gale, A. (2020, November 13). Asia-Pacific countries push to sign China-backed trade megadeal. *Wall Street Journal.*

Fallon, T. (2020, January 4). The strategic implications of the China-EU investment deal. *The Diplomat.* https://thediplomat.com/2021/01/the-strategic-implications-of-the-China-EU-investment-deal/

Flaaen, A., & Pierce, J. (2019). Disentangling the effects of the 2018–2019 tariffs on a globally connected U.S. manufacturing sector. *Finance and Economics Discussion Series 2019–086.* Board of Governors of the Federal Reserve System. https://doi.org/10.17016/FEDS.2019.086.

Fisher, M. (2020, April 8). Why Coronavirus conspiracy theories flourish: And why it matters.

New York Times.

Fuchs, M. H. (2020, March 31). The US-China coronavirus blame game is undermining diplomacy. *Guardian.*

Glaser, T., Dickel, N., Liersch, B., Rees, J., Süssenbach, P., & Bohner, G. (2015). Lateral attitude change. *Personality and Social Psychology Review, 19*(3), 257–76.

Global Times. (2020a, November 8). Editorial: Drop illusions over China-US relations, but don't give up efforts. https://www.globaltimes.cn/content/1206128.shtml

Global Times. (2020b, July 24). Editorial: Pompeo's speech full of ideological bias, Cold War mentality: Chinese FM. https://www.globaltimes.cn/content/1195546.shtml

Gottfried, J., & Grieco, E. (2019, January 18). Nearly three-quarters of Republicans say the news media don't understand people like them. *Pew Research Center.* https://www.pewresearch.org/fact-tank/2019/01/18/nearly-three-quarters-of-republicans-say-the-news-media-dont-understand-people-like-them/

Hartnett, S. (2011). Google and the 'twisted cyber spy' affair: U.S.-China communication in an age of globalization. *Quarterly Journal of Speech, 97*(4), 411–34.

Hass, R., & Denmark, A. (2020, August 7). More pain than gain: How the US-China trade war hurt America. *Brookings Institution.* https://www.brookings.edu/blog/order-from-chaos/2020/08/07/more-pain-than-gain-how-the-us-china-trade-war-hurt-america/

Herrmann, R. K., & Fischerkeller, M. P. (1995). Beyond the enemy image and spiral model: Cognitive–strategic research after the cold war. *International Organization, 49*(3), 415–50.

Hurd, I. (2020). *International organizations: Politics, law, practice* (4th ed.). Cambridge University Press.

Kasinitz, A. (2015, May 5). News outlets ramp up breaking news alerts. *American Journalism Review.* https://ajr.org/2015/05/05/news-outlets-ramp-breaking-news-alerts/

Kelion, L. (2020, September 28). US squeezes China's biggest chipmaker SMIC. *BBC.* https://www.bbc.com/news/technology-54324973

Khasib, N., & Ersoy, M. (2017). Citizen, mainstream and peace journalism relationship in covering Syria events: A content analysis of Aljazeera. *Quality & Quantity, 51*(6), 2647–64.

Lee, S. T. (2010). Peace journalism: Principles and structural limitations in the news coverage of three conflicts. *Mass Communication and Society, 13*(4), 361–84.

Lee, S, T., & Maslog, C. C. (2005). War or peace journalism? Asian newspaper coverage of conflicts. *Journal of Communication, 55*(2), 311–29.

Leng, S., & Wan, L. (2020, March 25). US urged to release health info of military athletes who came to Wuhan in October 2019. *Global Times.* https://www.globaltimes.cn/content/1183658.shtml

Leskin, P. (2019, October 10). Here are all the major US tech companies blocked behind China's 'Great Firewall.' *Business Insider.* https://www.businessinsider.com/

major-us-tech-companies-blocked-from-operating-in-china-2019–5

Lin, C., Salwen, M. B., & Abdulla, R. A. (2004). Uses and gratifications of online and offline news: New wine in an old bottle? In M. B. Salwen, B. Garrison, & P. D. Driscoll (Eds.), *Online news and the public* (pp. 241–256). Routledge.

Lu, Y., & Lee, J. K. (2019). Partisan information sources and affective polarization: Panel analysis of the mediating role of anger and fear. *Journalism and Mass Communication Quarterly, 96*(3), 767–83.

Lu, Y., Ray, R., Ha, L., & Chen, P. (2020). Social media news consumption and opinion polarization on China's trade practices: Evidence from a US national survey. *International Journal of Communication, 14*, 3478–95.

Lynch, J., & McGoldrick, A. (2010). A global standard for reporting conflict and peace. In R. L. Keeble, J. Tulloch, & F. Zollmann (Eds.), *Peace Journalism, War and Conflict Resolution* (pp. 87–104). Peter Lang.

Martin, P. (November 16, 2020). Kissinger warns Biden of U.S.-China catastrophe on scale of WWI. *Bloomberg*. https://www.bloomberg.com/news/articles/2020–11–16/kissinger-warns-biden-of-u-s-china-catastrophe-on-scale-of-wwi

Matney, L. (2020, April 30). Apple News hits 125 million monthly active users. *Techcrunch.com*. https://techcrunch.com/2020/04/30/apple-news-hits-125-million-monthly-active-users/

McGregor, G. (2020, September 1). China parties as it plots an anti-decoupling strategy. *Lowy Institute*. https://www.lowyinstitute.org/publications/china-parties-it-plots-anti-decoupling-strategy

Mitchell, A., Gottfried, J., Kiley, J., & Matsa, K. E. (2014). Political polarization & media habits. *Pew Research Center*. https://www.journalism.org/2014/10/21/political-polarization-media-habits/

Müller, P., Schemer, C., Wettstein, M., Schulz, A., Wirz, D. S., Engesser, S., & Wirth, W. (2017). The polarizing impact of news coverage on populist attitudes in the public: Evidence from a panel study in four European democracies. *Journal of Communication, 67*(6), 968–92.

Myers, J., Chang, A., Gringlas, S., & Yu, M. (2020, October 10). Has the trade war taken a bite out of China's economy? Yes—But it's complicated. *NPR*. https://www.npr.org/2019/10/10/768569711/has-the-trade-war-taken-a-bite-out-of-china-s-economy-yes-but-its-complicated

Ng, T. & Wu, W. (2020, August 25). China boosts macroeconomic cooperation in 'constructive' trade talks with US. *South China Morning Post*. https://www.scmp.com/print/news/china/diplomacy/article/3098682/us-china-trade-talks-resume-phone-after-trump-ordered-delay

Peter, C. (2019). The people's voice—the people's choice? How vox pop exemplars shape audience judgments as a function of populist attitudes. *Journalism and Mass*

Communication Quarterly, 96(4), 1004–24.

Pompeo, M. (2020, July 23). Communist China and the free world's future [Speech at the Richard Nixon Presidential Library, Yorba Linda, CA]. *Department of State.* https://2017-2021.state.gov/communist-china-and-the-free-worlds-future-2/index.html

Qu, T., Feng, C., & Xin, Z. (2020, September 17). TikTok becomes a case study for Chinese companies planning global expansion. *South China Morning Post.* https://www.scmp.com/print/tech/apps-social/article/3101747/lessons-learned-tiktok-becomes-case-study-chinese-companies

Simpson, A. (2020, July 20). Farmers in Upper Midwest hurting: 'I don't see an end in sight.' *Star Tribune.* https://www.startribune.com/farmers-hurting-and-i-don-t-see-an-end-in-sight/571793472/

Stamps, D., & Mastro, D. (2020). The problem with protests: emotional effects of race-related news media. *Journalism and Mass Communication Quarterly, 97*(3), 617–43.

Swanson, A., & McCabe, D. (2020, September 20). U.S. judge temporarily halts Trump's WeChat ban. *New York Times.*

Tankersley, J., & Bradsher, K. (2018, September 17). Trump hits China with tariffs on $200 billion in goods, escalating trade war. *New York Times.*

UNCTAD. (2019). Trade and trade diversion effects of United States tariffs on China. *United Nations Conference on Trade and Development.* https://unctad.org/en/pages/PublicationWebflyer.aspx?publicationid=2569

United Nations. (2020, March 31). UN tackles 'infodemic' of misinformation and cybercrime in COVID-19 crisis. *UN Department of Global Communications.* https://www.un.org/en/un-coronavirus-communications-team/un-tackling-%E2%80%98infodemic%E2%80%99-misinformation-and-cybercrime-covid-19

World Health Organization (WHO). (2020, November 22). *WHO coronavirus dashboard.* https://covid19.who.int/

World Trade Organization (WTO). (2020, October 6). *Trade shows signs of rebound from COVID-19, recovery still uncertain.* https://www.wto.org/english/news_e/pres20_e/pr862_e.htm

Yang, G., and Wei, W. (Eds.). (2021). *Engaging social media in China: Platforms, publics, and production.* Michigan State University Press.

Yang, Q., & Liu, Y. (2014). What's on the other side of the great firewall? Chinese web users' motivations for bypassing the internet censorship. *Computers in Human Behavior, 37,* 249–57.

York, E. (2020, September 18). Tracking the economic impact of U.S. tariffs and retaliatory actions. *Tax Foundation.* https://taxfoundation.org/tariffs-trump-trade-war/

Contributors

Hamilton Bean (PhD, University of Colorado) is an associate professor in the Department of Communication at the University of Colorado Denver. He also serves as director of the University of Colorado Denver's International Studies Program and routinely teaches at the International College Beijing. He specializes in the study of communication and security.

Steven Beckman (PhD, University of California–Davis) is retired associate professor in the Department of Economics at University of Colorado Denver. His specialty is experimental economics. In 1996, he began teaching American and Chinese students through the University of Colorado Denver's International College in Beijing, where he taught international trade and international finance, and conducted experiments assessing attitudes toward inequality, uncertainty, and risk. His work has been published in the *Journal of Risk and Uncertainty*, *Social Choice and Welfare*, *Journal of Economic Education*, *Journal of Economic Organization and Behavior*, and *Journal of Money, Credit and Banking*, among others.

Nicky Chang Bi (PhD, Bowling Green State University) is an assistant professor in the School of Communication at the University of Nebraska–Omaha. Her research interests are social media effects, public relations, strategic communication, and advertising.

Peiqin Chen (PhD, Fudan University) is a professor in the School of Journalism and Communication at Shanghai International Studies University. Her research focuses on international journalism and communication.

Ke Guo (PhD, Fudan University) is a professor and dean in the School of Journalism and Communication at Shanghai International Studies University. His research focuses on global communication, public opinion, and media studies in China.

Louisa Ha (PhD, Michigan State University) is the former editor-in-chief of *Journalism and Mass Communication Quarterly*, the oldest journal in mass communication, professor of research excellence in the School of Media and Communication, and the founder and leader of the Emerging Media Research Cluster at Bowling Green State University. Her research interests are audience research, media technology, online advertising, and comparative international communication. Her 2007 edited book, *Webcasting Worldwide: Business Models of an Emerging Global Medium*, was the recipient of the 2007 AEJMC Robert Picard Book Award; it has been translated by Tsinghua University Press. Her latest edited books include *The Audience and Business of YouTube and Online Videos* and *Asian Women Leadership: A Cross-Sector and Cross-National Comparison*. In addition to the books, she has more than one hundred publications, including seventy-three refereed journal articles, twenty-two book chapters, three invited essays, and six non-refereed journal articles, three encyclopedia essays, and many miscellaneous publications.

Stephen J. Hartnett (PhD, University of California–San Diego) is a professor in the Department of Communication at the University of Colorado Denver. He served as the 2017 president of the National Communication Association and is the founding editor of the Michigan State University Press book series, US–China Relations in the Age of Globalization. His most recent books are the co-edited *Imagining China: Rhetorics of Nationalism in an Age of Globalization* (2018) and *A World of Turmoil: The United States, China, and Taiwan in the Long Cold War* (2021).

Yanqin Lu (PhD, Indiana University) is an assistant professor in the School of Media and Communication at Bowling Green State University. His research interests include political communication, media effects, and communication technologies. His work has been published in journals such as *Journalism & Mass Communication Quarterly*, *New Media & Society*, *International Journal of Communication*, and *Journal of Media Psychology*, among others.

Nan Lyu (PhD, Hong Kong Baptist University) is a lecturer in the School of Journalism and Communication at Shanghai International Studies University.

Frankline Matanji (MA, Bowling Green State University) is a doctoral candidate at the University of Iowa, specializing in international and development studies. His research interest ranges from China–Africa international relations, the empowering role of participatory communication for directed social change, political communication, and the effects of digital media use especially in the Global South.

Rik Ray (MA, University of Calcutta) is a doctoral student at the Institute of Communications Research at the University of Illinois at Urbana–Champaign. Prior to his doctoral study at the University of Illinois, he studied at the doctoral program of School of Media and Communication, Bowling Green State University. He is primarily interested in using computational methods to study the architecture of social media platforms and internet policy issues in the Global South.

Jian Shi (MA, Tianjin Normal University) is a doctoral candidate in the S. I. Newhouse School of Public Communications at Syracuse University.

Shuo Tang (PhD, Indiana University) is a postdoctoral research fellow in the S. I. Newhouse School of Public Communications at Syracuse University.

Lars Willnat (PhD, Indiana University) is the John Ben Snow Endowed Research Professor in the S. I. Newhouse School of Public Communications at Syracuse University. He was previously the director of the School of Journalism and Media at the University of Kentucky, and earlier taught at Indiana University in Bloomington, George Washington University in Washington, D.C., and the Chinese University of Hong Kong. In 2015, he was awarded the prestigious Thousand Talents Plan Distinguished Professorship by the Chinese government. His research interests include journalism studies, media effects on political attitudes and behaviors, cross-national and comparative survey research, and media in Asia. He is author of numerous journal articles and book chapters and coeditor of five books: *The American Journalist in the Digital Age* (2017), *Social Media, Culture and Politics* (2014), *The Global Journalist in the 21st Century* (2012), *Political Communication in Asia* (2009), and *Empirical Political Analysis: Research Methods in Political Science* (2018, 9th ed.). Professor Willnat has lectured and conducted research in more than thirty countries, has been a Fulbright scholar and lecturer, and a guest professor at leading universities in China, Hong Kong, Germany, Japan, Malaysia, Poland, Singapore, South Korea, and Switzerland.

Yang Yang (MA, University of Sheffield) is a doctoral candidate at the School of Media and Communication at Bowling Green State University. Yang's area of interest lies at the intersection of advertising on social media and intercultural communication regarding the translation process of American pop culture to Chinese pop culture. She is currently researching the social media influencer on TikTok (also known as Douyin in China) about influencers' persuasive power and the parasocial relationship between influencers and followers.

Ning Zhan (PhD, Zhejiang University) is an associate professor in the School of Journalism and Communication at Shandong University, Jinan, China.

Ruonan Zhang (PhD, Bowling Green State University) is an assistant professor in the Department of Communication and Theatre at Auburn University at Montgomery. Her research focuses on intersections between public relations, social media, and intercultural communication.